THE
WAY
AROUND

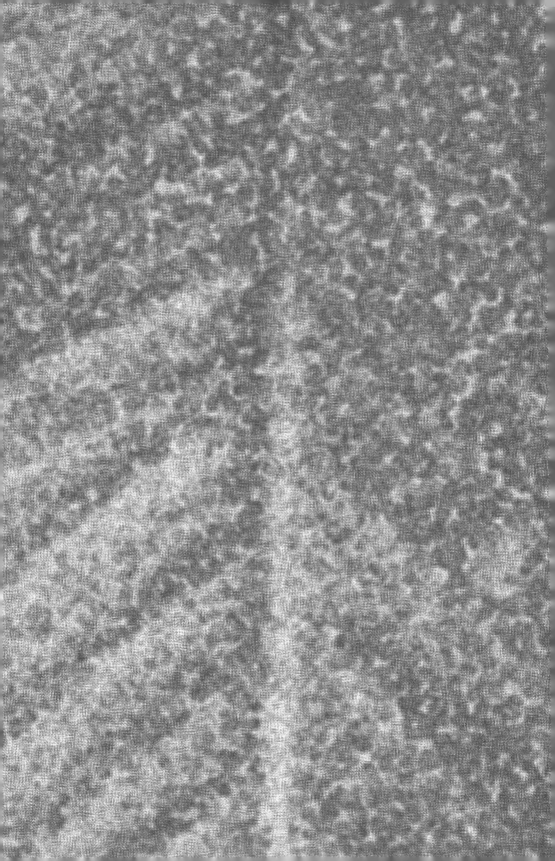

THE
WAY
AROUND

FINDING MY MOTHER AND MYSELF
AMONG THE YANOMAMI

DAVID GOOD

WITH **DANIEL PAISNER**

DEY ST.

AN IMPRINT OF WILLIAM MORROW PUBLISHERS

DEY ST.

All photos courtesy of the author.

HarperCollins books may be purchased for educational, business, or sales promotional use. For information please e-mail the Special Markets Department at Spsales@harpercollins.com.

FIRST EDITION

Designed by Paula Russell Szafranski

Library of Congress Cataloging-in-Publication Data has been applied for.

ISBN 978-0-06-238212-2

15 16 17 18 19   OV/RRD   10 9 8 7 6 5 4 3 2 1

To my daughter, Naomi —

may you grow up with a foot in both worlds,

and a heart big enough to hold your entire family

"Science is nothing but the finding of analogy, identity, in the most remote parts."

RALPH WALDO EMERSON

Contents

September 9, 2011: 5:43 a.m. 1

ONE   How I Got Here 7

September 9, 2011: 8:04 a.m. 33

TWO   Reunion, Union 37

September 9, 2011: 8:32 a.m. 55

THREE   Jungleland 59

September 9, 2011: 9:21 a.m. 89

FOUR   Taking Time 93

September 9, 2011: 10:27 a.m. 137

FIVE   Home 141

September 9, 2011: 11:12 a.m. 169

SIX   My Yanomami Ways 173

SEVEN   Returning 219

EIGHT   The Good Project 257

Acknowledgments 271

THE
WAY
AROUND

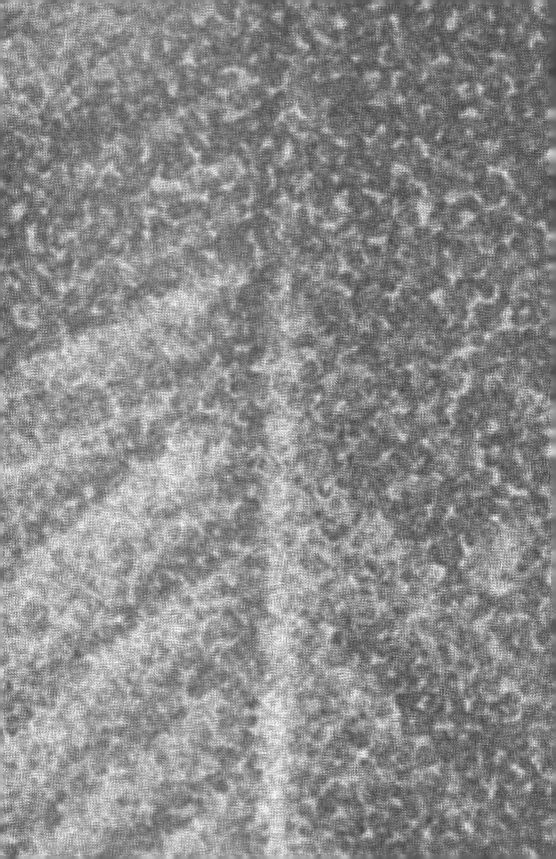

UPPER ORINOCO, YANOMAMI TERRITORY

We were trekking through a thick of jungle, past our old village. The deserted shabono still stood, but it had been swallowed up by grass and brush that had not been cleared in over a year. This was to be expected, of course. This part of the jungle, this deep in the territory, the flora of the rainforest can choke a clearing in no time flat.

Set your machete down for any stretch and it is like you were never there.

As we passed, I could see the left-behind artifacts of village life: gathered stones, clotheslines, abandoned hearths, broken cooking implements, tattered pieces of Western-style clothing. This had once been the center of activity, the focus of a people—my people—and now it was like a ghost town.

Irokai. I used to live here and play here, my mother said. Well, not in this exact spot, not in this same shabono, but in this general area. I used to lie in my mother's hammock and laugh and laugh.(Okay, maybe it wasn't the very same hammock she uses now, but another one just like it.) I closed my eyes and imagined what our family's area would have looked like many years ago, but I could not picture it. I

1

had seen photographs—but, still, I could not picture it. I looked around and around but could find no touchstones, no markers to take me back twenty-plus years—something, anything to let me know I had walked this ground before.

Irokai-teri. The people of Irokai. The people of my birth. The Yanomami of my home village, scattered now throughout this jungle, many of them clustered in and around the village they had once called home. The village of my mother, my cousins, my tribe. . .

They are a seminomadic people, the Yanomami, and so it often happens that when a village moves they must make return trips to pick clean the gardens they have left behind while the new gardens take root.

We had set out from the riverside village earlier this morning, at first light, to see what we could see. I could not think how to tell my mother I wanted to visit our old village. I could only say, "Irokai-tekeprahawe." ("Irokai, far away.")I could only make a going motion with my hands.

Somehow, my mother understood.

I was allowed to believe the trip was my idea, but it was time for a group to head out to the garden anyway. Irokai-teke. The garden of Irokai, where there was work to be done. They were going with me or without me. We would be gone for several days. There was a group of us, fifteen or so, and we would splinter into smaller groups as we made our way—usually with the men out in front.

It was a long haul, but I could not put a clock on it. This part of the world, there was Yanomami time and there was outsider time. For an outsider, even for some of the missionaries familiar with the region, it could take an entire day to cover this ground. But for this group—oh, man, they plowed through the rainforest like nothing at all, cutting a new path where the old one was meant to be. Like they were walking on a city sidewalk. Barefoot, no less. Me, I was wearing sneakers, which actually were a kind of hindrance once they *became wet and soaked through with mud, but the soles of my feet had not been toughened to withstand the uncertainties of the rainforest floor.*

As I walked at the butt end of our group, trailing my mother and a small cluster of women who seemed to take pity on me and slow their pace so I wouldn't fall too far behind, I wondered if my bare feet would ever be tough enough for the rainforest floor—probably not, I feared. And it was not just the hard earth that caused my feet such trouble. No, there were roots and fallen branches, rocks and creepy-crawly things— all the jungle-variety nuisances you'd expect. But there were also thorns, muddy slopes, protruding sticks that could pierce the soles of your feet, bloodsucking parasitic fleas, snakes, and spiders and about a hundred different dangers, a hundred different ways I could trip, cut, or otherwise hurt myself as I scrambled to keep up. I needed a second set of eyes just to look down and watch where I stepped, while the first set of eyes could look up and ahead.

The garden just beyond the communal living area still yielded its share of crops, so the Irokai-teri visited the abandoned area from time to time. This explained why there was at least the semblance of a trail. We had been this way before—we, as in my people; we, as if I belonged. It also explained how the trip came about in the first place. See, it made no sense to go on a sightseeing mission, just so I could visit the place I had once lived, but it made all kinds of sense to organize this trek in search of food. Plantains, mostly, but there were also various fruits. We would bring back what we could carry to the people of our village. The women had brought along several empty baskets for just this purpose— the jungle equivalent of bringing your own eco-friendly bags to the grocery store, I guess.

I thought it was remarkable that the garden continued to thrive, after being neglected for so long. It spoke to me of the strength and resilience of my people left alone in this same jungle, untended. In this one small way, the area still lived and breathed and continued to provide.

In our core traveling group there was me, my mother, my two "wives," and another woman from the village who'd brought her infant child along for the adventure. Even the woman with the child was making better time than me. The men were way, way ahead, but they carried a much lighter load—just their bows and arrows. The men were meant to be quick on their feet, agile, able to quickly draw their weapons in case an animal appeared that might make a suitable dinner, or in case the group was attacked by enemy raiders. The women were burdened with baskets and clothes and firewood . . . and, me.

It was hot—not crazy hot, the way it can get in the middle of the day, but hot enough. I was bone tired. I was twenty-four years old, in reasonably good shape, but my mother and these other women were running me into the ground. I was dragging, flagging, spent. At one point, one of my wives saw that I was having some difficulty and stopped to wait for me. She motioned to my pack, as if she meant to carry it. I responded with bluster. I said, "Yanomami keya!" ("I am Yanomami!")As if I had something to prove—to myself, to the people of my village . . . to my mother.

"Yanomami keya!"

The others, they could see that I was struggling, so it was decided that our core group would stop for a rest beside a narrow creek, and as we set down our few things my mother reminded me in broken English and the generic, universal hand gestures that had quickly become our primary means of communication that this wasn't the first time I stood on this very spot. She pointed to me. She pointed to the creek. Then she smiled and pointed back to me, and back to the creek, and I understood that I used to splash in these waters as the village elders fished, as the women washed our clothes and cleaned our pots. I had seen pictures of this very spot, I now *realized. Home movies, too—shot by my father when I was only a year or so old. But my memories were once-removed. I could not recall ever being in just this place, in just this way.*

Here again, I could not close my eyes and picture the scene from so long ago. I could only picture the pictures I had already seen. There was nothing in my view to take me back to how I was as a child, to where I was as a child, other than my mother's constant gesturing, and the corresponding images I could recall from the thousands of photographs my American anthropologist father had taken during his time stationed here.

Still, it was a good place to be, just then, and as I set down my pack and rested along the muddy creek bed I was overwhelmed by a sense of satisfaction. That is all it was, contentment, but in that moment it was everything. To know that as a small boy I had breathed this air and splashed in these waters . . . to know that I had traveled from half a world away and then some . . . to know that I had arrived in the place where I began, reunited with my Yanomami mother and reentangled with the many branches of her family (my family!) after more than twenty years . . . It was enough to just lie out by the water and listen to the thrum of jungle activity.

I thought back to what I knew of my father's first visit to this part of the world, as a graduate student. He had come to this jungle in 1975 on a $250,000 grant from Pennsylvania State University to monitor the protein intake of the Hasupuwe-teri. He traveled with steamer trunks, medicines, food, trade goods—and enough gear to stock an Eastern Mountain Sports outlet. I was here with a backpack and a couple thousand dollars scraped together from my hourly-wage jobs. I had a machete, a hammock, maybe a tube of Neosporin., My father was concerned about my safety, of course; but he also told me I was nuts, to head this deep into the jungle with such limited resources; he told me I had no idea.

He was right, of course, but I couldn't afford to listen to him—meaning, I didn't have that kind of money to mount an expedition of such size and scope. Meaning, I couldn't go against my own instincts. My gut told me I was meant to make this trip—my heart, too. I had everything I needed, I stubbornly thought, and so I set out for the jungle. Yeah, I was afraid, but I accepted that I would be afraid. I was cool with it. Yeah, I was in over my head, but I'd decided early on that whatever obstacle, whatever uncertainty would come my way, I would compartmentalize my fear and find a way to power past it. I would keep laser-focused on my mission to find my mother and rediscover my indigenous roots. And here I was, in the thick of the rainforest, doing just that.

I closed my eyes for a moment, and in that moment I think I fell asleep. I cannot be certain, but I believe I drifted off for a beat or two, listening to the music of my two wives, chattering in a tongue I could barely understand. The admonishing tones of the young Yanomami mother speaking to her restless child. The familiar sound of my own mother, calling to me from the other side of the creek in the sweet, singsong voice I thought I might never hear again.

It felt to me like home.

CHAPTER ONE

How I Got Here

MY STORY BEGINS IN SOUTHERN Venezuela but it does not begin with me. It was my father's story first—and then, of course, my mother's—and yet for the longest time it wasn't a story I wanted to hear.

Later on, once I was old enough to figure things out and my father filled in some of the blanks for me, it wasn't a story I wanted to share, but I'll get to that.

As I set my story to paper now, I'm reminded of the ways we learn the back stories of iconic comic-book heroes. Stay with me on this: I wasn't big into comic books as a kid, but I grew up in a time when larger-than-life superheroes and action figures were in the air and all around. Superman, the Incredible Hulk, Spider-Man . . . they were all over the movies, and in every one of these movies there was a scene or a storyline that filled in the blanks of how the hero came to be—how he got his superpowers, where he came from, what was driving him, what made him vulnerable. Only it was never *just* a where-they-come-from type deal. Other than being superheroes and saving the world, these characters all had some dark emotional troubles buried way down deep. There were layers and layers of turmoil. They struggled with their identity, with their sense of self, with the memory of a childhood trauma—like Bruce Wayne trying to make sense of the senseless killing of his parents when he was a small boy and going on to become Batman. It was all presented in a neat little package, and I used to think about this type of thing when I was a kid. A lot. I'd think about people and their back stories. I'd see someone do some incredible something on the news, or meet a new person in school and wonder how they got that way, and it was the same at the movies. I'd stare at the big screen and imagine myself into the scene—not because I saw myself in such big, bold strokes, or because I thought there was anything heroic or epic or even a little bit interesting about my life. Actually, the opposite was true. I looked in the mirror and saw a regular American kid, nothing special—just . . . *me*. I played baseball. I had a paper route. I messed around and got into my share of trouble, clashed with my father, picked on my little sister and little brother, left my dirty clothes and wet towels on the floor.

Larger than life? Me? No way. In fact, I longed to be a typical American kid, to blend in. But in the back of my mind I knew the world looked at me and saw something different . . . something *other*. Folks around town, they knew my story. My teachers, the other kids at school, our neighbors . . . they knew my story. Journalists, academics, social scientists of various sizes and stripes . . . every once in a while we'd hear from one of them, too, because *they* knew my story. At a time in my life when all I wanted to do was hide, there was no way to do that. For years, I walked around thinking people were always whispering about me and my family, trading some detail or other in hushed, *Canyoubelieveit?* or *Just-lookatthosepoorchildren!* tones, going silent whenever I entered the room, stopping just short of telling my story. My *origin* story, as I came to think of it—just like in the comic books, only it didn't leave me feeling bigger or better than anyone else. If anything, it left me feeling smaller . . . *less than*. And so I tuned it out, best I could.

But I couldn't tune it out forever, so here it is.

(Dim the lights, cue the drumroll, wait for it . . .)

My father, Kenneth Good, was an American anthropologist, studying at Penn State University under the guidance of
his field director and advisor, Napoleon Chagnon. Chagnon was
known for his work studying an isolated tribe of Amazonians
known as the Yanomamo, or the Yanomami, or the Yanomama—
phonetically they are all incorrect, so I'll just settle on one spell-
ing and run with it, Yanomami. He was a controversial figure,
then as now, but back in the middle 1970s Chagnon was considered a leading authority on the region and its people, and as
much as any other anthropologist of his time it was Chagnon
who brought the Yanomami tribe to world attention. He was
the first American anthropologist to shine meaningful light on
this part of the rainforest. He wrote an ethnographic account of
the Yanomami, initially titled *The Fierce People*, which became
a bestseller. According to Chagnon, the study of the Yanomami
people revealed the full, rich history of the human condition. He
tied the group's evolution to his ideas about evolutionary theory,
and pioneered a kind of scientific anthropology through which he
advanced his notions on social behavior and genetic relatedness.

A little history is helpful here: Sustained Western contact in
the Yanomami territory dates to the early 1950s, when Protestant missionaries established the first mission-based settlements
in the area, followed soon after by a group of Catholic (Salesian)
missionaries. The Protestant mission was known as New Tribes,
and that was the jumping-off point for Chagnon as he began his
research. Soon Chagnon's work brought a ton of attention to the
Yanomami, attracting a diverse group of social scientists who
sparked at the chance to study a civilization relatively untouched
by European colonialism, and to observe the interaction of man
and nature as it might have appeared for hundreds of years.

There's no room in these pages to discuss the nuances of Chagnon's theories and the nature of the controversy that attached to
his work, so I'll just cut right to it. The important takeaway, for
me, was this: Chagnon's depiction of the Yanomami as a kind of

"fierce" people was the dominant view of this indigenous tribe, scattered across hundreds of villages in the Orinoco drainage basin straddling the border between Venezuela and Brazil—an isolated, lowland-dwelling group predisposed to chronic warfare.

It was a view my father shared, for a time—until he visited the region in 1975 as part of Chagnon's research team. What he found was . . . well, a *revelation*.

Before I elaborate on my father's take, it's probably a good idea to set the scene. Back in 1975, when my father first traveled to the jungle, southeastern Venezuela was a federal territory, although these days it's an official state of Venezuela—the Amazonas. Yanomami territory, an area that covers approximately thirty-eight thousand square miles, stretches across Venezuela and Brazil in the western parts of what is known as the Guiana Shield. It's an undeveloped band of unbridled wilderness, and despite the encroaching forces of globalization it remains one of the most pristine, biodiverse regions on the planet—a gloriously vast swath of land largely untouched by the industrialized world. Indeed, the unique ecosystem of the rainforest has stamped Yanomami culture for centuries. Its boundaries had put a kind of cap on the acculturation process for much of the Yanomami people; some parts of the territory were so remote and impenetrable that it was difficult for outsiders to enter. Because of this "chronic isolation"—a term I picked up from the American anthropologist Jared Diamond— the diffusion of technology and ideas and other ways of thinking couldn't really reach the remote Yanomami villages, so that the conquistadors, explorers, and scientists who roamed the region for centuries were never able to truly conquer the territory.

As a result, much of the Yanomami lived as they had always lived. They had no written language. They only counted to two—in fact, they only had words for "one," "two," and "many." (As my father would remind me throughout my childhood, those bigger numbers only led to trouble.) They had no calendar. Their customs and traditions could only flourish in their own way—meaning, there was limited opportunity to learn or grow in a way that might lean toward the influences of the outside world. The way things were done, the way the Yanomami interacted with each other was the way things had *always* been done, the way they had *always* interacted with each other—year after year, generation after generation, century after century.

In the mid-twentieth century, when anthropologists and missionaries began making sustained contact with the Yanomami in Venezuela and started to study their ways, the world paid closer attention; the lessons of the Yanomami, it was widely believed, would help scientists to understand, in an oversimplified sense, a piece of the evolution of human behavior. Plus, it was just plain fascinating, like stepping through some time-travel portal—a real-life version of *Land of the Lost*—only it wasn't always talked about in the most sensitive way. In the 1960s and 1970s, we were using words like *primitive* and *stone age* and *Indian* to describe the Yanomami people—descriptions that have now given way to more accurate terms like *indigenous* and *traditional*.

But a picture was worth a thousand words and when *Science* and *National Geographic* and other publications started showing images from these jungle villages virtually untouched by Western civilization, the space between the developed world and the undeveloped world became a little less huge.

As a graduate student in anthropology at Penn State, my father was tasked with studying the diet of the Yanomami tribe—specifically, to see if there was a link between protein deficiency and this supposed tendency toward "warfare." Napoleon Chagnon was out to prove that the Yanomami fought and raided in order to increase their reproductive fitness. For example, it was argued that the shortage of women was one of the main causes of lethal violence and raids; consequently, a raid would result in a counterraid, resulting in a chronic, endemic state of intervillage warfare.

On the other side of the argument was Chagnon's professional nemesis, Marvin Harris of Columbia University. Harris wasn't buying Chagnon's explanation for Yanomami warfare; he believed that the tendency toward warfare had more to do with basic elements of sustenance, such as the scarce availability of meat—more of an ecological explanation, really. Harris believed that when the Yanomami battled it was like any other turf war over resources, waged by any other groups of people in conflict—the same way we fight in the Middle East over oil, say. As I came to understand it, Harris's thesis was that man, even "primitive" man, might indeed be inclined to fight over food, but only to satisfy a base hunger, or to ensure access to a steady food supply—specifically, game and the territories in which to hunt.

Basically, you had the classic nature versus nurture debate, played out in the jungles of the Amazon, and my father was caught in the middle. Since Chagnon was his thesis advisor, my father's unstated objective was to support Chagnon's theories, but even before he embarked on his research my father had his doubts. How could a people be hardwired for aggression?

Going in, the enterprise didn't make a whole lot of sense to my father, but this study was his ticket into the territory, and his doctoral degree, so he signed on—and if you ask him now, he'll say he signed on with an open mind. He traveled to the region with Chagnon and two other graduate students, who scattered to other villages on arrival. It was a well-funded operation, and each party traveled with an ample supply of medicines, trade goods, and research tools. Whatever my father needed to make his time in the jungle more comfortable, whatever he needed to complete his work, whatever he needed to help him make friends and form alliances with this exotic, seminomadic group of people . . . it was all within reach.

All he had to do was keep his head down, follow the protocol, and collect the data he needed to reinforce his director's thesis. Piece of cake, right?

TO LOOK AT PICTURES of my father now, diligently charting the diet of the Yanomami villagers, is to see a man on a mission. He was prepared to be won over to Chagnon's way of thinking, but that's not what happened. Instead, my father spent months dutifully recording everything the Yanomami consumed in Hasupuwe, a small village of less than one hundred inhabitants and hundreds of frogs. That was the first thing my father noticed when he initially arrived there, the incessant calling of the frogs, and it's how the *Hasupuwe-teri* got their name. *Hasupuwe* is the Yanomami word for frog—so these were the frog people of the rainforest.

In his time in the village, my father weighed everything the *Hasupuwe-teri* ate—not just meat and fish, but berries and nuts and plantains. The people in the village didn't know what to make of my father at first, with his industrial scale and his careful note keeping. Their endless curiosity left my father bereft of any privacy or peace. Once the novelty of having a foreigner around wore off, they left him to do his thing, pretty much, but after a while it began to feel to my father like he was spinning his wheels. Chagnon had also left him alone in this part of the jungle after a short while and once his mentor was gone it didn't take long for my father to see that his fieldwork would be incomplete if he didn't develop a better understanding of Yanomami culture in a broader context. You can't just measure protein intake and try to extrapolate some theories on human behavior based on a bunch of numbers, he was realizing. He wanted the bigger picture, so he turned his attention to the people of the village—not *just* what they ate. He learned the language. He studied their ways.

He had been living in a mud hut the villagers had helped him to build, but it was at some remove from the heart of daily village life, so as soon as it was feasible he moved his hammock a little bit closer to the *shabono*, the communal roundhouse structure where village life was centered. There were no walls, no doors, no privacy—just an open expanse where the villagers ate, slept, laughed, and played, surrounding an open-aired center. My father set up camp inside the *shabono*, by his very own hearth—a sweet little perch in the middle of all the action.

The Yanomami had looked at my father warily when he first

arrived. At five feet, eleven inches, he towered over the other men of the village. (On average, the adult Yanomami male stands about five feet even.) There had been missionaries and relief workers in the territory, so the village elders had some experience interacting with *nabuh*—men and women from the outside world. But over a period of months, my father's relationship with the *Hasupuwe-teri* took on a different tone. He went from being a circumspect interloper to a trusted, familiar presence, and at some point he looked up from weighing peccaries and studying his field notes and found a people laced together by purpose and lineage and common good. He could see no evidence of a people biologically predisposed to "chronic warfare." In its place he found a mostly peaceable civilization free from the woes and stresses of modern life: bills, taxes, career advancement . . . for him, even the pressures of family life were softened in the rainforest. He had thought that generalizing the tribe as ferocious was a gross misrepresentation.

That said, my father certainly witnessed episodes of violence during his time in the jungle, even *lethal* violence. However, he could not accept the notion that the Yanomami are an inherently violent people. Often, these violent incidents were isolated affairs, an exception to a baseline behavior that was mostly civil, collegial, collaborative.

As a kid, when I listened to my father talk about his experiences in the rainforest, he compared the occasional violent outbursts among the Yanomami to a mugging in Manhattan. It would be unfair and off-point to categorize *all* New Yorkers as violent, just as he believed it was unfair and off-point to generalize about the Yanomami in this way.

One thing that strikes me about the isolated acts of violence described by my father and other anthropologists is how they're held out as standard, business-as-usual type behavior—although here in the United States, by contrast, we find the same isolated acts of violence being perpetrated every day, in every community.

The difference, really, is that the Yanomami live in an open society. Their communal living structures, their routines, their interactions leave nothing to the imagination. Everything's just so *out there*, in every sense of the phrase—so these intermittent examples of violence must have been jarring to an outsider.

And just as these outbursts might have been jarring to my father, I imagine my father was a pretty jarring presence in the village, at least initially. As a young man, he could be a little arrogant; he bristled at authority, even arguing with his professors and advisors in ways that were clearly against his interests and his better judgment. Socially, he'd always been a bit of a misfit; even as a kid I could see he was a little awkward in certain social situations, but here among the Yanomami he was freed of the small talk and polite conventions he'd struggled with back home. He was more himself, he said. He fell in love with the people, the culture, the pace and pulse of a simpler, cleaner, more organic way of life.

As his fieldwork was drawing to its close, my father started thinking he didn't want to leave—so he set about looking for reasons to stay.

He found them.

When my father first arrived in Hasupuwe, the people called him *Aka porebi*—or, "Ghost Tongue."(Typically, the phrase is used to refer to a Yanomami child who has not yet learned to speak.)But soon he was able to communicate effectively, almost fluently. He had a great gift for languages, my father, and here it proved enormously useful. The villagers took him in—as a novelty at first, but eventually as one of their own. He learned to act like a Yanomami, defend himself like a Yanomami, joke like a Yanomami, tease like a Yanomami.

My father wrote about his transformation in his book, *Into the Heart*, which was published in 1991 and became a bestseller. His story is not mine to tell—but like I said, it does set the stage for my arrival, so I'll hit some of the highlights here. One of the most indelible scenes from his book, for me, came early on in my father's stay, when the *Hasupuwe-teri* would gather around as he logged his field notes each day. It was a welcome routine, but it meant something far different to the villagers than it did to my father. The concept of writing was completely foreign to the Yano-mami, of course. To them, my father was just making squiggly lines, drawing on pieces of paper, so they'd take turns doing the same, making designs, scribbling. "Although they'd never held a pen before," he wrote, "they would take mine and draw some-thing—as likely as not right over my page of notes."

While still on the first leg of his rainforest odyssey, my father acclimated to village life—and yet even as he became more involved in the community, he continued to look on as something of an outsider. He was a trained anthropologist, after all, and he was therefore conditioned to remain at least somewhat on the periphery. He was there to observe, but in order to observe fully he believed he needed to participate as well.

This clash between the roles of observer and participant came to a head for him one afternoon in a harrowing way—a moment he also shared in his book. What happened was my father was awakened one afternoon while he was taking a nap. Appar-ently, he took a lot of naps during his time in the jungle, prob-ably because his days began each morning with the sun. He was not alone in this; it was hot in the rainforest—like, ridiculously, insanely, oppressively hot—and during the heat of the day many of the Yanomami tended to laze around in the shade, to escape the worst of it. On this one afternoon, my father woke to a series of screams—terrifying, agonizing screams. Best he could tell, they were the screams of a woman, and they were accompanied by sounds of struggle. He went to see what was going on, walk-ing from his hammock in the *shabono* past a tableau of ordinary village life—women and children who seemed to take no notice of the disturbance. But once he got to the other side of the *sha-bono*, what my father saw was alarming. There appeared to be two groups of young men, pulling violently at the arms and legs of a young woman, like she was a human wishbone. The woman was howling with fear, and it appeared to my father that she was also in pain, and yet all around, just a few yards from where this woman was being attacked, other Yanomami were going about their business: there were two women roasting plantains, and another woman weaving a basket, and another woman nursing a sick child.

Now, it's important to mention here that the Yanomami do not in any way condone rape or the violent behavior of men toward women. Let's realize, however, that these things are not acceptable in our culture, either, and yet they still find their way into our lives. According to my father, many Yanomami women did leave their place by their hearths or hammocks and attempt to help this woman and free her from her assailants. And many did not. What was most disturbing to my father, really, was how public this scene was—and now, all these years later, we must consider this in context. As we've noted, everything is out in the open in Yanomami culture. There are no walls to hide behind. Imagine if we lived in this way, in our Western world, with scenes of domestic violence played out for the entire community. Husbands yelling at wives in front of their neighbors. Mothers smacking their children as they prepare dinner. So I want to be careful here, as we ease into my story, that I don't present a picture of the Yanomami as an ugly, brutish band of thugs. Yes, this was an appalling act. And yes, many in the community seemed to shrug it off. But, again, it must be considered in context.

As my father pulled closer to this horrifying scene, he realized with a start that he knew the woman in agony. She had been helpful to him on a recent visit to a neighboring village, and had recently come to Hasupuwe seeking refuge from her husband, and now here she was, at the center of a peculiar brand of violence my father could hardly understand. This was not violence for the sake of violence. No, this was something else entirely—a brutal piece of reality my father's Western sensibilities could not come close to understanding. He inched closer and was astonished to see that the woman herself was hardly struggling. She'd gone limp, resigned to whatever fate had in store for her. It turned out it was a group of three or four young men my father knew from the village, the *huya*, trying to cart this woman off in different directions, pulling against three or four elderly women he also knew.

For the longest time, my father stood in horror. He could not think what to do, what was expected of him. He could hardly process what he was seeing. Finally, he noticed another woman returning from one of the gardens with her child. He knew her well enough to flag her down and ask her what was going on.

"Oh, that," the woman said, almost dismissively, like it was nothing. "Those boys are trying to drag her into the forest to rape her. And the women, they are trying to stop them."

She said this in a matter-of-fact way, as if this type of exchange was an ordinary occurrence, a simple fact of jungle life, an unfortunate display of what the villagers might have thought of as mischief, but it was nevertheless upsetting to my father. He'd been living among these people for several months by this point, and knew them to be kind, compassionate, and even generous. He'd never seen this type of behavior, played out just a stone's throw from the communal heart of the village. An unprotected woman—that is, a single woman who had passed the onset of her first menses; or, a "married" woman whose husband was away from the village for an extended period of time—was vulnerable, the same way a female college student might be vulnerable walking home alone from a frat party. It was an abomination, but it was so. It was the way of the jungle.

(Just to be clear, my father had yet to shed his Western perspective on a bunch of Yanomami social issues, but these too would fall away over time.)

And so the woman continued to struggle. My father stood, still and silent, as yet another teenage boy joined the scrum to help his friends, and eventually they managed to pull this poor woman from the futile grasps of the elderly women who had been trying to save her from this particular piece of trouble. They proceeded to drag her into the jungle.

My father followed, tentatively, not sure how to act in this situation.

"I had no doubt I could scare these kids away," he later wrote, reflecting on this moment. "They were half-afraid of me any-way, and if I picked up a stick and gave a good loud, threatening yell, they'd scatter like the wind. On the other hand, I was an anthropologist, not a policeman. I wasn't supposed to take sides and make value judgments and direct their behavior. This kind of thing went on. If a woman left her village and showed up some-where else unattached, chances were she'd be raped. She knew it, they knew it. It was expected behavior. What was I supposed to do, I thought, try to inject my own standards of morality? I hadn't come down here to change these people or because I thought I'd love everything they did. I'd come to study them."

So what did he do? Nothing. After another long while, he retreated back to the *shabono*—disgusted with himself for not interfering, sickened by what he had just seen, and confused by the indifference the other Yanomami seemed to express over the same situation. The "last straw" in his decision making actually came from a small boy my father knew from the village, who hap-pened by as my father was considering his next move. The boy followed my father's gaze to the gang of teenagers—some of them his brothers and cousins, perhaps—rutting and grunting over this helpless woman. Then he looked up at my father and said, "Don't go out there."

"Why?" my father wanted to know.

His response: *because they are eating her vagina*—a jungle idiom that was certainly not meant to be taken literally but instead to indicate that these wild teenage boys were sexually devouring their female prey, having their way with her.

And so my father slinked back to the *shabono*—defeated, deflated, disgusted with himself for not coming to his friend's aid, and yet at the same time a part of him wondered if that was even expected of him in these parts. It gnawed at him for the lon-gest time. It would take months—years, even—for him to fully shed his Western mind-set and learn to take this type of behavior in stride, maybe even longer for him to reconcile the man he had been back home with the man he was now expected to be in the jungle. Along the way, he struggled through a bout of malaria that nearly killed him—and a disastrous spill from a dugout canoe as he shot the Guajaribo Rapids that nearly killed him all over again. And yet he adapted. Slowly, he was transformed, and it was in this very transformation, this cultural transition that a foundation was laid for my mother to enter my father's life, and as I look back on my father's time in the jungle I realize that if he hadn't eventually made this leap, this shift in his thinking . . . if he hadn't come around to shedding his role as an anthropologist and embracing his role as a full-fledged member of the *Hasupuweteri*, there would be no "origin" story for me to tell.

SOME COUPLES MEET CUTE. Some couples meet obvious. My parents met weird—at least, that's the way many Westerners see it, before they learn the full story. That's how I saw it when I was a kid, growing up in New Jersey, with a family tree that didn't look like anyone else's in my neighborhood. Even my father saw it this way early on, I think, probably because he'd made several trips back home to reconnect with his old ways of looking out at the world. He first returned to the United States in June 1977, after a little more than two years in the jungle. Upon arrival, he went to Penn State to end his association with Napoleon Chagnon, determined to resume his studies with Marvin Harris at Columbia University, where he'd been admitted as a PhD candidate.

Before heading to New York to begin his work at Columbia, however, my father took a little detour, traveling to the Max Planck Institute in Munich, through which he would have an opportunity to continue his fieldwork with the Yanomami people. The position allowed him to return to the Amazon almost immediately; if he had gone directly to Columbia, it could have been another year or longer before a follow-up expedition could be set underway, and Marvin Harris agreed that this was a good opportunity for my father to further establish his contacts in the region.

This was where my mother came into the picture, although the picture was hardly clear just yet. She was still a young girl at the time—maybe eleven or twelve, but impossible to know for certain since the Yanomami didn't have a concept of things like birthdays and calendars. Time in the rainforest is not cyclical or compartmentalized, as we tend to consider it in the Western world. It is not measured in years, so there's no Yanomami equivalent to describing the year 2015, say, or to reflecting back on what life was like in the 1960s. The Yanomami are not bound by numbers; they don't measure their progress or growth numerically. Unlike the Western world, they are not obsessed with numbers. You don't have to be eighteenth smoke, or twenty-one to drink, or have a 3.0 GPA to graduate. You don't have to pay your taxes by a certain date on the calendar.

So nobody knows how old my mother really was when my father first met her. The answer would have held no meaning. What *was* meaningful was how my mother appeared in my father's story—and, soon enough, in mine. She was sitting with her mother by the communal hearth one afternoon, about a week after my father had returned to the village. He was deep in conversation with a man known a Yanomami name that loosely translated as Longbeard—the headman of the *Hasupuwe-teri*. Longbeard spoke to my father about a matter of great importance.

"*Shori*," he said, using the familiar Yanomami kinship phrase that loosely translates as brother-in-law, but can be used to refer to a close friend or trusted companion. "You have lived among us for a long time. You have gone away and now you have come back. You are now one of us. The time has come for you to take a wife."

Right away, my father thought something must have been lost in the translation. He had lived in the village for those two years, leading up to his last trip back to the United States, and in all that time no one had ever mentioned the idea of marrying him off to a female member of the tribe. And more to the point, my father never wanted for companionship in this way. He had his work to keep him busy, he said. Life in the jungle was enough of a challenge without adding a relationship into the mix. His sex drive was fairly nonexistent, distracted as he was by the oppressive heat, the incessant mosquitoes, the communal sleeping arrangements, the strange foods, and on and on. So he stiff-armed the idea, tried to redirect the conversation, but Longbeard was firm on this. If my father was to live among the *Hasupuwe-teri*, he must take a wife. It was the way of things.

Now, to take a wife in Yanomami culture can mean simply stringing your hammock next to the hammock of an available woman. That's the extent of a marriage ceremony in that part of the world—done deal. It can mean sharing a wife with another Yanomami male, which my father knew from observation could get complicated.(As long as I'm on it, let's be clear: The Yanomami are predominantly monogamous, although it's not uncommon to see a man with two wives. However, it's rarer still to see a woman with two husbands, but it does happen from time to time.)And it can mean a marriage in name only, because as often as not a Yanomami "betrothal" can amount to nothing much at all.

The way it works, typically, is that once a man is betrothed to a Yanomami woman, he begins to spend time with her and her family. Very often, these types of arrangements are made between families, in much the same way an "arranged" Western marriage might take place. Once the betrothal is set, nothing changes. The young woman continues to live with her family and go about her routines, as before. The young man does the same. Sometimes the younger generation isn't even aware of the arrangement their parents or older relatives might have made on their behalf. It is only talked about when there is something to talk about.

Next, there is a kind of trial period, as both sides get to know each other, not unlike the way things happen in a Western court-

ship, only in *that* part of the world it's known as dating. The Yanomami betrothal period can last for months, even years . . . it can
even begin before a child is born.

(My younger sister Vanessa—you'll meet her in a bit—was
betrothed to a local man while my mother was still pregnant with her!)

There is no notion of romance in Yanomami culture—anyway,
nothing that resembles our Western ideal. Yanomami women don't
swoon over their men or pine for them when they are away; they
don't write love songs or poems; the union between husband and
wife is based more on companionship and proximity and family
than it is on love and chemistry and any other Western ideal. Obviously, if two people don't like each other, if they're not compat-
ible, there won't be a marriage, but it's a relationship of practicality,
really. You need a woman to fish and cook and bear children. You
need a husband to hunt, and to protect his family. They are two
parts of a necessary whole.

My father's first thought was to laugh off Longbeard's sugges-
tion, but he wanted to be respectful of the village headman. He
valued his friendship with Longbeard and was careful not to do
anything to upend his place in the community. Still, he thought it
was a preposterous notion. How could he, a Westerner, seriously
consider accepting the betrothal? It would be one thing to begin a
romantic relationship with one of the women of the village—but
this, too, could be problematic. She could be pledged to another.
She could have certain expectations he was not prepared to meet.
But to commit to a marriage as he understood the term, the institution, the relationship . . . it was out of the question. It was absurd,
really, in every way imaginable, but especially in logistical ways.
His "tour of duty" this time around was scheduled to last only a
couple of months, so the thought of entering into a long-term relationship was out of the question.

And yet, there it was. Longbeard was persistent. Whatever
objections my father raised, Longbeard batted them aside, like he
was shooing flies. However my father tried to resist, Longbeard

pushed back. Finally, my father threw up his hands, in a *what the hell* kind of way and said, "Fine. I will take a wife."

"Then it is decided," Longbeard said, and as he made the pronouncement he caught sight of my mother and grandmother, cooking over the fire. He pointed toward my mother and said, "Take her."

As it happened, my father knew my mother and her family. He was friendly with her older brother; they often fished together. He was friendly with her mother; she often cooked for him. He was even friendly with my mother. She often kept him company as he went over his notes and had lately fallen into the welcome habit of bringing him food from her mother's hearth. In this way, they passed many enjoyable hours together. Sometimes my mother joined my father on one of his fishing treks with her brother, climbing on my father's giant back and clasping her hands around his neck as he carried her on piggyback into the jungle.

It was a friendship, nothing more—a *family* friendship.

As it also happened, my mother was already betrothed to another man, but among the Yanomami this was pretty standard, a way to keep your options open.

MY FATHER CALLED MY mother *Yarima*, although that wasn't her real name. In Yanomami culture, a given name is rarely spoken out loud. It's considered taboo—a huge insult, actually. To say someone's real name, it is believed, is to leave them vulnerable to attack by the evil spirits. They are always lurking, these spirits, always listening, so it follows that if these spirits learn your name they can somehow inflict harm or cause sickness.

There are a lot of superstitions that attach to the naming of a child. Most Yanomami parents don't even name their children for months, sometimes longer, and when they finally do the child has taken on some trait or characteristic that has already lent itself to a nickname. It is this nickname that becomes their handle. Before a child is named, a parent or grandparent, aunt or uncle might refer to him or her in kinship terms such as my Nephew, or my Older Sister(*Hekamaya*; or, *Pataye*). Even after a child is named, he or she will continue to be called by these kinship names by their parents and relatives. But once you are given a nickname and grow into it that is how you are known.

Yanomami nicknames are not always flattering. My father told me he once knew a man in a neighboring village who went by the name of *Shamaposiwe*—A Tapir's Asshole. And once he learned the language and began to speak fairly fluently, my father traded the Ghost Tongue name he'd carried since arriving in the village for *Hukopata*—Big Forehead.

(Just to be clear, to the Yanomami my father *did* have a big forehead, and I can only assume that *Shamaposiwe* likewise resembled his namesake.)

As long as I'm talking about names, I'll slip in a word or two about my own, before returning to my parents' story. In the rainforest, I was often called *Davi*—a sweet diminutive of my American name. Or by some other kinship term. My mother called me *Moka*, a term of endearment a mother might offer to her son, or a wife to her husband—only, I had a little trouble with the literal translation of this one. According to my father, *Moka* can also mean Head of a Penis, so all this time my mother was calling me dickhead.

To the villagers, I was known by the Yanomami name of *Ayopowe*, which roughly translates as "walkabout" or "detour." The name was given to me by mother's brother, an uncle I called *Shoape*. He was one of the few people remaining in the village who remembered my father, from twenty years earlier, and when I arrived in the village, after spending the first night in the jungle with my mother in Hasupuwe, Shoape greeted me with a force field of emotion. He was an old man, even by Western standards—by the math of the jungle, he was practically ancient. He had once been the headman of the *Hasupuwe-teri* during my father's time and now he was a respected elder. He approached me, with great ceremony and great kindness. I did not know how to respond, so I tried to respond in kind. Whatever he would do, I would do. He put his hand on my shoulder, so I put my hand on his shoulder. He smiled, so I smiled. He patted me on the back, so I patted him on the back, all while he was talking a million words a minute in Yanomami. I'd been studying words and phrases, but he spoke so fast I couldn't make out a thing.

Hortensia Caballero, an anthropologist from Caracas who organized my return to my mother's village, and *Sor* Antonietta, one of the Catholic missionaries who accompanied us on this leg of the trip, took turns helping to translate, and here is what they told me Shoape was saying:

This is the truth. You are Yanomami. You are a part of this village. You are Irokai-teri. *You are my nephew. You are a part of this village, nephew. You are Yanomami.*

(The Yanomami tend to repeat themselves, I was learning.)

The headman became so emotional in his welcome that even a jungle-toughened scientist like Hortensia was moved to tears—a sight, frankly, that reinforced for me the deep connections my father had made in the territory, the rich history we all shared.

Shoape proceeded to dub me *Ayopowe*, suggesting that I had taken the long way around, reminding me that I had come from this place and had now returned to it, a journey that had taken many long years.

The name fit: *Detour.* The long way around—the story of my life, really. It takes me a while to get where I'm going, but eventually I find my way.

IT IS IN MY nature, apparently, to take my sweet time—as I am doing here. I've taken the long way around in telling my parents' story, so let me get back to it. My father was good to his word to Longbeard and accepted the betrothal. Nothing would come of it, he felt sure.

In the meantime, there was the matter of bride payment, the flip side of what we know as a dowry. In Yanomami marriages, the man offers gifts and services to his wife's family, almost like a formal transaction to seal the deal, so my father provided pots and pans, machetes and fishhooks. Already he had been providing these things to the villagers as trade items in exchange for their many kindnesses, but now he made them available directly to my mother's family as well. They were like a down payment, an indication of his intent to marry—although at this stage my father had no idea what that might mean or if it would ever come about. If anything he was sowing the seeds for a future relationship, and in the present moment he was cementing his close ties to this one family group as a way to make him feel at home in that remote part of the world.

Things went on in this way for the next while, and over time there was a deepening relationship between my mother and father. Typically it was a full-on family affair. As a unit, they spent more and more time together; in groups of three, they spent more and more time together; one-on-one, they spent more time together. My father came and went—returning to the United States to complete his studies and prepare for his next trip. Sometimes he was gone for months at a stretch, sometimes for years, and as he spent more and more time away from the jungle, he found himself thinking more and more of Yarima, who despite my father's initial disinterest in a romantic relationship was growing up to be a beautiful young woman.

Was he drawn to her at this point, in a romantic way? It wasn't the sort of thing we discussed around our house when I was growing up, and my father's book offers no absolute clues, but I have to think he was fond of her. There was affection, of a kind. She was becoming a woman—especially in the eyes of the Yanomami men in her village. And so I believe my father's feelings of fondness and affection began to turn in this way as well. He began to see her as other men in the village began to see her—to think of what was possible between them instead of what was impossible between them.

When he was away for long periods, my father spent a lot of

time looking at pictures. He traveled with a photo album, and hundreds and hundreds of slides. In some of the pictures, Yarima wore some of the Western-style clothes he had given to her—a red shirt, pants, sneakers—the first clothes she had ever worn in her life.

On one return trip, my father journeyed up the Orinoco and began to suspect that the *Hasupuwe-teri* were no longer on the river, that they had moved farther inland. There was a stillness on the water my father could not at first understand or explain away. He stopped first in the village of Patahama, in part to rest up for the next leg of his journey, but also to inquire about the *Hasupuwe-teri*. More and more, he was thinking of Yarima and her immediate family; more and more, it was *his* family now, and he longed to reconnect, so he was surprised to find himself anxious about their well-being. And what he found in Patahama was distressing; the village had been hit by an outbreak of malaria— what the Yanomami called *prisi-prisi*. Many of the *Patahama-teri* were lying in their hammocks, deathly ill. The ones with the strength to walk were thin, haggard, moving slowly.

Perhaps the malaria explained the *stillness* my father had felt. Perhaps it was the spirits, warning him away.

My father, together with a friend from Caracas who accompanied him on this trip, gave medicine—500 mg tablets of chloroquine—to the *Patahama-teri* they thought they could save, but it was too late for many of them, and as he made his way through the village he could see the shamans chanting over the bodies of the dead and dying. These people were sick, and he was traveling with medicines that could potentially cure them of that sickness, so that became his focus, his purpose.

The Yanomami death rituals were elaborate, and here my father got to see them take on a sickening hue. The family keens and moans and mourns around the body of the deceased all night long. In the morning, they dress the body with ceremonial paint and feathers. Typically, they'll burn the body at this point, and after the village shamans perform their ceremonial chants any remaining bones of the deceased are collected, ground, and mixed with a plantain or banana drink. Then close relatives imbibe the sacred mixture, returning the body to its source, strengthening the bodies of the living with the spirit of the departed. But when a body dies from a sickness like the *prisi-prisi*, the Yanomami worry it's contagious; they worry that the smoke from the burning corpse will infect them, too, so here the few healthy *Patahama-teri* were carrying these decorated dead bodies into the jungle, where they were wrapped in mats and placed on a raised platform. There the bodies would remain for a period of time until the shamans determined that they were free of the poisonous spirits and could be cremated.

As he looked on in this clinical way, my father caught himself thinking of Yarima and her family— *his* family. He saw his thinking become less clinical, more personal. He could only hope that the *prisi-prisi* had not infected the *Hasupuwe-teri*. He knew what it meant in this part of the world when density-dependent diseases like malaria spread through a community; he knew that one of the ways the Yanomami had learned to deal with an epidemic was to essentially abandon ship—to quit the *shabono* and disperse into the rainforest, a basic social buffering measure to stop an outbreak from spreading any further.

My father had himself felt the devastating ravages of malaria, so he knew how these good people were suffering. He worried— more, perhaps, than he would have expected himself to. He could not get to her quickly enough—and yet, when he finally arrived at the *Hasupuwe-teri*'s inland *shabono* and learned that Yarima and her family were not sick, he did not go to her immediately. He noticed her across the way, but they did not talk. It was not the Yanomami way, to make a big deal out of greeting each other after a long journey—even after a separation of eight long months. Instead he hung his hammock, unpacked his few things, and tended to the people of the village who had gotten sick. It wasn't until later that night, after the evening meal, that he and Yarima greeted each other and began to get reacquainted.

Over the next few weeks, my parents found ways to reestablish their friendship—that was all it was, at this point, and it was a tentative friendship at best. They had been apart for so long, they treated each other like strangers for a time, but they fell into an easy rapport soon enough. The fact that many of the villagers were gravely ill lent a certain intensity to their relationship during this period, as my father continued to dispense his supply of medicine and the village shamans gathered each day to chase away the *prisi-prisi* spirits. Probably, too, my father could see the way the other young men of the village looked at my mother, but he could not think in this way or pursue any new type of relationship because within a short while he was struggling with a second bout of malaria. He came down with a fever, and right away, he knew. This time, he realized sheepishly, he'd foolishly given away the last of his chloroquine. Instead he gave himself a healthy dose of Fansidar—a relatively new antimalarial drug that was said to have severe side effects.

By his symptoms, he determined that he had *Plasmodium falciparum*, a particularly lethal strain of malaria that left its victims feeling like they were tied to a yo-yo string, suffering through cycles of paroxysms, high fever, and exhaustion. One day they'd feel like they were about to make a miraculous recovery; two days later they would take a turn for the worse. This would go on for weeks, so as the disease passed through my father's system, there were moments when he was able to work—able, even, to trek back to Patahama to witness the funeral ceremony for the malaria victims whose bodies had been hung in the jungle to allow the evil spirits to exit the corpse as it putrefied— followed by moments where it felt to him like he was about to die. He was in and out of sleep, in and out of fever dreams, and then up and about like there was nothing wrong with him. This went on for weeks, and during this time Yarima and her mother came to him and tended to him alongside the village shamans, but in his moments of relative strength my father could only focus on his return to health.

Happily, mercifully, my father survived this second bout of malaria, and when he was well enough to travel the *Hasupuwe-teri* made a bed for him in a canoe and sent him downriver with a guide, to make his way out of the territory. Yarima came with her mother and brother to see him off, but there was no display of emotion, no grand farewells. Again, it was not the Yanomami way. He was going, and soon he would come back. Or, not.

UPPER ORINOCO, YANOMAMI TERRITORY

We continued our trek—my mother very often leading the way, and me just as often the last in line. I struggled to keep up. From time to time, I'd drop so far back I couldn't see the person up ahead of me—a momentary flash-worry because I couldn't always be sure where I was going.

This deep in the rainforest, the trails were unlike anything I could have recognized back home. Typically, there was only a thin sliver of clearing to mark our way, but the Yanomami knew precisely where they stood. They would get where they needed to go.

The person in front would hack away at the brush with a machete, and the others would follow, but by the time I'd catch up the jungle seemed to swallow this fresh trail and leave me wondering. At times I could only listen to know where I was going.

After a while, we reached a larger clearing—another creek, this one accented by two giant boulders reaching up from the water. Two women had begun to fish from these boulders—a tricky business since the slopes of the boulders were fairly smooth and slick with moss. One of the women was my mother's sister—my aunt, who was a few years older than my mother, which by Yano-mami standards made her one of the village elders.

We used worms for bait, which we collected from the creek bed. I was still fighting with the language, so most of my communication happened through pointing, through pantomime. One of the women showed me what to do and I followed along.

Since my father's time in the region, many Yanomami villages had moved more and more to the river, where they fished by hook and line, so we fished in this way as well, hand-casting from the big, slippery boulders. I had only been in the jungle a couple of weeks by this point, and I was still acclimating to the region, to the routines. I had no real experience in the wilderness. I couldn't start a fire without a matchbook or a lighter, and I was deathly afraid of bugs. (In fact, ever since I'd announced I wanted to return to the rainforest to find my mother, my fear of bugs was a running joke in my family; nobody could understand how I planned to survive in the Amazon if a ladybug frightened me.) And as for the patience you needed to fish . . . well, mine was in short supply.

Wherever possible, I tried to mimic the others and fit myself in, but my unfamiliarity and my unease gave me away. Clearly I was no outdoorsman. There was one moment, as I stood on one of the moss-slick boulders and waited for a nibble, when I noticed a small spider crawling across my ankles, and I tried my best not to shriek. I waggled my foot, to shake the thing away, but the spider held fast, so I called out to one of the women closest to where I was standing. I pointed to the spider and nervously asked, "Wai-teri?" Loosely translated, it meant "fierce," and I hoped that if I said it over and over, lifting my voice each time as in a question, it would be like asking if the spider-thingy was dangerous.

"Wai-teri! Wai-teri!"

It was the best I could manage, and the only response that came back was some pointing and snickering, which of *course was the only response I deserved. When the others were through laughing at me, they returned to their tasks, and it was then that I noticed my mother was nowhere in sight. I didn't think anything of it at first—no doubt she'd slipped away for a beat to complete another task, unknown to me. The others continued to talk and fish and make themselves busy, as before, so I returned my attention to the fish line in my hand and tried my best to keep my balance on that slippery rock. The continuing conversation may or may not have had anything to do with me, or my mother, or my apparent fear of spiders, but I couldn't help but think it might. In the few weeks I'd been living among my rainforest family, I had learned to tell when the others were talking about me. It wasn't hard since usually the talk was accompanied by snickering and pointing in my direction.*

For now I seemed to be in the clear. Whatever kind of fool I had just made of myself, I was no longer the center of attention. In fact, something else had come up—a turn in the weather. All of a sudden the skies began to darken. The trees began to rustle. The rainforest floor went from lush to ominous. This was a cause for some alarm—at least to me. The others, they were used to the flashstorms that shook the jungle with such a surge of violence it would feel for a few terrible moments like the world was coming to an end. Already I had been on the downspout end of a few of these storms, but each time I had been in the safety of the mission compound, or the shabono. Here I was out in the open—separated, I now realized, from the one person in the rainforest I could turn to for protection, for reassurance.

My mother. My lifeline.

Just then, just as the sky turned darker still and the wind kicked up a couple of notches more, I heard my mother's voice. It seemed to come from the thick of jungle on the far side of the creek. It came through faintly at first. It wasn't a scream so much as a trill, but it pierced the stormy sky.

"Twee!"

It was not a word I recognized from my limited Yanomami vocabulary, but there it was again.

"Twee!"

I followed the sound of my mother's voice and turned just as she appeared through a curtainlike opening along the bank of the creek. She was running, with her hands in the air, like she was being chased by a bad guy, determined to show she was unarmed.

"Twee! Twee!"

I could not imagine what was going on.

CHAPTER TWO

Reunion, Union

MY FATHER WAS THINKING CLEARLY as he set off on the Orinoco, but even he could not say when he might return. There were a lot of personal, professional, academic, and financial issues he had to take care of. He needed to develop a source of income. He needed to spend some time in the United States. He needed to make his way to Munich, to discuss his ongoing (and increasingly tense) relationship with the Max Planck Institute, but the first order of business was to meet with Marvin Harris, who had by now moved from Columbia University to the University of Florida, in Gainesville.

Basically, my father needed to get his act together. He was a thirty-six-year-old graduate student; his career was very much in a state of flux and he realized he had to kick things up a notch and complete his doctoral degree. Believe me, if there's anyone who can understand my father's mind-set during this period, it's me. In and out of graduate school, back and forth to the rainforest, with no clear path to a certain future . . . it's become *my* story now, right down to my money worries, my career worries, my relationship worries, but like everything else it started with my father, and it felt to him like he was treading water, running in place.

37

With Harris the closest thing he now had to a mentor, it made sense to follow him to Florida, so that's what my father eventually did, and as he put the pieces of his life in the developed world back in order he thought back on this last frustrating visit to my mother's village. He was there for only three months, and during most of that time he was sick as a dog, delirious, in and out of his hammock. He did not have the energy to devote to my mother, and now that he was back on American soil this was looming as a great regret. A part of him wished he had not even made this last trip—it nearly killed him, and it brought him no closer to Yarima. It surprised him that he kept thinking of my mother in this way—but, clearly, he was developing feelings for her.

As things played out, my father would not return to the jungle for almost two years, and in that time he was all over the place—literally, figuratively, and every way in between. The next time he saw Yarima it was December 1980. A lot had changed in her part of the world; and yet, on a purely personal (and biological) level, a lot had remained the same. My mother still hadn't reached the age of maturity (meaning she had yet to menstruate), so the relationship they shared was not about to become sexual. It wasn't even a prospect, as far as my father was concerned. Again, there was no way to know Yarima's exact age, except to compare her physical development to Western girls of about the same age, although even here there would be mitigating factors such as psycho-social differences, family history and diet, exercise and sleep habits, so that a true comparison was impossible. Anyway, my father wasn't thinking along these lines, even as he was beginning to look on his time with Yarima as one of the more important relationships in his life—a friendship that served to knit him to the Yanomami people, and one that awakened in him a part of his personality he himself didn't recognize. With Yarima he found that he could laugh in ways he had never laughed before; he could be more like himself and less like the serious, guarded, results-oriented graduate student he was pretending to be.

Even so, he could not understand the place he had made for
Yarima in his heart. She was exotic and beautiful, this was true,
but at that time he did not think of her in a romantic or even a
sexual way. At least, he didn't *think* he thought of her like this,
even as he was strangely drawn to her.

The relationship between my mother and father was very much
a Yanomami relationship; it sprang from a society where young
women were given a great deal of responsibility and treated in
many ways as adults; it came about organically, rooted very much
in time and place. When my father was in the United States, or
in Germany, his feelings didn't make a whole lot of sense to him;
when he was in the jungle, he didn't even consider them—they
were just the sweet by-product of his time there, so of course he
found himself longing to return.

Soon enough, he did—to continue his research through the
auspices of the Max Planck Institute.

In the years my father had been away from the rainforest, there
had been a kind of fission in the village of Hasupuwe. This is a key
aspect of Yanomami village life and it rates an explanation here.
What happened was the two main lineages of the *Hasupuwe-teri*
had had a falling-out and went their separate ways. Here the two
sides of an escalating conflict simply agreed to disagree; it was
like the story of the Hatfields versus the McCoys, only without
the bloodshed and blind hatred. Whatever was at issue, it was
resolved with this somewhat amicable separation, as in a civilized
divorce. One group moved deeper into the jungle and built a new
shabono. Of course there were family ties that would always bind
one group to the other. Individuals from one group would often
visit friends and family in the other group—for a day, a week, or
longer—but in almost every respect they were no longer a single,
unified community.

And yet even this description of the rift among the *Hasupuwe-
teri* is filtered through my own ethnocentric view. The reality of
what transpired in the village during my father's time away can
never be truly known to a Westerner, because there's no true

cross-cultural corollary. About the best I've come up with is the following scenario: Let's say you're married, with several children. You and your wife live with your cousin, who stays in the basement. You come to rely on your cousin's contribution each month to keep up with the rent and other household expenses. He is also married, with several kids of his own. You find out that your cousin is having an affair with your wife while you are away at work. Because of your financial situation or other outside factors, you have no choice but to allow your cousin to remain in your home. Things go on as before—you share food, heat, water. You are forced to see him every morning. On its face, this seems like it would be an untenable situation, doesn't it? Wouldn't you want to kick him to the curb? Or move away with your family? But imagine that these options just weren't possible. Imagine that you and your cousin and your two families were so tightly and inextricably bound to each other that separating was out of the question. There would be a growing resentment and anger. There would be fistfights and quarrels. Who knows . . . in a heated moment, you might even reach for your gun and shoot your cousin—an extreme outcome that also happens in the jungle.

You see, the Yanomami are not immune to isolated incidents of domestic violence, which is why I've come to look on this type of village fission as an elegant social adaptation to mitigate conflicts and keep them from escalating to lethal violence. Over time, the remaining family ties would fall away with the generations, ever more so as these newly established villages moved through the jungle and continued on in their nomadic ways, but in the years immediately following a break the points of interconnection were many—and deep. Their interests remained aligned, for the next while. This was the situation that greeted my father when he was finally able to return to the region. As soon as possible, he made his way to Hasupuwe, but my mother and her immediate family had moved on with several other family lineage groups to establish a new village a few miles away. He immediately sent for them. It was nothing for them to travel the short distance to reunite with him here, so that's what happened.

Once again, my parents kind of circled around each other when Yarima and her family made their way back to Hasupuwe from the nearby village of Irokai. Once again, there was no tearful reunion. In fact, they barely acknowledged each other across the *shabono*, only to approach each other slowly, tentatively as the day wore on.

Here is how my father described their time together, once they were reunited:

We went fishing and gathering together, sometimes with her brother, sometimes just the two of us. In the evening she would roast plantains for our dinner and prepare whatever meat might have been brought in from a hunt and distributed. During the night I would see her get up to tend her fire, adding wood to keep the sleepers warm. I felt I wanted to squeeze each day, to keep it from ending. But the time slipped by like magic, and as hard as I tried to put our return out of my mind, it loomed closer and closer. . . .

The way it worked out, this was one of my father's shortest stays in the territory—a period of mere weeks. During that time my father had a kind of fission of his own with Professor Irenäus Eibl-Eibesfeldt of the Max Planck Institute; the two had been at cross-purposes for some time leading up to this trip, and the situation came to a head in the jungle, to the point where my father believed he had no choice but to remove himself from the program. Specifically, my father broke with Eibl-Eibesfeldt over his approach to the work. My father could be prickly about his professional relationships, I learned years later as I read over his notes and talked to him about his fieldwork, and here had had no patience for the research methods of Irenäus Eibl-Eibes felt. Ultimately, he decided he could no longer continue to work with Eibl-Eibesfeldt, and to remove himself from the study, which in turn meant my father would have to remove himself from the jungle as well, since of course he was there on the institute's dime.

(I had the chance to meet with Eibl-Eibesfeldt and my father many years later, and the two of them got along like long-lost pals, with no signs of the rancor or professional frustration that had marked their time as colleagues, so I guess even a prickly anthropologist like my father was able to soften over time.)

Leaving the jungle was one thing, but leaving Yarima . . . well, my father wasn't quite sure what to make of it. It might have been unavoidable in this instance, even inevitable, given the tensions between him and Eibl-Eibesfeldt, but it still troubled him. Unlike his previous departures from the territory, this one was laced with an emotional uncertainty. All during this time, my father was having trouble sorting through his feelings about my mother. She was on the verge of womanhood, no longer a child, and yet he could not tell if the affection he felt for her was familial . . . or something else, something more. He worried about Yarima's safety. This was a related worry, because it tied in to the betrothal; Yarima was promised to him, but once she reached womanhood, that promise would disappear if my father wasn't there to protect her.

This prospect terrified my father. He had only to close his eyes and picture that horrifying scene from his first extended stay, as he stood and watched his friend hauled off into the jungle and raped by the *huya*. He knew this sort of thing could happen to Yanomami women who had no husband or family to protect them, and it sickened him to think Yarima might be vulnerable in this way if he wasn't around. And he also knew that just being around wasn't enough to keep Yarima from the clutches of the young Yanomami men. He would need to be present *and* vigilant. He would need to guard her and protect her as she bathed, as she gathered food, as she chopped firewood. Whenever she left the safety of the village, he would have to watch her.

He could never rest from watching her—until she bore him a child.

Still, he thought perhaps if he and Yarima were married—*truly* married—she might be spared, out of respect for his position in the community. And he knew the time to act on this thought was now, before he left the territory. But knowing it was time to act and knowing *how* to act were two different things, so he sought out his good friend Red for advice. Red was probably his closest, most trusted friend in the village. My father met him early on during his first extended stay; he dubbed him Red because he was wearing a red T-shirt the day they met. More than anyone else, Red had helped my father learn the language and customs of the *Hasupuwe-teri*. Red spoke slowly, syllable by syllable, so my father could take his time with each word. And once my father was able to speak pretty well, Red patiently helped in other ways. Basically, he was my father's guide to all things Yanomami, and over the years my father came to trust Red's insights on village life.

Red's advice was to make a speech, a *patamou*, in front of the entire village, during which my father could state his intentions and let everyone know Yarima was to be his wife. This made sense to my father, who by this time had been on the receiving end of dozens, maybe even hundreds of such speeches. They were a common occurrence; whenever someone had something important to say, he stood up and said it—loudly, with great conviction. It would be an honest, forceful, emotional speech, during which my father would make his farewells but vow to return. In a way, he would be staking his claim to a certain role within the community going forward—not only in regard to his relationship with my mother, but also to his place in the village.

The two friends worked on the speech together; my father practiced what he was going to say, and Red listened and gave his opinion on what parts to take out, what parts to leave in. Finally, the night before he was due to leave, my father stood beneath the *shabono* in the central area usually reserved for the headman to make his pronouncements—what amounted to center stage or the town square. Everyone was in their hammocks. My father had their full attention. And then he just went for it—whipping himself into a kind of frenzy as he spoke, slamming his fists repeatedly against his sides for emphasis.

Here is what he said, as he reported it in his book:

Today I am going away. But I am coming back. I am coming back. I am coming back. No one is to break into my storage house. If you do, when I come back I will be very angry. Very angry. And her [pointing to Yarima]. No one is to touch her. No one is to touch her! No one! She has been given to me! She is my wife! I have never touched any of your wives! You do not touch my wife! You do not touch my wife! If I come back and find out that someone has touched her, I will know! I myself have never touched her! And no one else is going to! No one!

As I read that passage, it made me think of that great iconic scene from *The Terminator* when Arnold Schwarzenegger utters that famous line: "I'll be back." I imagined my father's impassioned appeal had the same kind of chilling effect, especially the way he kept repeating himself, in classic Yanomami style.

He'd made his point.

IT WAS ALMOST A year before my father found another path back to the jungle—and for a beat or two, he almost didn't take it. At the end of 1981, he was offered the opportunity to conduct a Yanomami census on behalf of the Venezuelan government, so he felt he had to consider it carefully. The work itself would be unexciting, routine, but it would be a chance return to the territory—this time for a project that would come with a budget, a salary, and the luxury and convenience of helicopter travel, which would put the whole of the Venezuelan rainforest within reach. He would be responsible for an area in Yanomami territory known as "sector six," a vast region that stretched between the Orinoco and Siapa rivers and included my mother's village as well as a great many neighboring villages my father had already visited. So that was another argument in favor of taking the gig.

The one worry here was that he'd been away from my mother for too, too long, and this was the main argument against accepting the census job. After so much time, my father felt certain that his opportunity with Yarima was lost. She would be married to another by now. The thought of her with another man, perhaps even with a child by that other man, was almost too much for him, but the thought of never living among these good people he had come to love was equally depressing, so in the end he signed on for yet another Amazon adventure. Where it would lead him, he could not guess; he couldn't even be sure it would lead him back to my mother.

My father's job with the census bureau was to identify all the villages in the indigenous territories by air, and then to spend some time in each village and count and categorize the inhabitants— simple enough for someone with his experience in the region. One of his first stops on land was the village of Patahama, which he'd last visited in the midst of that terrible malaria outbreak. My father told me he pretty much raced through his work, took a quick head count, and continued inland to Hasupuwe.

Sure enough, Yarima had moved on. In fact, her entire lineage had moved on, so my father's heart sank. His good friend Red was in the village, but he was strangely silent about Yarima. My father didn't want to bring her up, and Red didn't offer any information, so the two men talked about other things. My father went about his work, reacclimated to these familiar surroundings. He stayed for three days, and in all that time Red didn't mention Yarima, so by this point my father was feeling frustrated and confused. It was a curious stalemate. My father didn't want to be the one to bring her up, but he didn't know how much longer he could last in her old village with no word of her.

Finally, my mother arrived in the village. It was a great and welcome surprise. Everyone in the village seemed to stop what they were doing when she appeared through an opening in the *shabono*. The others all knew her circumstance, of course. They knew of her betrothal to my father. They knew, too, that Yarima had at last had her period—what the Yanomami call the *yiipimou*. There's a whole ceremony for it, so they definitely knew—it's the jungle equivalent of tweeting about it, or posting it on Facebook. When a woman starts to menstruate for the first time, she is cast out into the jungle in a special house built just for this occasion, made from the leaves of what the Yanomami called a *yiipi* tree. The women in her family bring her food while she stays in this special house. When she is finished with her period, the women return and dress her in ceremonial garb, while the others in the village gather by the family hearth and welcome her back to the community.

So, clearly, it's a great big deal—and, also clearly, Yarima returning to my father after all this time was a big deal, too. Really, it was just one big deal piled on top of another, and it was different from all those other times, all those other reunions. This time, my parents didn't circle each other awkwardly. This time, they didn't complete their chores and go about their daily business before seeking each other out. This time, my mother walked straight to my father. She was carrying a kind of bouquet—a fistful of roots. And she was crying.

They did not embrace—it was not the Yanomami way. But it was a joyful, tearful reunion. Then my mother hung her hammock next to my father's and they were married. Just like that.

It would be some time before the relationship was consummated—but here again, I'm a little sketchy on the details. At this point it was expected that she marry and become pregnant and start a family; it was the way of things, and my father had lived long enough in the territory to understand that it was the way of things, and that he was now a part of that.

Still, my father wanted to make sure he and Yarima were comfortable with each other, that my mother didn't feel rushed. Yanomami couples don't share a bed, or hammock, the way couples do in most Western societies. This appears to be a tradition born of practicality, more than anything else: the typical Yanomami hammock can barely hold one adult body, so the idea of two people getting comfortable enough to sleep in such a cramped sling doesn't even occur to them. That's one of the great innovations my father brought to his time in the jungle. He traveled with a big, roomy cotton hammock, so my parents developed the habit of sleeping together—a first in that part of the world. They did this even before they consummated their relationship, and that kind of closeness, that kind of intimacy, played an important part in moving their relationship to a physical one.

(I'm betting it also raised a few Yanomami eyebrows, because no one in the village had ever seen a husband and wife behaving in just this way. They were a regular pair of trailblazers, my parents.)

This having-sex-in-broad-daylight in the jungle was another aspect of Yanomami marriage my father had to take his time with. Red actually advised him on this—the same way he advised him on most things. He told my father to take my mother swimming, or fishing, or gathering. This was where the action was, apparently—so much so that the Yanomami have even developed a kind of euphemism to describe the marital act. A husband might say to his wife, *We have not been out gathering for a long time. A*nd she will take his meaning.

Curiously, the Yanomami are not inclined to this kind of subtlety in their language. To be clear, they have a terrific sense of humor. They love to laugh and joke. But a Yanomami sense of humor has more to do with slapstick and silliness than it does with clever wordplay, so euphemisms like these are uncommon—or maybe it's just that some of the layers of meaning are lost in translation. Whatever it is, it's more likely you'll hear men and women speak bluntly about personal subjects, instead of talking around an issue in a suggestive way, so here I have to think the colloquialism is not meant as euphemism at all. It's not some coy expression. It means exactly what it means, on its face. It must be that to a Yanomami woman, the sex act is somehow tied to the act of swimming, or fishing, or gathering, or whatever activity she is asked to participate in alone with her husband that provides the opportunity for the sex act to take place.

As long as I'm on it, let me just share another few thoughts on sex among the Yanomami. Typically, it's the husband who will initiate this type of outing, seeking to create one of these private moments. I don't know this from firsthand experience, but this is what I've learned from the ethnographies I've read, from my father, from my Yanomami brothers and cousins. In my father's book, I learned the word *waikou*—meaning, to hump—only it is most often used by the young men of the village who cannot imagine what it must be like to have sex with someone who moves with her partner, whose enthusiasm matches their own.

SO THERE WERE MY mother and father, living as man and wife, at long last. They were finally married, in every sense, but their routines were very different from the routines of other Yanomami couples. The most obvious difference was that my father was required to leave the village every so often to work on his census-taking project. This kind of behavior was so far removed from the norm, the Yanomami didn't even have the language to describe it. Sometimes my father left the territory entirely—once or twice, to return to the United States to deliver a paper or to pursue some aspect of his doctoral work. This was an adjustment for both of them, I think. For my mother, there was no model for this type of "marriage" in her village; with the exception of brief hunting or gathering trips inland or upriver, husbands and wives were together, so she struggled to understand these long separations. For my father, the time apart was troubling for the same reasons as before; until she gave birth to a child, Yarima was considered fair game, so he made sure to keep these trips short and to make his presence known each time he left and then again each time he returned - not unlike the way an animal might mark his territory.

Soon he was able to set some of these worries aside because Yarima became pregnant, in the spring of 1983—at least, my father *thought* she was pregnant, but he had to return to Caracas before it could be confirmed. It was a time of great consequence for him, but my mother and her family and the other villagers would have taken this sort of thing in stride. My father tried to take this possible development in stride, too, but in his mind it was too big for that. The idea of a child forced him to think more permanently about his time in the jungle. His marriage to Yarima had never been a passing union; he was committed to building a life with my mother, whatever that life might entail, wherever it might unfold. But with a baby on the way, he found himself thinking of ways to remain in the village in an open-ended situation; he thought in traditional Western terms about things like providing for his young family and building a future. In Yanomami terms, there was no such thing as building for the future—at least, not as a Westerner would perceive it. There was only the present; a child simply meant that you continued on as before, with another mouth to feed, that's all.

If Yarima was in fact pregnant, he would no longer have to worry about her safety when he was called away for his work, but the pregnancy just replaced one set of worries with another, and another, and another—whole *subsets* of worries, really. The one constant worry that seemed to touch on all these others was work. As his census project neared completion, my father started having all kinds of trouble with his working papers—that's why he'd had to head back to Caracas. While the project was underway, he had a special permit issued to him by the president's office, but with the project at an end that permit would expire. He could apply for another one, through Venezuela's Bureau of Indian Affairs, but it involved a mess of bureaucratic red tape and assorted nonsense. It could take months for the paperwork to come through—or, after a long wait, it might not come through at all. He would have to come up with some other options to continue on in the territory in an open-ended way, but for the time being he was coming up empty, so he stayed in town and did what he could to move the permit process along in a face-to-face way.

For weeks he was stuck in Caracas, trying to navigate all that government bureaucracy, and he wasn't doing such a great job of it; he was no closer to solving his permit problem than he'd been in the beginning. Before he'd left, he only suspected my mother was pregnant—she'd missed her period, was all. And now there was this: the longer he was away, the more he wanted to believe Yarima was in fact pregnant. It surprised him that he found himself wishing for a baby in just this way. They had hardly had time to discuss it, to consider what a baby might mean. And yet the more he wanted to believe it, the more it killed him not to know, either way.

Here I believe it's instructive to point out that certain factions of the Venezuelan government were not particularly welcoming to American involvement with the indigenous tribes of the rainforest. If a Venezuelan native from Puerto Ayacucho fell in love with a Yanomami woman, it would not have been seen as such a big deal; however, an American anthropologist like my father was not given the same kind of free pass. That said, I don't think he worried too, too much about the political or logistical consequences of his relationship with my mother. He followed his heart, even as it led him down a precipitous path. The same could be said about how the anthropological community might have perceived his actions, and he didn't give a shit about those people, either.

At one point, he met a Yanomami man he knew on the streets of Caracas. He did not particularly like this man, but he stopped to greet him anyway. The man remarked that my father looked thin compared to the last time they had seen each other. The man said there was a reason for this: his wife must be pregnant.

The Yanomami, we know this truth, the man said. A *pregnant wife makes the husband skinny.*

In this way, my father knew.

Sadly, my mother had a miscarriage, in about her sixth month of pregnancy, according to my father's best guess. It was more of a stillbirth than a miscarriage, that's how far along she was, but the result was the same: there would be no child, after all. My mother had told my father she was pregnant when he finally returned to the village—by this time, she was clearly showing. She had done some best-guess calculations of her own. She pointed to her swollen belly and explained it the best way she knew: *Two moons and two moons*—meaning, she was about four months along.

My father had been overjoyed with the news, and now he was devastated. But my mother's reaction to losing this child was more typical of the Yanomami. She simply said, *We will make another baby.*

Soon enough, they did . . . and that baby was me. It happened about a year later, about a month or so after my father finally received word from the Bureau of Indian Affairs that he had been granted a one-year permit to continue his work in the region. It was a year of turmoil. My father was grieving for this unborn child and stressing about a way to remain in the territory, and underneath all that he was facing a series of scandalous charges brought by the Venezuelan government that he had somehow "stolen" the wife of another Yanomami man. Specifically, the charges were brought by Venezuelan Bureau of Indian Affairs. As far as my father could ever determine, the charges stemmed from a vengeful move made by an acculturated Yanomami who had taken it on himself to charge outsiders a "toll" every time they came in and out of the territory. When my father refused to pay, the man looked to trip him up in what ways he could—and he was helped along in this by a sympathetic functionary in the bureau who also had it out for my father. This was just one way government officials tried to make my father's life so difficult he would eventually leave the country. If you read between the lines of every allegation, my father was cast as a kind of interloper, a *nabuh* who'd set upon these unsuspecting members of the Yanomami tribe and tried to insert himself where he did not belong.

The upshot of this year of turmoil and all these crazy,

unfounded charges was that my parents were being tugged and pulled from the simple pleasures of village life, forced to confront the harsh, perhaps prejudicial realities that seemed to flow from their transparently "mixed" marriage. Beneath the tug and pull was the lesson that the outside world was not meant to mix with the indigenous people of the rainforest.

Somewhere in there, my mother was issued a national identity card, which my father believed she needed to move about the country freely, and as she did she was removed more and more from the only world she had known. She went with my father and her older brother to Puerto Ayacucho and then on to Caracas, to clear one bureaucratic hurdle after another. The disconnect between these major metropolitan areas and their simple *shabono* in the thrush of the Orinoco was incomprehensibly vast. Really, it cannot be overstated. She'd never been out of the jungle—to her, the whole world was the rainforest. If she was told she was moving to another place, another village, she could only assume it would be another village much like her own, with another *shabono*, another garden. She had no frame of reference for what she was about to see and experience: skyscrapers, elevators, armed policemen (and women!), traffic, a teeming mass of people . . . it was all impossible to consider, impossible to take in.

My mother looked out at all those people on the busy streets of downtown Caracas and said to my father, *They are like the ants that travel through the forest.*

The availability of such an abundance and variety of food was one of the hardest things for my mother and her brother to comprehend. It made no sense to them that there should be such plenty, and my father recalls taking my mother to a restaurant during this period and seeing her become frustrated when the waitress came by to ask my mother in Spanish what she wanted to eat, waiting impatiently for my father to translate.

"It aggravated her that someone would ask something so ridiculous," he wrote in his book, "and instead of answering she'd tell me to make whoever it was stop talking such nonsense."

But such nonsense found my parents and my uncle at every turn. For a while during my their short stay in Caracas, a friend loaned my father a motorcycle so he could get around town, racing to appointments with lawyers to see about his permit status and to clear the various charges against him—and, to academics and conservationists to see about the many grant requests he had pending. Once she got over the fear of the motorcycle and understood it for what it was (she'd thought it was some sort of beast, at first!), my mother used to climb on the back and hold tight to my father's waist as he raced with it down the Turgua mountainside. Oh man! What an odd picture that must have made! And yet it was a clear indication of my mother's openness and courage that she would make such a leap from her familiar routines into such unknown territory—and a testimony to the trust she'd placed in my father, the tall, ghost-tongued *nabuh* with the big forehead who seemed about to whisk her away, away, away.

As soon as it was feasible my parents returned to their village, together with my uncle. For a while they lived as they had lived before—simply, organically, peacefully. Soon a small grant came through, allowing my father to remain in the jungle for another few months; soon after that, another permit was granted. Life was allowed to continue—permit to permit. And yet for all those beautiful forces that had brought my parents together, there was now an ugliness that threatened to tear them apart . . . and it was into this environment that I was finally conceived.

UPPER ORINOCO, YANOMAMI TERRITORY

My mother came tearing out of that brush like her hair had been set on fire. She was waving her arms, yelling, dashing back and forth. It was almost funny, the way she was flailing around, but she moved with such a sense of urgency and purpose it was clear we were all in some kind of danger.

The others, I could see, were not laughing.

I figured out soon enough what my mother was trying to say. She was pointing to the branches of the high trees, motioning for me to get out of the way, shouting a word she half-remembered from her time in the States twenty years earlier.

"Twee! Twee!"

Tree! Tree!

Her warning was not just meant for me, of course, but she said it in a language she hoped I could understand, even if there was a little something lost in the translation. Her body language helped to fill in the blanks, and I soon joined the others as we scrambled for cover in the narrow shelter made by the two giant boulders. The rocks were about ten feet tall. They formed a natural lean-

to at the point where they touched, and I huddled beneath with my mother, my two wives, the other woman, and her child. Imagine five or six people crouching beneath a dining room table—that's the picture we must have made. We were pressed close to each other in this tight space—so close I could hear my mother's breathing. I could smell her smells, feel her heat. She was not out of breath, the way I might have been if I'd sprinted out of the jungle like that. She smiled, in a satisfied way, and as the skies opened up and dumped down on us she touched my wrist, sweetly.

We all sat there silently for the next while, waiting for the storm to pass—me, plainly terrified; the others, less so. Our makeshift lean-to didn't do such a great job protecting us from the rain, which hit us hard in a sidelong way, but we were safe from falling tree limbs and other debris.

It was a violent, microburst-type storm. I'd never experienced a storm like this in the middle of the jungle; it was nothing like the flash thunderstorms you'd sometimes see back home. It was upon us in an instant, and it lasted only a few instants more. The rain pelted down on us in an aggressive way—at least, that's how it felt to me when I was in the storm's middle. For a terrifying few moments, the still waters of the creak ebbed and rippled like a stretch of rapids, the thin trees leaned away from the wind like windshield wipers, branches cracked and fell to the rainforest floor. Absolutely I was scared, but I held my mother's gaze throughout. She could only touch my wrist and smile.

The whole time, there was nothing to say.

I was super-aware of my environment, in awe of the raw power of the rainforest, trying to analyze the precariousness of our situation, unaware of the extent of the danger we could have been in. The others didn't appear too worried; they were calm, chill. Me, not so much. I huddled in the small space made by these two boulders. I pulled off my shirt and wrapped it around my camera, thinking it would protect it *from the rain, but as I looked down I was freaked out by all the bugs crawling at my feet—I guess they were a little put out by the storm, too.*

I looked around at my Yanomami "family" huddled with me in this makeshift shelter. The women were all topless. Their faces were variously decorated with tribal markings; their noses, pierced with hii-hi sticks. The child was completely naked. Outwardly, I tried to play it cool, but in my head I was saying, "Holy shit!" I imagine now that the others were anxious too, but they did not show it.

Despite the differences in our clothing and demeanor, despite the differences in our approach to adversity, our features looked very much the same. At least I looked the part, for now. I could stare into these same-seeming faces and feel as if I were looking in a mirror. My mother's face especially. There was no mistaking the fact that we were all connected, even as we fit together awkwardly beneath the shelter of these boulders. Even as we soldiered past these tense moments in the middle of this tropical storm.

At one point, during the worst of it, I looked over to my mother and caught her staring off into the trees. I wondered what she was thinking—if she was thinking anything at all. I imagined myself in her situation, just then. I considered her stoicism, her sense of calm, and tried to attach these aspects of character to my own worldview. Even out here in the rainforest, my mind wandered to mundane details like school, taxes, bills piling up at home. I thought of the perils of the storm. I thought of a dozen different scenarios that might keep us from returning to the relative safety of the shabono, and another dozen ways we might catch a break and continue on, as before.

And then there was my mother, soaking in the moment, her head very likely filled with nothing much at all beyond a certainty that this perilous moment would soon pass. She wore a kind of inadvertent smile. It didn't seem to indicate happiness or even contentment. For all I knew, it didn't indi-cate anything at all, but I took it to mean that all was right and good. I allowed myself to think that a piece of that small smile was meant for me; it was there because her son, her Davi was here by her side, home again after all this time.

At long last.

Once again, my mind reached back to a time twenty years earlier, when I might have splashed and played and sunned myself in this very spot. I closed my eyes and pictured my mother how she was then—young, playful, almost child-like herself. And yet I could not make the connection, to how things were for me as a child, in this rainforest, to how they were at just this moment. I worried that too much time had passed. I wondered if the time lost could ever be recaptured, if I could truly fit myself in—to this place, to these people.

For now, we appeared to be safe, but the harsh, wet wind hurried past the spaces between these two boulders and slapped us around. Through it all, my mother's expression remained unchanged—an absent smile, as she gazed off into the distance, studying the wind, studying the rain. She was unafraid. I had no idea what she was looking at, what she was thinking, but I could only look at her. I could only think of her. I could only think, This is my Amazonian mother, Yarima. I could only feel an enormous sense of pride, an overwhelming sense of disbelief . . . that I had come from this place, from these people.

And then I surprised myself. I spoke—to no one in particu-lar. To the rainforest, perhaps. I said, "Yanomami keya!" (I am Yanomami!)

CHAPTER THREE

Jungleland

THE WHOLE TIME HE WAS in the rainforest, my father was being pulled back to his life in the States. There were money issues, academic issues, visa issues—basically, a whole lot of issues. He resisted the pull at first, and kept looking at ways to remain in my mother's village, but reality kept getting in the way. He might have been "married" to my mother in Yanomami terms, but in the eyes of the Western world their union did not grant Yarima any rights or privileges, and while in the indigenous territory it only gave my father a kind of limited hall pass, allowing him to move about as if he belonged . . . but not really.

In the beginning, he thought that if he and my mother were man and wife they could build a life together and find happiness. It did not matter if they lived in her world or in his, as long as they were together. I don't think he thought things through that far. But then, with my mother pregnant a second time and with all these issues weighing down on them—on *him*—it started to matter. Dad could not bear the thought of losing another child, he told me later; he did not want my mother to go through another pregnancy without receiving proper medical attention—not that this had anything to do with my mother's miscarriage; this was my father's Western sensibility shining through. And he did not want to bring a child into this world without being able to count on a steady income and a certain career path.

For all these reasons, and many more, my father persuaded my mother to travel with him to his *nabuh* village—and in Mom's mind, that was all it was.(*Caraca-teri*—that was how my mom used to refer to Caracas.)Most likely she thought Dad just lived in another part of the rainforest—a part she had not yet seen or heard about. She could not imagine the culture shock awaiting her once she left the territory, because it was beyond the realm of her experience. My father could imagine it for her, but it would be filtered through what he knew and understood. He could explain that there would be more people, but he could not begin to get Mom to grasp what that might mean. He could explain that the buildings in his home village would be larger than she was used to seeing, but in Mom's mind that would have simply meant a more elaborate *shabono*. And you could just forget trying to explain any of the conveniences of modern life like washing machines, or computers, or satellite technology.

Mom had already had a taste of city life when she visited Puerto Ayacucho. But that was just a small sampling of what lay in store. When my parents' story became well-known, a lot of people seemed to miss the fact that between the jungle and the United States, they spent this transitional time in Caracas. Dad was looking for grants, looking for ways to stay in Venezuela, but there weren't a whole lot of opportunities, and there were still those government forces conspiring against him. America wasn't a *done deal* in my father's mind until the very last moment, like a last resort. It wasn't until deep into my mother's pregnancy, when he started to feel he had no choice but to return to the United States with his new wife and a baby on the way.

Professionally, academically, he couldn't catch a break, so that's when the idea of traveling with Mom to America took final shape. Dad felt he was out of options, but in his mind it was only a short-term solution. His goal all along was to buy a piece of land in Puerto Ayacucho—the capital of the Amazonas state, and during my father's time a small shantytown with dirt roads and only one gas station, and which has now grown to become a small, burgeoning city—which would have left him strategically positioned between Caracas and the indigenous territory, allowing him to live a life with one foot in the developed world and the other foot in the undeveloped world. From a base in Puerto Ayacucho, it would have been easy for Mom to return to her village for extended visits, and for Dad to find a way to pursue his research; or they could live in a more permanent way among the *Hasupuwe-teri*, with Dad "commuting" to whatever academic gig he was able to line up in the city. But none of that ever materialized, and with the clock ticking on my mother's pregnancy my father thought it was time to head home. Once there, he thought he could regroup, finish his doctorate, line up an appropriate grant, and make his way back to the jungle in a more open-ended way.

Anyway, that was the plan.

Once in the States, my parents stayed in my grandparents' dining room in Pennsylvania. They were married almost immediately in the courthouse in Media, Pennsylvania—the county seat of Delaware County, just outside Philadelphia—and I always thought it was a fitting name, for the harsh spotlight of attention that quickly attached to their marriage.

There's a telling moment from my father's book about their wedding ceremony, which took place on October 22, 1986. Obviously, my father had to translate everything the judge said so my mother could understand, and then he had to translate everything my mother said so the judge could understand. At one point, when Mom went to answer the "do you promise to love, honor, and obey your husband?" part, Dad tried to get her to just nod her head, but Mom had something she wanted to say.

"*Pata*," she began, using the Yanomami honorific for *big man* to address the judge, and then she went into a long response that Dad loosely translated in this way: *Tell the* pata *that I am your*

wife. Tell him that even if you become sick, I will still be your wife.
If you cannot leave our hammock, I will go down to the river and
get you water. I will harvest plantains and roast them for you on
the fire. Tell the pata *that I will gather fruit and honey for you.*
I will cook your meat. I will care for you and do all these things,
even when you are very old. Even then, I will be your wife.

The judge had a sense of humor, apparently. He said, "I pre-
sume that's a *yes*."

To say that my grandparents weren't thrilled by my father's
choice of bride would be an all-time understatement. They were
completely shocked, dumbstruck . . . maybe even a little ashamed.
As far as I ever knew, my father never told them the full story of
his relationship with my mother until they all met at the train
station in Philadelphia. They knew he'd married a Yanomami
woman from Venezuela; they knew he was expecting a child;
more than that, I guess my father figured they'd pick it up on a
need-to-know basis. Plus, some things are just too hard to explain
long-distance.

At first my grandparents didn't take the news all that well. My
grandmother had said, "Kenneth, it's one thing to go down to the
jungle and *study* these people, but to marry one of them?" She'd
make it sound like a joke, but to my father it rankled.

Mostly, though, my grandparents held their tongues and did
what they could to make my mother feel comfortable in their
home. However, that was almost impossible once I was born—a
week and a half after the wedding, on November 2. Can you imagine the scene? My mother, an Amazonian tribeswoman, nursing
her newborn child in the dining room of her American in-laws?
It sounds like the premise for a really bad sitcom.

For a while, my father thought my birth would play out like
we were still in the jungle. You see, my grandparents lived in a
caretaker's house on a grand estate, so their backyard was this
great big field, and as my due date drew near my mother kept
saying she would just wander outside and give birth to me in this
suburban wilderness. My father was only a little troubled by this

prospect—and only in a worst-case scenario. If the birth went well, and I turned out to be a healthy baby, it would be a way for my mother to keep connected to her Yanomami traditions. But if something went wrong? Dad thought Mom would just toss me into the woods and come back into the house—a simple display of natural selection that might have been routine in the jungle but wouldn't exactly fly in Pennsylvania.

Eventually, my grandmother warmed to my mother—or, at least, she found a way to relate to her: shopping. Their favorite store was a fabric store, and Mom would pick out yards and yards of fabric, which she'd take home and stitch into clothing. In the jungle, yarns and fabrics were at a premium; the women used whatever goods the missionaries were able to supply, or whatever they could collect in trade. In the rainforest, making a fashion statement didn't go much beyond the decision to wear an item of clothing—*any* item of clothing. But in Delaware County, there was every imaginable color, every imaginable pattern, so Mom used to come home with one of everything. That was how she decided, by not deciding.

My grandmother also helped my mother learn her way around the supermarket, and to manage in the kitchen, but I'm told Mom had a hard time understanding how the microwave worked—to her, it was like it was lit by magic.

We didn't stay too terribly long at my grandparents' place. Dad started getting a bunch of phone calls. He'd begun work on his book, and he was on and off the phone with agents and publishers and producers who wanted to option his story, and his father seized on this one piece and held it out like a final straw. I guess it was okay to bring a jungle woman to sleep on the floor of your parents' dining room, where she would nurse your jungle baby, but it wasn't okay for the phone to keep ringing for you.

Soon we moved from my grandparents' dining room to the living room of my father's good friend Joe Simoncelli, in North Scranton, and then down to Florida, where my father finished his doctoral thesis and continued work on his book. The movie option money was the first meaningful payday in my father's professional life. He used a good chunk of that money to pay of his debts and keep ahead of his young family's expenses, and another good chunk to keep his promise to Mom—to return to her village as soon as possible.

While in Florida, Dad relied on the kindness of his academic colleagues to help Mom adjust to her new surroundings—specifically, to the *wives* of his colleagues, who made it a special point to look in on us and show us around. Or, at least, to make an effort. For the first time my parents had what could be considered a circle of friends, although I'm sure these friendships were a little one-sided. Mom could understand just a few words of English, and most of the social conventions were lost on her.

This culture clash led to some odd moments—and one of the oddest was also one of the most typical. To set up the story, I should mention that Mom had no taste for cheese—for dairy products of any kind, in fact. Dairy isn't a part of Yanomami diet, so naturally Mom found things like cheese and milk and butter a little stomach-turning.(Whenever we went out for ice cream as kids, she'd always order a rainbow sherbet.)Still, she was in Dad's *nabuh* village, determined to experiment with new foods, so whenever they shared a pizza Dad would eat all the cheese from Mom's slice and leave her with the crust—the *outer* crust, because the dough at the bottom had been touched by all that cheese. That's just how they did it. But here among this group the way they ate pizza set some people off.

Dad had finally passed his orals and earned his PhD, and a small group got together to celebrate. Dad wasn't up for a big party; he was more interested in the fact that I'd gone to the bathroom on the toilet for the first time that same afternoon, but he joined in as they ordered a bunch of pizzas. Without thinking about it, without realizing how his behavior must have appeared, Dad attacked the pizza in his usual way. He dug in and ate his fill and left the crust edges for Mom. Sure enough, a wife of one of his professors was looking on, horrified. She said, "Oh my God. Is that how you treat this poor girl? You just throw her the crust?"

The woman didn't much care for my father or approve of his marriage to my mother, so of course she saw this admittedly unusual way of sharing food as a flashpoint. It signaled to this indignant woman—and, I guess, to the rest of the room—that my father was mistreating my mother in some way, throwing her these table scraps like she was a household pet.

My father tried to explain the reality of the situation and move past it, but it pissed him off that he had to take the time to do so. Really, he had no patience for this sort of thing—the way he was always forced to explain himself; the way the cultural divide left him feeling like he was being judged; the way he tried to *anticipate* any misunderstandings before they came up—and yet, when he was out and about with Mom, helping her to learn the ways of *his* world, this sort of thing happened all the time.

ALL TOLD, THERE WERE several trips back to Mom's village after we'd begun our life in the States, but this one took place about a year after I was born, in November 1986. Mom was pregnant with Vanessa—four or five months along. The plan was to spend several months in the jungle, and to return home in time for Mom to give birth in an American hospital, but Vanessa had a different idea. She arrived about two months ahead of schedule, in February 1988; she was born on a banana leaf. Oh, man, she was tiny! I don't have any firsthand recollection of Vanessa's birth, but I've seen pictures, heard stories. She was so small, my father worried she wouldn't make it. Had she been born in a hospital setting, Vanessa would have been placed in a neonatal ICU, probably for several weeks, but there's no such thing as a neonatal ICU in the jungle. All you can do is hope she makes it—and, happily, she did.

I imagine Vanessa's arrival was a traumatic event for me as well as for my parents, because it pushed me from my mother's breast. That's how it goes in the jungle—one child is breast-fed until the arrival of another. My father used to tell me how Yanomami women would breast-feed their young much longer than, say, an American woman. However, when another child was born, that was it for the older sibling. No weaning process. No warning. My dad recalled Mom putting the quits on breast-feeding like some sort of embargo had been placed on me. I cried for the boob, but to no avail. Once Vanessa was born, my breastfeeding days were over. I had to quit cold turkey.

We were in Hasupuwe for about six months on this trip—enough time for me to pick up bits and pieces of the Yanomami language, and to move about the village with a level of autonomy and familiarity, but I was way too young for any of those influences to stick in any kind of lasting way. I was curious, outgoing, open to the ways of my Yanomami family . . . qualities that would leave me in time, but I'll get to that.

MY *FIRST* FIRSTHAND MEMORIES? They all take place in and around our apartment in Rutherford, New Jersey, where we moved when Dad got a job on the faculty at Jersey City State College, where he continues to teach, only now it's known as New Jersey City University. When I close my eyes and picture my early childhood I see myself and my sister, Vanessa, in the bottom apartment of the two-family house we rented there.

I can remember Mom getting us ready for bed in Rutherford—saying, "Go toothbrush." She used to say it really fast, like it was all one word—*gotoothbrush*. It was a catch-all term, although to be completely accurate it's not like she had any concept of "bedtime" or what it meant to get a child ready for bed. There is no "putting your kid to bed" in the jungle, but this was just one of the ways she learned to adapt to the Western world. She took her mothering instincts, and what she had seen and learned by observing other mothers in her village, and attached them to what was expected here in the States.

Vanessa and I shared a room, with bunk beds, and on some nights we gave Mom a hard time at bedtime, especially if Dad wasn't around. What kid wants to go to bed? So we'd get on Mom's nerves, and she'd reach into her ever-expanding Western bag of tricks to get us to cooperate. One of the ways she disciplined us and kept us in line was to pin us down and pour pepper in our mouths. I don't think she'd had any experience with pepper in the jungle, unless it came from a *nabuh* visitor or from one of the missionaries, and once in the States she saw it as more of a weapon than a spice. It was crazy hot . . . it really burned our tongues! I can remember doing something to set Mom off one afternoon and she took off after me across the front lawn, barefoot, holding the jar of pepper high above her head. I was scared as I ran, and Mom was laughing as she ran after me, but it wasn't so funny when she finally caught up to me.

She never lost some of her jungle ways, which she passed down to us kids—like the way she used to peel plantains with her teeth. She'd chomp into the plantain on one end, like she was biting into an ear of corn, and she would work her way across. She'd do this several times, until the skin had been loosened, and then she'd finally twist it off.

Also, she was constantly barefoot—a habit that was passed down to my sister. To this day, Vanessa walks around the house and yard without shoes, and if someone calls her on it or teases her, she'll say, "Hey, I got it from my mom, okay?"

I can remember romping around in the snow with Mom and Vanessa, and looking back I have to think my mother had a hard time adjusting to winter. How do you make the leap that takes you from an indigenous tropical environment, with no knowledge in meteorology, and find room in your thinking for a phenomenon like snow? For wind and ice and frigid temperatures? But somehow she found a way to adapt, and soon she was trudging around our neighborhood in boots and a ski parka, rolling around in the snow like a kid on Christmas morning. It got to where she loved the snow; she thought it was so cool, so much fun, so unlike anything she'd ever seen or experienced; she even helped with the shoveling.

And I can remember walking down Main Street to Dunkin' Donuts, which became almost a daily ritual. By the time Danny was born—in May 1991—I was going on five, and I would help Mom push my little brother in the stroller as we walked on the side of the road. Dad used to give Mom twenty dollars a day, out of which she was supposed to pay for our food and whatever else we'd need on our outings, but Mom had no concept of money. It was just a piece of paper to hand over in trade. She had no idea what things cost—what it even *meant* to conduct a transaction of this type. We'd ask for our donuts by pointing, and when the kid behind the counter told Mom how much she owed, she simply handed over this piece of paper and waited for the kid to hand back another few pieces of paper and some coins. This was Economics 101, as far as Mom was concerned: you hand over a piece of paper and in exchange you get what you want.

There was a Burger King on our daily route as well, and this was another frequent stop. Mom just loved those Burger King french fries—and with all those donuts, all those fries, all that processed food, she started to gain a lot of weight. Nobody noticed this or talked about this at the time—at least, not in a way that filtered down to us kids—but if you look through our family photos you can see a dramatic change in Mom during her time in New Jersey.

This routine continued on until Danny's first winter, when I helped to push his stroller through the snow because I thought Mom was having a hard time walking on the snow herself—in much the same way I'd have a hard time years later, trying to walk in bare feet over the uncertain terrain of the rainforest floor. But it turned out Mom was surprisingly adept at walking through snow with the stroller; as a grown-up I now see that she didn't even need my help, but she was helping me to achieve a measure of independence and responsibility by letting me think otherwise.

The Mom I remember from those early days in Rutherford is happy, smiling, wide-eyed at the unfolding wonders of the world. Outwardly, she looked like any other suburban mom—she even went out and got a perm, in the style of the day. But underneath the outward appearance there was the restless spirit of a curious child. She used to sit with us for hours watching television. She loved Barney and Pee-Wee Herman. She loved merry-go-rounds. She loved to jump up and down on the bed with us to the music of Gloria Estefan or Michael Jackson, which we played really, really loud when Dad wasn't home.

Actually, it was often the case that Dad wasn't home—he worked a lot in those days, like any young professor. He was low man on the departmental totem pole, which meant he taught a heavy course load and kept long office hours. And when he wasn't teaching, grading papers, or meeting with students, he was trying to advance his own research.

Mom could never understand Dad's work schedule; even the *idea* of a work schedule made no sense to her. The concept of going to work, for most of each day, was completely foreign to her. Here in Dad's *nabuh* village, the men would fairly disappear, for many, many hours. Dad tried to explain that his going to school each day to teach was the same as a Yanomami man heading into the jungle to hunt; he needed to work, to earn money to buy food and other necessities; this was the way he hunted and gathered. It was not the same, of course, but Mom could not appreciate the distinction. She'd never had a reason to count past two back in the jungle, and now here in the States she couldn't put two and two together and figure out why my father was out of the house for so long each day.

Over time, we later learned, Mom started to feel pretty isolated, pretty lonely. There was no one around for her to talk to, other than us kids. For a while my father arranged for someone to come to the house and help Mom with her English, but she wasn't the most motivated student. Dad had picked up Yanomami fairly easily when he first went to the jungle, but he was good with languages and academically motivated to learn. Plus, he had that whole total immersion thing going on. Mom also had that total immersion thing, but she had no such motivation. She could get by with a few words and phrases, and us kids learned to understand a good deal of Yanomami, but she began to ache for the active life she left behind in the jungle.

Looking back, I have to think Mom didn't see any reason to learn English, other than these few words and phrases she needed to get by. All along, she'd been led to believe her time in the States would be short—an extended stay while my father sorted out a next move for our family. In her mind, perhaps, she was just biding time until we all returned home—to her *real* home.

When my father's book came out, he started doing a lot of interviews. At first my father only spoke publicly about his situation when he was asked to give an interview or make an appearance. That all changed when his book came out, and he began actively seeking these opportunities. He wanted to sell books. Often my mother would join him on camera during this second wave of media attention. From time to time, a reporter would ask Mom how she liked living in New Jersey, and she would smile politely as if to indicate that she liked it very much, but at the same time she would shake her head *no*. Sometimes she would answer in English. "No," she'd say—meaning, *I do not like living in New Jersey*. But then my father would answer for her, and helpfully explain some of the difficulties Mom was having, the tough time adjusting, concluding that it had not been an easy adventure but that it was all shaking out to the good.

I don't think Mom minded doing these interviews with Dad—but at the same time, I don't think she fully understood what she was doing. She was simply along for the ride.

I SUPPOSE IT'S POSSIBLE my parents would have stayed together if it hadn't been for the making of a documentary for National Geographic called *Yanomami Homecoming*. Nothing against National Geographic—the tensions and difficulties that came up during this time could have happened on any shoot, for any production company. I guess I should back up and explain. Producers from National Geographic persuaded my father that it would be a good idea for the entire family to trek back to the jungle to record footage for a planned documentary about my family and life in our rainforest village. The documentary that came out of this association was an important marker in the life of my family, chronicling the story of my parents' unique relationship and showing the world what it was like to raise such a colossally "mixed "family; *Yanomami Homecoming* got great reviews, although some scenes were misrepresented or taken out of context. It also presented my father in a controversial way—at least among the anthropological community, where many colleagues thought my father had married my mother to somehow advance his career. This made no sense; if anything, his marriage to my mother probably cost my father professionally; it hurt his standing in the academic community and it got in the way of his ability to publish in a scientific way. He'd be the first to tell you it killed his career, but he didn't care. His focus was on my mother—helping her to adjust to life in New Jersey, teaching her, helping her to raise three children.

Still, the making of that documentary was a kind of tipping point, the way my father remembers it. It came about nearly four years after our last trip to the jungle, when Vanessa had been born. What happened was we flew down to Venezuela as a family to participate in this shoot, which had been in the works for months. To Mom and us kids, however, it seemed to come up on its own. One moment we were in New Jersey, walking by the side of the road to Dunkin' Donuts, Mom pushing little Danny in the stroller while Vanessa and I toddled along behind, and the next we were frantically packing and making ready for the long trek back to the rainforest. Dad discussed it with us, of course, and the logistics of the trip must have taken a long time to plan, but we weren't involved in any of the long-term planning. He told Mom that she was going home. And he simply told us kids that we were going on a great adventure to the rainforest, to visit with Mom's family.

We hadn't been to the jungle in four years—a stretch of time that must have been interminable for my mother, but also immeasurable. Remember, my mother's time horizon was pretty much tied in to her limited sense of numbers and quantity. *Time*, to her, meant today and tomorrow, one moon and two moons, forward and back. There was no room along that limited time horizon for a sense of longing. Beyond a day or two, a week or two, a season or two . . . she could not begin to contemplate, and yet after living so long in the suburbs the days away from home must have strung themselves together and started to mean something. The time away probably began to weigh on her, even if she couldn't fully understand it or measure it. In the beginning, Mom could think of her time with my father in his *nabuh* village as a kind of *wayumi*—a really long trek. It fit with the nomadic lifestyle she'd known her entire life. There had been a return trip to the jungle that first year, and then another, so there was a coming-and-going aspect to their lives, a balance between *here* and *there*, and once it became clear to my mother that we were all traveling to her village she was superexcited. Those four years away suddenly became like two moons and two moons more, that's all, but there was nothing in Mom's frame of reference to prepare her for the short, quick-hit trip my father and the National Geographic producers had in mind.

We were only in Mom's village for five days, and yet the National Geographic cameras were able to capture our lives in the rainforest in a compelling way, managing to make it seem like they'd followed us around over a period of weeks and months. There were images of me and Vanessa playing in the muddy creek water with other Yanomami children—and to this day, if I watch that footage, I'm taken back to those snapshot idyllic moments, splashing around without a care in my head, feeling like I belonged. The kids of the village were a lot like the kids in my kindergarten class back home, in every way you'd expect a little kid to notice, except they were mostly naked and I didn't understand most of what they said. At five years old, I didn't pay much attention to any cultural differences, but we threw a ball around, chased each other in the mud and rain, wrestled, held hands, laughed . . . basically, found a way to be *like* each other instead of *unlike* each other. In the documentary, you can see my mother crabbing and gathering firewood, my father helping to make repairs to the *shabono* or deep in consultation with one of the village elders. There we are by the communal fire, laughing and playing and eating. Taken together, it comes across like one of those montage sequences you see in a movie, where a bunch of scenes are stitched together to show the passage of time in a *business as usual* sort of way. It's amazing, really, the semblance of daily life the National Geographic producers were able to cobble together in such a short stretch of time. They were able to take five days' worth of footage and find the *business as usual* underneath . . .

And then, once the cameras had captured everything they needed, once they'd interviewed Mom and Dad with the village in the background, it was time to go. Just like that. And to hear my father tell it now, it's like the rainforest floor was pulled from beneath my mother's feet.

She was not expecting to have to leave; we had only just arrived.

You have to realize, my father wasn't keeping our itinerary from my mother, but there was no good way to explain it. Also, there was no avoiding it, from his perspective. He had three children to support; he could only take a short leave of absence from his job; there was only this narrow window in his academic schedule and in the producers' schedule to set up this five-day shoot in the jungle. Also, I was already in school and my father felt that he could only keep me away for a brief period.

Mom didn't understand any of this, of course. She knew only that we were finally traveling this long way, on that big bird in the sky, with her three small children. She could only assume that after such a long time, after such a long journey, there would be another long time before the next long journey, before the *here* and *there* could rebalance itself, so when it became clear to her that we would be picking up and leaving her village so quickly after we'd arrived, she was pissed.

I'd never seen Mom pissed, or sulking, or seething with resentment, so I probably didn't recognize this emotion for what it was, but even as a little kid I could see she was not herself as she stomped around in a thick, black funk, completely shocked and unhappy and miserable.

There's actually a Yanomami term that gets close to describing how my mother was probably feeling: *Hushuo!* I think that summed up my mother's reaction to our brief stay in the jungle.

The other reason my father saw this experience as a kind of tipping point was that during those five idyllic days in the jungle a poison was introduced into our family life in the form of a local facilitator/interpreter/*motorista* who was part of the National Geographic crew. I won't give his real name here, because the man is well-known in the territory, and I don't want to cause my family any trouble by calling him out in a public way. Let's just say his name was Armando, and let's just say he was bad news. It's tough to point to any one specific thing this man did to disrupt our family dynamic in the short time he spent with us during the filming. But he clearly made some kind of important connection with my mother; he clearly started to gain her confidence, and offer his in return, and in the exchange I believe he took advantage of my mother's newfound resentment and began feeding her all kinds of ideas, convincing her she was being abused by my father and somehow exploited by her life in the United States. He wasn't Yanomami, he was from another tribe in the territory known as the Ye'kwana, but the producers hired Armando as an extra set of eyes and ears on the ground. He was there to help the production run smoothly, efficiently, to help with transportation and translation, but my father began to feel he was overstepping his authority. Armando knew the territory; he worked as a field guide, spoke Spanish, so he was a valuable part of the National Geographic team, and from all outward appearances he did his job well. But there was something sleazy about him, something suspicious. My father used to pull us aside and say things like, "Stay away from Armando."

So from the very beginning, Dad knew not to trust this guy.

I was just a little kid, so I couldn't see what my father saw, couldn't guess what he didn't like about Armando, but it was clear he saw *something*. What I've put together since is that Armando must have seen some kind of opportunity with my mother, some way to step inside whatever sliver of spotlight she may or may not have had in the territory. That's the way of the acculturated jungle, I'd learn. The folks with a little bit of education, a little bit of exposure to the modern, developed world are often the first to exploit their own people. Everybody's working some kind of angle—only here, Armando's angle was not yet known. My father couldn't quite figure him out, and I guess it's possible that one of the reasons Mom was so noticeably upset at our quick turn-around was that this guy had started filling her ear with ideas about separating from my father and remaining in the village.

It might have been nothing, this suspicion of Armando, except he didn't go away—and even when we *did* finally separate from him he didn't stay gone. We said goodbye to him as we made our way out of the territory and back to Caracas, and there was no reason to think we'd ever see him again. But Mom wasn't right after that. She seemed sad to us kids—like, all the time. She didn't laugh, the way she used to *always* laugh. She didn't smile, the way she used to *always* smile. She went through the motions of taking care of us, of helping with the packing, of breast-feeding little Danny, but her head was someplace else. Her heart, too. It's like she was broken.

Once in Caracas, we stopped for a couple of days and stayed with some friends of my father. At some point during this visit, Mom started chasing after me with a stick. I don't remember what I did to set her off, or even if I did anything. Maybe she was just taking her anger and frustration out on me, although I don't know that it registered that way to me at the time. Back in New Jersey, she used to throw shoes at us kids and we would playfully taunt her, but throwing stuff was a typical Yanomami gesture. (When I returned to Mom's village as an adult, there were a lot of times when my family members were sitting around the fire throwing plantain peels at pestering dogs and monkeys who wandered too close to the hearth.) We always turned it into a game. But my father and his friends saw this behavior as something different ... something *other*. Here she was, chasing her child around a friend's apartment with a stick, in a menacing way; it was an embarrassment and a worry to my father, particularly since Mom clearly meant to strike me with the stick, not just scare me.

Dad told me years later he did not know how to make Mom understand that it was necessary for them to return to his *nabuh* village. It wasn't a language barrier, he said, so much as a cultural barrier—of the kind you can't always get past.

His friends actually suggested a path to understanding. In a million years, my father would never have come up with this plan, and as I think back on it now I'm amazed it didn't take another million years for him to agree to it. However, someone suggested that my mother needed to remain in the jungle a little while longer. Dad's friends pointed out that Mom had been apart from her family for four long, confusing years, cut off from the only world she had ever known. Indeed, there had been many births and deaths in her lineage in the time we'd been away, and many other changes, and Mom had only this short time to adjust to the new realities of her village. Dad agreed, of course; he loved my mother, loved the life she lived in the jungle, hated that the life he needed to live in the States put her in conflict. His friends all seemed to believe it would be too much for my father to manage us on his own. Since Danny was still breast-feeding, it was decided that he would return to my mother's village with her.

As these plans took shape, these friends told my father of a German family they knew in Caracas with three little girls, all around Vanessa's age; the family knew of my parents' story and would be willing to take Vanessa in for a short time, allowing Dad to go back to New Jersey with me, where he could finish out the semester while I returned to kindergarten.

This wasn't the best plan in the world, but it was definitely a plan. It was *something*—a way to give Mom what she needed. A way to set things right, at least for the time being. I can't imagine what was going through my father's head, though, as he thought this through. There was a lot to take in, a lot to consider. It couldn't have been easy for him, just as it couldn't have been easy for my mother. He was frantic with worry—for Mom, for us kids, for his career, for our future as a family. And Mom, she was just frantic.

And so it was decided. Vanessa would remain in Caracas with this German family. Mom would return to her village with Danny. In Dad's head this was just a temporary thing—you know, like taking separate vacations. We would find our way back to Caracas at the end of the semester, collect Vanessa, and continue on to Hasupuwe or Irokai or Wawatoi or wherever the *Hasupuwe-teri* happened to be living and spend the Christmas break there with Mom and Danny. By then Mom would be refreshed and back to herself and we'd return as a family to New Jersey. All would be right in our little world.

But that's not exactly how it went down, and this is where Armando entered the picture again. For some reason, my father hired him to escort my mother back to the territory. Already, Dad had some big-time suspicions, he knew this guy was toxic, but my mother needed a guide for the journey back to Yanomami territory and Armando seemed like a logical choice. Dad wasn't thinking clearly. Or maybe he wanted to leave Mom in the care of someone she knew, even if *he* didn't trust him—a classic devil-you-know versus the devil-you-don't-know dilemma. Also, there weren't a whole lot of options and Dad didn't have the time to coordinate my mother's return trip to Hasupuwe.

Whatever his thinking, we'd just gotten rid of this asshole and now he was back in our lives, back in Mom's ear, back filling her head with his destructive, self-serving ideas. Of course, Dad didn't know just how destructive or self-serving this guy was, but he could only imagine. He also imagined that there was something else between Mom and Armando—something close to what we'd consider an affair. That's a major deal in our Western culture, but in the life of the Yanomami, it rates only a shrug. To Dad, it was everything; to Mom, if true, it was nothing.

And yet even with all his doubts and suspicions and concerns, my father hired Armando to take Mom back to her village, inviting this poison back into our lives.

I don't remember the return trip to the States with my father or what life was like without my brother, sister, and mother. I do recall that Dad busied himself with his work when we got back, and that I went back to my routines. Life went on as before, except now there were some huge pieces missing.

Vanessa, meanwhile, had a tough adjustment. To this day, she remembers this as a traumatizing time in her life, but I've never been able to press her on specifics. Bottom line: this German family wasn't as warm or welcoming as Dad had been led to believe, although I guess it's possible a lot of that had to do with the fact that Vanessa was only four years old, left to live among this family of strangers—of course, they couldn't have been warm or welcoming enough to replace her own family.

Also, Vanessa's continued presence in Caracas raised some concerns in the Venezuelan government. As the cross-cultural child of a Yanomami woman, she was a natural flashpoint of public attention. As my parents' story became more and more known, certain government functionaries seemed to be more and more concerned that Vanessa had been left in the care of this family. The host family began getting menacing phone calls from bureaucrats, asking after the child of Yarima and Kenneth Good. The family believed they had to conceal Vanessa from public view, which probably contributed to her feelings of isolation and loss. It got to where the father called my dad in New Jersey some weeks into this arrangement and said, "This isn't working out. You need to come and get your daughter. I can no longer keep her safe."

This distress call came in over a weekend, and in those days my father had a Monday, Tuesday, Thursday teaching schedule, so he slogged through his classes on Monday and Tuesday and hopped a flight to Caracas that night, returning to New Jersey in time to teach his class that Thursday. There was no time on that tight turnaround to head out to the jungle to check on Mom and Danny, so this was just a quick-in, quick-out trip to collect Vanessa and bring her home.

It's a wonder my father got through this uncertain time. No, the decisions he made on behalf of his family didn't always shake out to the good, and they didn't always make sense in retrospect, but they were made on the fly, with a sense of desperation—one Hail Mary pass after another. He couldn't face the thought of losing my mother. He was up against it . . . and scrambling.

This next part I actually remember—at least, from the narrow point of view of a child. I remember being reunited with Vanessa and how it was to put back some of the missing pieces of our family. This was no tearful reunion (our family didn't do tearful reunions), just as there had been no tearful goodbyes (we didn't do those, either). But I did have a sense that the picture of our family was coming back into focus. With Vanessa now in the mix, a lightness returned to our little family. I remember what it was like to once again have a playmate, someone to keep me company while Dad was busy planning one of his lectures or grading papers. I remember that Christmas season approaching, and Dad making plans to leave us with our uncle while he went to Venezuela. I can even remember that conversation—Dad saying, "I'm going to the jungle to get Mommy and Danny." And me hearing it like this was a completely normal thing to say to your kids, like telling them you were going down to the corner store to get a quart of milk.

Since it was Christmas, Dad loaded up on gifts to bring along with him—gifts for the villagers and for Danny. The holiday holds no meaning for the Yanomami, naturally, but my father was in the spirit of the season, excited to knit his family back together, so he purchased the usual supply of pots and pans and machetes and other trade goods and bundled them up in a great big bag, like he was a *nabuh* Santa Claus. He got gifts for Mom and Danny, too, and these he took the trouble to wrap. Mom understood Christmas from her time in New Jersey and she came to love it—the lights, the spectacle, the good feeling in the air and all around. But after lugging all this stuff with him to the rainforest, my father wasn't exactly greeted with open arms. He told me the story years later and tried to give it a funny spin, but it was more sad than funny—*way* more sad than funny. What happened was he stepped off the boat and made his way to Hasupuwe after yet another ridiculously long journey, and he came upon a pack of little kids, playing. They saw my father, this giant *nabuh*, loaded down with these giant trash bags. He must have looked terrifying. And, who knows, maybe they'd heard stories about my dad and had been taught to fear him, just as they were taught in those days to fear any outsider.

Now, here's the part my father tried to spin as funny: Among the kids who scattered in fear as he approached the village was a naked little boy Dad recognized immediately as Danny. Dad hadn't seen Danny in months, at an age when toddlers undergo dramatic physical changes, but there was no mistaking him. His skin was noticeably lighter than the skin of the other children, but there he was, screaming his little head off, running in the opposite direction, spooked by the sight of his own father.

It must have been a crushing thing for my father, to have come all this way to put his family back together, and to have his own son be afraid of him like this, but in the retelling Dad just laughed it off—tried to, anyway.

THERE WAS ANOTHER CRUSHING piece to this return visit: Armando was still hanging around. Or, if he hadn't been there all this time, he was there now, and this was unsettling to my father. True, it was my father who had invited this man back into our lives when he hired Armando to accompany my mother from Caracas back to her village, but he thought the relationship would end there—and yet here Armando was. Whatever doubts my father had had about Armando's agenda, whatever suspicions he'd had about the rainforest version of an "affair," they were all now ratcheted up a notch in his mind, so by the time Mom and Dad circled each other in the *shabono* a time or two and finally came together in greeting, things were tense between them.

Little Danny came around soon enough. He returned to the *shabono* a short while later and eyed my father warily for a beat before jumping into his arms. Unfortunately, the tension and uncertainty that hung in the air between my mother and father could not be gotten past so easily.

Here's something it helps to realize: when my father returned to Hasupuwe, it was generally understood among the villagers that Yarima would be returning with him to his faraway *nabuh* village. The one would follow from the other—a Yanomami if/then scenario. If my father returned, *then* Yarima would return with him to his village in New Jersey. She would be with her children, even if she ached to remain in the jungle, even if her family, her lineage wanted to keep her close. This was the life she'd sort of chosen—and my father, he was the man she'd sort of chosen. Armando seemed to understand this, too, and when he was with Yarima and my father in the communal area he appealed to her to go and be with her children. He said all the right things—in a way that may or may not have been duplicitous, scheming. Who knows what he was saying to my mother in private, but in public he was encouraging Yarima to accept my father, to return with him to his home village.

Still, the awkward tension between my parents lasted the entire time my father remained in Hasupuwe; Dad had only meant to stay in the territory a couple of days before heading back out, and in that time he had to gather Mom's belongings and Danny's things and make other preparations to leave. Even under the best circumstances, if things had been "right" with my parents, this would have been a difficult time, because Dad felt the pain of leaving the village each time he left, but now it was exponentially difficult. Despite the tribe's recent history with Mom's long absences, Dad had a hard time explaining to the village elders how long it might be before their next visit.

The Yanomami understood coming together, and they understood coming apart; it's the space between that held no meaning for them, and it was in this space between that my parents' drama unfolded.

But Mom knew what it meant to separate, and she moved about with a heavy heart. She helped with the packing, she helped with Little Danny, but it felt to my father like she was doing these things in a grudging way. That funk she'd been in, some months earlier in Caracas? It hadn't gone away—or perhaps it had, but now it was back. Dad understood this, he later explained, but he believed Mom's mood would brighten when she returned to the States to her kids; he *had* to believe this, he said, because this was the woman he loved and this was the life they had made, the family they had made.

Soon they made it to Platanal. Something had changed since my father first arrived in the territory some years earlier; the forces of the outside world were encroaching. Here in Platanal, for example, the *Majecodo-teri* were busy building a new *shabono* using the *Hasupuwe-teri* as hired hands to assist in the building—suggesting the emergence of a class structure, where a village of haves can find a way to exploit a village of have-nots. To my father, this was a big shock, a cultural revolution, a troubling indication that the reach of the outside world, the forces of supply and demand were making their way into the jungle.

Meanwhile, Armando wouldn't go away. It's like Dad had stepped in shit and couldn't scrape the stuff off his shoes, the way Armando kept following them. Dad couldn't quite grasp this man's intentions or ulterior motives.

Finally, a plane arrived on the tiny Platanal airstrip to take them to Esmeralda—a small settlement on the shores of the Orinoco, and a central meeting point for military personnel, doctors, missionaries, and other relief workers in the region. The arrival of a plane was always a cause for great excitement in the jungle. It's like a holiday, a parade. The Yanomami gather on the airstrip at the sound of the engines, and as the plane rolls to a stop it's escorted by dozens of villagers running alongside. Always there is a tremendous scrum of activity, children running this way and that, and on this day that's pretty much what happened. Dad was busy organizing several pieces of luggage—there was no one around to help him. Mom was moving slowly toward the plane, her steps so tiny and tentative it must have seemed to anyone watching that she never really wanted to get where she was going. There was a lot of heat and haste and movement, my father remembers, and at one point Dad noticed that the flow of excited villagers seemed to suddenly stop and start moving in the opposite direction. It was the strangest thing—like a switch had been flipped. First these dozens and dozens of whooping and hooting villagers shot past him, headed toward the plane as it taxied to a stop; and next, these same villagers were shooting past him going the other way. He followed the action like he was seated at center court at a tennis match.

His first thought was that there had been a raid. Or maybe there'd been a fight and the people were scattering every which way. He couldn't worry about it, though. His focus was on getting all that luggage on board, and seeing to his paperwork, so he kept moving toward the plane. Mom and Danny had continued on ahead of him on the short trail from the small shelter they'd been staying in by the airstrip; he'd had to double back a time or two to collect another few pieces of luggage and he'd lost sight of them in the commotion.

When he got to the plane he could not believe what he saw. There was Danny on the grass airstrip, sitting all by himself, screaming his little head off. His hands were in the air, like he was reaching, reaching, reaching . . . for *what*? And Mom was nowhere to be found.

Dad looked left and right and all around and could see no trace of my mother, and as he frantically surveyed the scene his eyes kept coming back to this screaming child all alone in the middle of this jungle airstrip. Poor Danny was plainly terrified—and Dad, he was mystified. He couldn't understand what had just happened, what it might mean, what to do next.

QUICKLY, MY FATHER REALIZED that my mother had fled. She knew he would find Danny on the airstrip and bring him home to our village in New Jersey. Now my father had to decide whether or not to go after my mother. His mind was racing.

Complicating things (or at least confusing them) was the presence of Armando, going through the motions of consoling my father—counseling him, even, telling him to run after my mother, to find a way to bring her back. The man was playing him, but my father could not see that.

Poor Dad didn't have a whole lot of options—and he didn't have a whole lot of time to think them through. It felt to him like the entire village was against him. The plane was due to take off. He had two small children waiting on his return, a job to get back to, a local government that had been trying for years to bust his chops and make him pay for marrying an indigenous tribeswoman and removing her from the territory in the first place. He was afraid that word would get out that Yarima had left him and that the government would find some way to use this against him.

So what did he do? He grabbed little Danny and boarded the plane. He knew that if word of this "separation" traveled across the jungle canopy to the big city there could be trouble waiting for him in Caracas. Some bureaucrat could get it in his head that Dad was kidnapping Danny, forcibly removing the child from his mother, and Dad could be detained, or jailed, or worse. There was no telling how the authorities would react to this latest turn, so Dad's new desperation plan was to get to Esmeralda as quickly as possible, talk to his missionary friends there, make sure they understood the full story of what had happened, and then catch the next flight out to Caracas. It was essential, my father thought, to take full advantage of his time on the ground in Esmeralda. He reached out to his missionary friends directly before any rumors or lies had a chance to find them ahead of the truth.

The layover in Esmeralda was anxious enough, but then Danny came down with a really bad case of worms, so the tough spot Dad was in got a little tougher. Poor Danny was shitting up a storm, and Dad worried he'd become dehydrated, which could have been a problem on the long flight home from Caracas to New York. The short hop from Esmeralda to Caracas wouldn't be a problem, he thought, so Dad talked to the people he needed to talk to and got out of town as quickly as he could. Once in Caracas, he holed up with Danny in a hotel room and hoped like crazy the diarrhea would pass before their flight out the next morning.

Happily, mercifully, it did—but Dad wasn't in the clear just yet. He'd have to wait for something else to pass: soon after he landed in the United States, he had a terrible attack of kidney stones. My poor father! Whatever could go wrong on this return trip from the jungle went completely wrong, and here the pain became so bad he pulled into a hospital emergency room on his way to my uncle's house to pick up me and Vanessa. He just kind of stumbled into the ER, holding Danny, and collapsed.

He was in the hospital only for one night, but when he *did* finally make it back to my uncle's house Dad didn't come completely clean with us about how things went down with Mom. What could he have said? How do you tell your kids their mother isn't coming back to them? How do you explain that the love she felt for her children was not enough to overcome the pain of leaving her family, her village, her way of life? How do you tell them your heart is broken because the woman you love, the woman you've built a life with, is not coming home?

And forget us kids—how do you admit these things to yourself?

There are no words—in English, in Yanomami—so Dad simply said Mom was still in the jungle, and that the plan was for her to stay in the jungle awhile longer. That's all. In just that moment, this made perfect sense to me; given the weird pairings and separations of these past months, this fit right in. And it never occurred to any of us—Dad included—that *awhile longer* might mean we'd never see Mom again.

THE NEXT CHAPTER IN Mom's life, the next chapter in our life as a family is a little unclear, and I'm afraid a lot of it will always be unclear. A great many of the details are lost in translation and others have been swallowed up by distance and washed away by time.

Here is what I know, from interviews and talking with friends: Armando continued to visit the village and hold a great deal of influence over my mother. I know that he tricked her into believing that her kids were in Caracas and that he could take her to us. Of course she went along with whatever Armando told her to do. We were her children, after all.

In this way, he convinced Mom to accompany him to Caracas. She went willingly, but once there she was more and more under his influence. She was known to be missing from her village, and occasionally spotted around the city by area missionaries and others who knew her or knew of her. She was not a hostage in the literal sense of the term, but she wasn't allowed to leave Armando's watchful eye. He kept her holed up in a room, where she was raped and abused. He had threatened to hurt her if she attempted to leave when he was out.

This period of "captivity" lasted for days, and from time to time Dad would receive a phone call from one of his Caracas friends telling him that someone had seen Armando treating Yarima harshly, or roughing her up, or threatening her in public. During this time, Armando also coerced Mom to appear on national television and radio and claim she had been abused and mistreated by my father— even to state that she had been kidnapped and forcibly removed to the United States, where she was held against her will for four years.

I know that Mom did not know whom to believe, what to believe. There were all these forces, all these outside interests trying to pull her in all these different directions . . . a sick propaganda effort to portray my father as an evil, imperialistic American, a white man who'd snatched an innocent Amazonian woman from the jungle and forced her to become a Westernized housewife. It's no wonder she basically snapped—and, in a tragic irony, the whole time she was being held captive, she was being abused by this asshole Armando. The reports my dad was getting showed him to be a manipulative, scheming menace.

I know that Dad did not at first think there was anything he could do to protect Mom from so far away. He was afraid to set foot on Venezuelan soil. A government agent had called my father at home in New Jersey demanding that he return to the territory to defend himself against any number of trumped-up charges. It was never made clear to my father what charges he was facing, only that he was essentially a marked man; if he tried to return to Venezuela, he would probably be jailed and tortured, and we kids would likely be thrown into an international custody battle.

Eventually, word got around that Yarima was being held against her will—a situation that did not look good for the Bureau of Indian Affairs, which was ultimately forced to instruct Armando to back away from whatever situation he'd made with my mother. She was returned to her village soon after.

Over the first stretch of months, possibly for a year and or more, Dad would sit us down at regular intervals to record an audio greeting to send down to the jungle. He had hoped that hearing the voices of her children would make Mom want to come back home to New Jersey. He bought a special tape recorder for just this purpose—actually, he bought two, so he could send one to Mom so she could have a way to listen to the tapes. Our messages were basic, cookie-cutter stuff:

We love you, Mommy.

We miss you, Mommy.

Please come home to us, Mommy.

Dad had some good friends in Venezuela—the Dawsons—and

he sent these tapes down to them in hopes that they would find their way up the Orinoco to my mother's village. We never knew if those tapes made it to my mother, but all this time later I can't imagine how she would have reacted to them. Think about it: She'd been raped and beaten. She'd been traumatized, and brutalized, and forced to go on national television to tell lies about her husband and her experiences in the United States. She'd become so fearful of outsiders that any time a *nabuh* approached her village she would dash into the jungle, to keep from being taken from her family. She trusted no one—not even the missionaries she'd come to know over the years. So to think of her playing these tapes, hearing our voices . . . it would have been terribly upsetting to her.

Still, the Dawsons kept trying—and, still, we kept reaching out, but as each month passed with no word of Mom, and after that each year, this new reality began to take hold. Mom was gone. She wasn't coming back.

And meanwhile, back home in New Jersey, life went on.

UPPER ORINOCO, YANOMAMI TERRITORY

The worst of the storm lasted for just ten minutes or so, and as the winds died down and the rain began to ease it occurred to me I should probably take on a more traditional male role among this group. I didn't like feeling so completely useless and redundant. I wanted to protect these women, in what ways I could.

I wanted to matter, to belong.

Of course, at just that moment there was nothing I could do, nothing any male member of the village could have done, but that didn't stop me. The rain was still heavy enough to keep us huddled beneath our boulder-eaves, but I remembered something my friend Hortensia Caballero had shared with me about how the men of the village would sometimes seek spiritual help during these tropical storms.

Hortensia was the Venezuelan anthropologist who had played such a vital role in getting me upriver to reconnect with the Yanomami, and during our long voyage into this part of the rainforest she told me of the village shamans who would dance and chant and blow away the storm clouds.

Like an idiot, I thought, Hey, I can do that!

So I did—anyway, I tried. Even though the storm had set-tled somewhat, there was still the danger of falling limbs from the ripping winds, so the others weren't planning to leave the safety of our cocoon just yet, but I sprang stupidly, fearlessly from beneath the rocks and sloshed out into the middle of the creek. The water was only shin-deep, so I moved about like I was tromping through a wading pool. I moved without grace and without hesitation. As I moved, I chanted—nonsense syl-lables, mostly, in a singsong voice that was my best attempt at an ancient incantation. I had no idea what I was doing, but I went at it with great enthusiasm. I thought that if I chanted loud enough, danced fiercely enough, attempted to blow away the storm clouds with enough force, I could somehow sum-mon the gods of the rainforest to dial down on this storm. I crouched low, and moved around on bended knees, like a sumo wrestler, which was probably something I had seen in a Discovery Channel documentary, now bent and twisted beyond recognition. Next, I turned my face to the driving rain and reached my arm to the heavens. And, finally, I cupped my hands around my mouth and tried to blow the clouds from the sky, the way Hortensia had described.

I must have looked like a fool—I get that now—but at the time I was determined. I thought I was helping, channeling the spirits to wish the storm clouds away, away, away.

My actions were so ludicrous, so far off the map of their shared experience, the others had no idea what to make of me. At one point I looked over and caught a glimpse of my two wives, with these stunned, blank looks on their faces. They'd never seen this type of behavior. And my poor mother, who only moments earlier had been staring sweetly into the violent storm, in her own way cherishing this point of pause with her long-lost son . . . she was probably ashamed of me, her cartoon shaman son. Who could blame her? Really, I was prancing and chanting and blowing like a clown. Even the small child was looking at me like I had just sprouted horns, like she was wondering what this crazy nabuh was doing, dancing like an idiot in the rain.

The whole time, I knew all that prancing wasn't going to do a damn thing, but it was something to do, a way to release some tension.

This went on for a few long moments—a few too long moments, until one of the women started to laugh. And then, as soon as one started to laugh, the others joined in, and soon all four women were doubled up, pointing, cackling helplessly. Once again I was on the receiving end of a whole bunch of pointing and snickering, and at this point I figured the only thing to do was join in.

For the next week or so, I was the village idiot. When we got back to the shabono, I'd look up and see one of these women—my mother, even!—aping my behavior, in all seriousness, trying not to laugh until her demonstration was over.

But in my defense, I'll say this: the storm eventually passed. And I chose to believe I had something to do with this. I was no shaman, I'll admit, but I wasn't about to sit idly by while the women of my village cowered in the shelter of two boulders and a furious storm threatened to do us in.

No way.

CHAPTER FOUR

Taking Time

WE DIDN'T OPENLY DISPLAY PICTURES of my mother in the house, not that I can recall seeing on a regular basis. As far as daily reminders went, there weren't any—at least, none that resonated in any kind of lasting way. This seems strange to me now, but at the time I don't think I even noticed. It's as if my mother vanished, erased from our lives like one of those drawings I used to make on my Etch A Sketch. Really, it was the same thing. There was this big shake-up, this big upheaval, and then there was this blank canvas where my mother used to be.

Eventually, I pushed any memories of my mother down so deep it's like she was no longer a part of me. Once I realized she wasn't coming home to us, I had no use for her, no place in my heart. I was angry, I guess. Confused. Probably a little scared. How do you deal with that kind of loss, when you're five or six years old? How do you help a child make sense of his mother's sudden and certain absence?

Once, a couple of years into our new reality, my dad shared Mom's comments from that bittersweet boat ride to Platanal, when she told him she wanted *real* Yanomami kids. It was a pretty messed-up thing to say—that my mother didn't think I was good enough to keep around.

93

But this was my father's parenting style, only to call it a *style* suggests it was something he thought through or worked on in some way. It wasn't really like that with Dad. He just talked to us like we were little adults, and here he shared this comment from my mother like it was nothing at all, unaware of the painful rejection underneath her words.

It never occurred to me until I decided to reclaim this part of my life that my father must have had his own reasons for letting my mother's memory fade from our household. It wasn't *just* that it went against his nature to pay extra-special attention to the emotional needs of his children regarding the loss of their mother. No, there was something more to it, I think. He was no doubt hurting from the upheaval of Mom's leaving, from the allegations made against him, from the unexpected separation from the woman he loved and with whom he had determined to make a life and raise a family—an unconventional family, yes, but a family just the same. The thought of decorating our house with pictures of his Yarima, with cherished keepsakes of their time together, with stories to keep her in our hearts and minds must have been too terrible, too painful to even consider.

In his own way, through his own heartbreak, my father did his best to help us kids talk through the situation, but I could only hear it as just talk. It didn't *mean* anything. Or, I didn't get what it might mean. Or care. Of course, I cared, at bottom, but I couldn't see bottom just then. I couldn't let myself care on the surface, so I shut down. I cut my mother off, blotted our relationship from memory. I was a pretty strong-willed kid, so I breathed deep and stuck out my chest and told myself I would have nothing to do with her. Ever, ever. I was dug in on this. I hated my mother, just then, wished she'd never been born.(And I was not thinking about what that would mean for me, of course.)

Whenever my father tried to bring up the subject of my mother, or to talk about some Yanomami tradition, or our time in the jungle as a family, I tuned him out. I was like those three "Hear No Evil/Speak No Evil/See No Evil" monkeys, all rolled into one—a little deaf, dumb, and blind to that side of my family, that aspect of my growing up. With my siblings I think it was more of an out-of-sight, out-of-mind deal. Danny, certainly, was too young to dwell in any kind of meaningful way on the excision of our mother from our lives, too young to remember the brief time he'd spent in the rainforest as an infant; and Vanessa . . . who knows what she was thinking, what she remembered, what she was made to endure when she was living with that German family in Caracas? From time to time, as adults, the three of us will get to talking about how things were for us as kids, but only in a surface way. We remember stories, but not the feelings that went with those stories. We remember moments, but not what those moments meant. And here I don't feel like I'm entitled to Danny's memories, to Vanessa's memories. I'm not here to speak on their behalf. I respect their privacy. Perhaps someday they will tell their stories—and it will be on their terms, not mine. For now I will include them in this story without imagining how the world we shared must have looked to them.

Here again, it never occurred to me that these were things my father needed to work through, that he needed to get past his own grieving for what he'd lost—for what we'd all lost. I only saw the situation as it related to me. It's not that I was selfish or self-absorbed, I don't think. Kids see the world based on their own hierarchy of needs, after all. And my father, his needs never even occurred to me. They were besides the point—to *me*.

Anyway, I had all this bottled-up anger, throughout my growing up. I told myself I had no mother. I refused to be Yanomami. I would get along just fine all by myself, thank you very much. I would make my way in *this* world . . . in *my* world. In New Jersey. And it's not like there was an occasional postcard in the mail from Mom, or special gifts from the rainforest, or a phone call on our birthdays, or any other way to keep us close or knit us back together. There wasn't even a way for us to pause and reflect on *her* birthday, because there were no such things as birthdays or calendars in the jungle.

In the jungle, when you were around, you just *were*.

In the jungle, when you were gone, you just *were not*.

THIS WAS HOW THINGS were in our house as we began to make our way without my mother. It was almost a clean break, except for those messages Dad used to make us record. As far as us kids ever knew, there were never any return messages from Mom—at least, none that ever trickled down to me, so we never knew if our "letters" from home ever made it to her, or if Mom was just ignoring us, or if something else was going on.

Eventually, these cross-cultural attempts to keep in touch melted away, and as they did Mom faded from our lives more and more. I do remember sneaking into my father's office in our basement from time to time just to see if I could find any trace evidence of her having been around. There was a kind of siren call to that mother-son relationship that was bigger than me, more powerful than me, and I was helpless against it. It left me reaching back to my mother without even realizing it. I might have been seven or eight, or ten or twelve. Maybe this was a regular thing, but I don't think so. Still, I have a few specific memories of sitting at my father's desk, paging through his book, looking through his files, stopping to stare at the tucked-away pictures of my mother—half-naked, in tribal paint, *hii-hi* sticks through her nose, looking nothing at all like any of my friends' mothers. Looking nothing like I remembered, even as I remembered less and less, but the picture that remained in my mind was of my somewhat Americanized mother, wearing somewhat normal Western clothes, hair done up in the style of the neighborhood, eating french fries at Burger King.

These stolen moments in my father's office looking at pictures of my mother as she truly was when she was happiest, when she was herself, happened with less and less frequency, and over time my mother began to seem less and less real to me. Less and less relevant, too. But here's the thing: my emotions must have been a little too heavy-duty for me to even consider. How do I know this? What do I mean? Well, years later, my father was down in the basement with my brother and they came across a pile of broken pencils. My father pressed Danny about this, because he was finding his pencils broken in half, and he figured Danny was the likely culprit. Each time my father would wonder about it, but then he'd get distracted and move on to something else, and now here they had discovered this pile of dozens of snapped pencils. It was a mystery my father hadn't even recognized as a mystery until just this moment. But Danny wasn't the one breaking all those pencils; it was me. Apparently, as I sat at my father's desk, looking at pictures, trying by turns to remember *and* forget the mother I'd lost, I'd fiddle with his pencils and break them in half. It was my release, my frustration. It was almost like a nervous tic, the way I kept mindlessly snapping these pencils, like I was easing up the pressures in my brain through this one action. I had all these thoughts, all these emotions, buried so deep within me that despite my inability to really acknowledge or act on them, they bubbled forth in this oddly aggressive way.

There's a lot of stuff like this that went unnoticed in our house—tucked away like these broken pencils, the hardly seen pictures of my mother. Once, long after my mother was gone, my father asked us kids if we needed "any of that so-called quality time." He said it in a tone of voice that made such a thing seem silly, so of course we picked up on that. I did, anyway. I made like I agreed with him. I said, "Quality time? Us? You're kidding, right?" It's like I was telling my father what I thought he wanted to hear, but the sad truth was that I'd been aching for just that. *Quality* time—with my father, with my mother, with both of my parents, together . . . all of that was missing from my life and I couldn't even recognize it.

I can only imagine how things must have been for my father. I mean, I'd lost my mom. Danny and Vanessa, they'd lost their mom. But my father, he'd lost his wife, his partner, the love of his life . . . it had to be a devastating thing. It wasn't a marriage of curiosity, the way it was often written about in the newspapers, or whispered about in our community, or even in my father's family and among his few friends and colleagues. It wasn't a novelty, a souvenir of his time in the jungle. No, my parents had a meaningful, almost spiritual kind of connection. They came from two vastly different worlds, but they were one . . . for a time. And now here he was, a single father, raising three small children, holding down a busy, demanding, intellectually draining job, doing the best he could.

For the first few years, we moved about in a shared silence, tiptoeing around the subject of my mother. Eventually it became clear to all of us kids that she wasn't coming back, but it was never really discussed—at least, not in an age-appropriate way. Certainly, not in a nurturing way. There were times when my father would let loose a volley of Yanomami expressions. Usually this would set me off, and I'd scream right back at him, "Stop with that stupid jungletalk!" That's what I used to call it, *jungletalk*—like it was shot through with black magic and dark, ancient tribal rituals.

Oh, and there was also this: for many years after my mother left, my father used to drag us to the annual meeting of the American Anthropological Association. One year when I was twelve, I stood in the hallway at one of these conferences with a good professional friend of his. We'd known this woman for many years and for whatever reason she had me huddled in conversation. These annual conferences were usually held toward the end of the year, in November or December, so naturally our talk turned to Christmas.

"Tell me what you want for Christmas this year, David," the woman said.

I was shy, didn't know how to answer. But this woman was persistent.

"No, really," she said. "Whatever you want, I'll get it for you."

I got all wide-eyed and superexcited, so I said, "I want a Nintendo 64 with Mario Kart!" I just blurted it out. I was like that kid in *A Christmas Story,* asking for his Red Ryder BB gun. For a few short moments, the thought that this woman had offered to buy this for me made me the happiest twelve-year-old on the planet—but as soon as I put it out there I looked up at this woman's horrified face and realized this wasn't about to happen.

She gasped—theatrically, like in a scene from a movie. Like she was horrified. She said, "David, I'm surprised at you. I'm very disappointed in you. You want a video game? You, of all people! You're just like every other American child. I expected something different from you."

Her voice was thick with disdain.

Holy shit, did that hurt! It felt to me like I was being teased on the playground at school by some kid who'd learned about my family background—but here it was coming from a grown woman. A family friend, no less! First she baited me into telling her what I really, really wanted for Christmas, told me not to hold back, and then she shot me down. And she didn't just shoot me down; she shot all kinds of holes in how I saw myself, in how I identified myself as any other twelve-year-old American boy. Of course, I was just like every other American child—that's how I was being raised!—but for some reason that wasn't good enough. That wasn't the role I was meant to play; in some ways, it wasn't even the role I was *allowed* to play.

All the time, I moved about with the unshakable sense that the world viewed us as an odd family—because, hey, back in the early 1990s, there weren't a whole lot of single fathers in our community, and among that small group there were hardly any who were raising three kids on their own . . . and only one who'd traveled all the way to the Amazon rainforest to find someone to marry and be a mother to his children.

Let's face it, our family was so far removed from the norms of our society that there was bound to be some finger-pointing, some whispering, and this became another thing for me to rail against, to reject. I hated the way we were scrutinized as a family. Probably one of the most uncomfortable examples of this was being forced to sit down with my kindergarten teacher, Mrs. M., who used to try to gain my confidence in a very sugary way. I remember despising this woman for this, not trusting her, thinking she was out to trip us up. She'd pull me aside while the other kids were playing, or keep me in the classroom after school or during recess, and pepper me with all these too-personal questions:

Do you miss your mom? Do you love your father? Does he ever hit you? Does he ever touch you?

At six years old, I could only mumble one-word answers, but it was clear to me even then what was going on. It was super-uncomfortable, super-unsettling. It was clear to me that people thought our circumstances strange and worrying and that me and my siblings needed protecting, in a child welfare department sort of way.

In response, I could only run through her questions with knee-jerk answers:

Yes, I miss my mom. Yes, I love my father. No, he never hit me. No, he never touches me. Leave me alone, you vile woman.

My teachers and other adults could sniff around all they wanted. They could go out of their way to look for ugliness, but there was no ugliness of any kind. About the only negative you could say about my father was that he didn't pick up on any of the clues that I was struggling with the loss of my mother, with an uncertain sense of identity. Every once in a while, he'd sit me down and tell me to be proud of my heritage, but only in response to some sort of outburst on my part—like me saying, "I am not Yanomami." Or, "I hate Mom!" Or, "Who wants to live in the jungle and eat snakes?"

Sometimes these outbursts came after an incident at school or with the neighborhood kids, who would occasionally press me about my mother. They asked a lot of questions. Our family's minor celebrity status didn't help things at all. There were articles in *People* magazine. There were talk shows, lecture appearances, book signings. There was talk of a movie, a documentary. Mostly, a lot of talk—some of it directed at me and my siblings, which I really, really hated. (Really!) So I tuned it out, best I could. I dug in a little more. Renounced my Yanomami heritage a little more forcefully. Buried my past in age-appropriate ways and determined to live a wholeheartedly American, same-seeming, attention-free life.

I don't recall the exact moment when I decided I no longer wanted to be Yanomami. There must have been a specific turning point that spun me from one side to the other on this. Whatever that moment was, however it came about, it's been lost to the years, buried beneath a lifetime of identity confusion and misplaced shame. These days I find myself wishing like crazy that I could undo the distance I put between myself and my mother's memory as I was growing up—but, of course, that's not possible, so I content myself with making up for lost time and looking forward.

And yet, as long as I'm on it, I believe it's useful and perhaps even instructive to look back and try to place my rejection of my Yanomami birthright in context. Why did I harbor such hatred and resentment? What was going on in my little-kid head? What made me think I could try to keep my family "secret" a secret from my friends?

There are no easy answers to these questions, and the questions don't end here, but there's a common denominator. The way I see it, I internalized my mother's leaving as abandonment, and this was probably why I rejected that part of my life. It felt to me like I wasn't good enough to be her son—like I wasn't *son* enough to get her to stay, or to want to take me with her back to the jungle. I never articulated these feelings, never even came close to recognizing them or acknowledging them in just this way, but this is how I've come to understand them. Yes, I was the product of an extraordinary marriage, the son of a Yanomami woman. And yes, this distinction set me apart in some way—at a time in my life when all I wanted to do was fit in.

As I reflect on that time in my life, I realize that these feelings of abandonment were based on my own Western ideal. I took an ethnocentric view—a view that railed against my mother's decision to abandon us. How else was I supposed to react? I was a child, an adolescent, a teenager, a young adult . . . I didn't have the tools or the world view to consider Mom's actions in context. Even so, those old feelings continue to tear at me as I think of my younger self. I close my eyes and picture my mother leaving my infant brother on that grassy airstrip, crying his little head off, knowing she might never see him again. I weep for little Danny, for Vanessa, for me. Intellectually, I understand that this was what my mother had to do to survive, to breathe . . . to *be*. And I get how mightily she must have struggled when she was in the United States, trying to make things work with my father and three small children.

But this is me, thinking with my head, as an adult. Back then, when I was struggling to make sense of my place in the world, I could only think with my heart.

WHEN I WAS IN the third grade, we moved to Long Valley, New Jersey—an upscale community that reinforced for me how different I felt in my own skin. Dad thought Long Valley would be a great place to raise his family, and on one level it was. However, the lily-white demographics forced me to be hyperaware of my physical characteristics and my identity as a Yanomami. The way I remember it, there were only three kids of color in my entire school. I stood out, absolutely—and I hated that I stood out. It's a wearying thing, a never-ending assault on your emerging sense of self, to know that no matter what you do or how hard you try, you will stand out. You will be noticed, picked on. And I was, constantly. The other two students of color, my compatriots, fared a bit better. They at least had "normal" white parents—both had been adopted—so their home lives were typical, and very much in line with the community.

Mine? Not so much. I was an outlier, in every way possible,

and every night as I fell fitfully to sleep I'd think of new ways to keep my secret from the other kids. As far as I ever knew, none of my friends knew about my jungle mom, but I lived in fear that I'd be found out and taunted on the school playground, that someone would call my mother a "primitive savage," or announce that she was "living naked in the jungle," with "freaky sticks in her nose." I'd hear those specific words in my head, in my dreams, and I was too ashamed, too afraid to ever bring this up with my father.

There was no denying my heritage, my unique place on the fault line between these two vastly different worlds, but I denied it just the same. I wouldn't even refer to my mother as "Mom" after she left us; I'd coldly refer to her as the woman my father married. Even after I'd flipped that on/off switch and vowed to grow up in the dark, my Yanomami past kept coming into the light, especially as I moved on in school. Throughout grade school, there was a long line of Mrs. M's who threatened to reveal my true identity, who pushed me to consider my family history in ways that suited *their* needs instead of mine, but I managed to stiff-arm the attention at just about every turn.

By middle school, though, this was a little more difficult. My teachers were more inclined to treat me as an adult—or, at least, a mini-adult who could be pushed and prodded to reconsider an admittedly narrow worldview. I can remember one crisis moment that found me as I was walking down the hall to my social stud- ies class. I was in the fifth or sixth grade, at Long Valley Middle School. I can close my eyes and picture it. I was walking past the dark blue lockers that lined the hallway. I was wearing my favorite pair of jeans and a faded T-shirt, my long hair parted on the left—a style that earned me a ton of teasing from Vanessa and Danny, who called it an old-fashioned comb-over. Still, by every other outward appearance, I fashioned myself to look like every other boy in the school, which was always my goal. Any day that I could pass unnoticed, just one of many typically American kids dotting the school landscape, was a good day. But this day was about to turn. It turned when I stepped into that social studies classroom and saw a pile of *Scholastic Journal* magazines, which came in every month or so. The drill was we would spend the first few minutes of class thumbing through the magazine on our own, and then the teacher would lead us in group discussion about whatever we'd just read, which was usually some fresh take on current events written for a middle school audience.

The class bell wasn't due to ring for another few minutes, so I grabbed my copy and started flipping through the pages, and as soon as I did my heart nearly stopped. The lead article that month was about the deforestation of the Amazon and how it was threatening the Yanomami. Accompanying the article were a dozen or so pictures—including (get this!) a picture of me! It was taken on our last trip to the jungle, when I was five years old; in the picture, one of my uncles was teaching me how to use a bow and arrow. I can't imagine anyone in that classroom could have made the connection, but there it was—the most unlikely, most incredible, most damning thing. Underneath the picture was a caption that read: "Yanomami boy learns to shoot a bow and arrow." I panicked—I felt like I was in a prison cell instead of a classroom.

I looked around the room and noticed a few of the other early-arrivers reading the same article, some of them turned to that very page. I studied their faces, but could see no signs to indicate they'd recognized me. There was no logical reason for anyone to make such a leap, but I worried anyway. I wasn't thinking clearly, could only imagine the worst, and the worst had some kid pointing to me and making jungle noises and everyone else joining in, laughing.

I scanned the article and noticed with great relief that it didn't include my father's name—but still, I was frantic that one of the other kids would discover my truth, that one side of my family was living naked in the jungle, shooting monkeys out of trees and eating bugs, that I was the little boy in the picture. Here in Long Valley, my secret was my own—at least among the kids in my class. Anyway, nobody said anything, and the classroom discussion that followed didn't give me away. The teacher had us read aloud from the magazine, and every time I heard the word *Yanomami* it was like a knife was being pressed into my back.

Finally, mercifully, class came to an end, and I stuffed my books in my backpack and tried to make a quick exit—but before I could make it to the door the teacher called me to her desk.

I felt defeated, deflated . . . found out. And I was. The teacher knew my story, of course—it would follow me all through school, a part of my permanent record. But she also knew that I was quiet about it. And here, to her great credit, she didn't advertise my story to the other kids in the room. She simply took the opportunity to press me on it privately—and to me, just then, this was agony enough. This was violation enough. I felt vulnerable, exposed. I didn't want anyone to see me weak, to see me as I did not wish to be seen, even my social studies teacher. But there was nothing I could do. I had to answer her questions, tell her everything she wanted to know, peel off another layer of myself and lay it out for her inspection.

That night, I lay awake in bed, feeling helpless, hopeless, pathetic, ashamed, depressed. I wanted to scream—but screaming would only bring my father in to see what the matter was. Screaming would only force me to peel off another layer and talk through my feelings . . . feelings I still didn't understand.

I'M NO PSYCHOLOGIST, SO I can't begin to imagine what was going on with me during those first couple of years after Mom left. I've logged a bunch of time in therapy as an adult, and even here I could only throw up my hands and wonder what was eating me as a kid, what I was railing against, why I was railing against it. But I do know this: I rejected my mother, in no uncertain terms. I know that a part of me felt like she had abandoned us because we weren't good enough, loving enough, Yanomami enough . . . *enough* enough. I know that my father didn't do the best job trying to turn me around in my thinking. Instead of *telling* me to be proud of who I was and to celebrate my Yanomami roots, he might have *shown* me these things. This is not a knock on him, not at all, because I know in my heart he was doing the best he could with the tools he had . . . but, *still*, he might have taken out those tucked-away pictures and helped to attach some stories to those mysterious faces. Oh, man . . . how I wish he'd picked up on some of those clues, those little red flags I couldn't help but wave, letting him know I was struggling. I wish he could have read my mind. That "quality time" he seemed to think wasn't necessary to the health and well-being of our little family? I wish we had some of that, too.

When I was twelve, we moved to Easton, Pennsylvania— and this would be another fresh start. Now I was old enough to strike out on my own a little bit, cut my own path, create a whole new identity for myself. This time I vowed that *no one*, not a single soul, would know my story. Not a teacher, not a friend, not a coach . . . no one. I would not be known as the son of an exotic Amazonian woman. No. I would be known as *me*. For *me*.

This strategy worked well enough, but there was some fallout to it—collateral damage, I guess you could say. By the time I got to high school, I had less and less to do with my father. We were emotionally distant, disconnected. Here again, a shrink would have said I blamed him in part, for the fact that I felt so constantly and desperately out of place, for the fact that there was nowhere to put all these confusing emotions and set things right. But in the end a lot of that blame was on me, because I didn't have the insight or the confidence to talk to him about it.

As I got older, I spent less and less time with my siblings, too. We had been close as kids, but I grew distant, and soon the three of us were living different lives. I found a good group of friends and started avoiding our house. I moved around our small town like I belonged no place else—like I'd come from no place else. I played a lot of sports, went to a lot of movies, hung out in my friends' kitchens, talking to *their* moms, imagining myself into *their* lives. I'd listen as my friends called out to their mothers and

I'd get crazy jealous—just the chance to say the word *mom* and have it mean something . . . that would have meant the world to me. A lot of times, there'd be a group of us at a friend's house, and everyone else would have gone in the other room to watch television or play video games, or maybe outside to mess around, and I'd be hanging back in the kitchen, helping my friend's mother make lunch or do the dishes or whatever . . . just soaking in a secondhand mom in this once-removed way.

This was me, hiding in plain sight, fitting myself in, passing myself off as a typical American kid.

One of the great hiding places for me during my childhood was baseball. I think I was drawn to it because it was such an all-American thing—the "national pastime." It represented what I so very much wanted to put out into the world . . . but there was more to it than that. I was also good at it. I was a decent athlete, and whatever natural ability I had was neatly matched to the game. I was fast—and not *just* fast, but quick as well. I could cover a lot of ground in the outfield, get a good read on the ball off the bat. Also, I could run the bases like a demon, and I had a laser-sharp eye at the plate. I hit in the leadoff spot, and I was a better-than-average spray hitter with a knack for getting on base . . . and once I was on base, I had a talent for rattling the pitcher and making things happen.

I'm not saying these things to blow smoke my way, but to set the scene, to show how it is that when you're encouraged in a thing, when you get a certain amount of positive feedback from it, you'll be drawn to it, big-time. And when that positive thing helps to blot out whatever pain or anguish or uncertainty attaches to your tucked-away life at home, you grab on and hold it close.

The other great hiding place I made for myself was a bold, hateful lie: I started telling people my mother died in a car crash. I was so crazy focused on deflecting attention from my jungle family tree, I decided Mom was better off dead. It shut people up, I'll say that. I realize now that I could have deflected that attention in a bunch of other ways—I could have simply told people she was from Venezuela, while sparing the details, or if I was feeling ambitious maybe even say she was from Italy, which would have explained my features. I could have said she had to go back home to take care of an aunt or uncle, which would have explained her absence . . . but that's not the way I played it.

I can still remember the first time I told someone my mother was dead. I was in the backseat of a car with my best friend Kyle. His mother was driving, making polite conversation. I don't know if she knew my family history, or if she was just playing dumb or being nice, but at some point she asked about my mother—something along the lines of "I don't think I've ever met your mom, David. Does she work out of the house?"

It might have been an innocent question, just something to say, but I heard it as an affront; it felt to me like I had to push back, so I said, "My mother's dead. She died in a car crash."

I didn't plan on saying this, didn't think it through beforehand. And I wasn't nasty or challenging about it, either. It just kind of came out in this matter-of-fact way . . . and once it did, I ran with it. There wasn't a whole lot Kyle's mother could say except to apologize profusely.

Soon as we got out of the car, Kyle punched me in the shoulder—said, "Dude, what the hell? I heard that your mom was, like, from another country. Said she had to go back home or some shit."

I punched him right back—said, "Shut the fuck up, Kyle."

And that was that.

From that day on, this became my go-to answer. It was like magic. It put an end to everyone's questions—even the innocent, well-meaning ones. And the great thing about this little white lie (okay, maybe it was a *big* white lie) was that there were never any follow-up questions. What do you say to a kid when he blurts out something like this? You certainly don't ask for details. You change the subject. But there was more to it than redirecting the conversation, I think. There was also this layer of revenge. In the way, way back of my mind, it gave me a little bit of power over a situation that had left me essentially powerless, and allowed me to take a measure of control in how I looked out at the world, how the world looked back at me.

From time to time, my two hiding places came into conflict— meaning, the one kind of canceled out the other, leaving me feeling lost, exposed. Once, not long after we'd settled into this new community, and I was feeling pretty good about the way I'd been able to keep my family history a secret, we had dinner with my baseball coach. He'd taken an interest in my game and was spending a lot of time with me, and it worked out one night that he took me and my father out for the best cheese steaks I ever had. My coach was one of those grizzled old baseball types, the kind of guy who looked like he'd been around a ball field his entire life. He told us a lot of stories about his time in the game, shared a bunch of tips on what I could do to be a better player, all of that. But then, in the middle of this great night, with these great cheese steaks, this great baseball chatter, my father tried to make a joke—and just like that, my world turned dark. He turned to my coach and said, "David here's not like the other boys you're used to coaching. The other boys, their moms are driving them back and forth to baseball practice. But David's mom, she's off in the jungle somewhere, naked, eating tarantulas."

It's a line I'd later steal and use in interviews, but back then it stung. It didn't strike me as funny . . . not at all. No, it was mortifying. All I'd ever wanted was to be like the other kids, to fit in, and here my father was calling me out to my coach in this embarrassing way, pulling the curtain back on how things were with our family . . . *joking* about it, even. I could have crawled underneath the table and died, and the worst part was that my father had left me ripped open like this in front of my baseball coach—a guy who'd had no reason to think of me as any different from all his other players up until this one low moment. Baseball was my thing, after all, my safe haven. For a while in there, it was the only place I felt truly at peace with myself, the only place I belonged, and here my father just kind of blew up my spot.

And it got worse from there. The coach, he thought this was

just about the funniest thing in the world—he wanted to keep the joke going the next day at practice, told me it would be great if I could show up to practice barefoot. "You can run the bases like that," he said, "and represent your people."

He was half-kidding, half-serious, but either way it added up to me feeling naked and ashamed in front of a man I admired, a man whose stamp of approval I thought I desperately needed. He didn't leave it alone, either. I tried to ignore him, shrug it off, but all season long Coach found a way to bring it back up. He'd take me aside and say stupid shit like, "Hey, Good, you don't really need those cleats. You can just run the bases in your bare feet."

It's tough for me to explain the special place I'd made in my life for the game of baseball. It's still a big deal to me, although I don't play much. I'm a Pennsylvania kid, so I root, root, root for my Phillies; toward the end of my high school career, they had a short, speedy Hawaiian outfielder named Shane Victorino, who used to remind me of the way I played the game—full tilt—so he became my favorite player. Still is, if you're keeping score at home. And I can still lose myself in the smell of the glove, the rhythms of the game, which I first felt playing catch with my father—so at least I can say my old man found *some* ways to connect with me outside the house. Dad was a good athlete with a strong throwing arm, so when we tossed the ball around it would pop into my glove with a sweet-hollow *thwack* . . . one of the signature sounds of my childhood.

What I remember best about playing back in middle school and high school was having all that room to myself out in centerfield. That was my position, and I *owned* it. I covered a lot of ground out there, and I loved that it was all mine. It was just about the only place in Easton, Pennsylvania, where I felt I truly belonged, where I had the power to do anything, accomplish anything . . . *be* anything. It was so peaceful out there, so calm . . . and here too this was part of the game's great appeal. The game itself is more of a mind game—as Yogi Berra so famously said, "Ninety percent of the game is half-mental." It's not all-out physical—at least not all-out all the time. There are bursts of action, interrupted by these great long pauses, all this time to think, and I tried to put that time to good use. I studied the other team. If there was a kid at the plate with a short swing, I'd make this or that adjustment in center. If there was a runner on second and our pitcher was holding him on, I'd try to anticipate his move. I'd try to think how Shane Victorino might react, might anticipate, might *will* himself to where the ball was headed a beat or two before it got there.

I was a good guy to have on your side, but I wasn't one of those kids who screamed their lungs out in the dugout, yelling "Hey, batter-batter!" or any of the other crap kids tend to yell from the bench. I didn't think cheering on my teammate would make him a better player, so I'd put my time to what I thought was more productive use. I'd study the pitcher. I'd check out his move to first base. I'd grab a bat and wait for my turn to hit, and to look at me, lost in the mind game inside the game itself, you'd have never imagined that my insides were churning, that there was this gaping hole in my heart . . . an emptiness in the place where my mother used to be.

So, yeah, baseball helped. But it couldn't help for long. Soon there were girls and alcohol and a whole mess of trouble lining up to set me off my game.

I WAS FOURTEEN YEARS old when I had my first taste of hard liquor. I'd found a stash of my dad's dry gin and wine in a cabinet in the kitchen. It wasn't any kind of big deal at first. Like a lot of kids, my alcohol consumption was limited by my limited access. But once I'd had my first taste, I only wanted more—a thirst that would change my life forever. I can remember the first time I got drunk. A few swigs and my fingertips began to feel funny. A few swigs more and I started giggling; everything was suddenly tranquil. This magical liquid took away my pain, lifted me from my worries. I didn't give a fuck about my problems—who I was, where I came from, who knew, who didn't know . . . All I cared

about, really, was when I could get my hands on another bottle—
the beginning of a dark, destructive path that nearly did me in.

There were distractions all around—enough to fool me into
thinking all was right with my little world. Soon enough, I had
found my first love. Her name was Sarah. I could talk to her about
my feelings, my emotions, my family. I'd never had that kind of
relationship before. All that buried shit, it started to come into
play. That's when I began to feel this hole in my life, in the place
where my mother was meant to be. Something was missing, you
know. Something I hadn't let myself see or feel until I started putting all this stuff out there with Sarah. Until I got drunk for the
first time.

We became super-attached—who knows, maybe in an
unhealthy way. I was pretty obsessed. I used to duck out of the
house at night and ride my bicycle to her house, a couple of town-
ships away. She'd sneak me up to her bedroom, and we'd talk and
fool around and talk some more.

One night, Sarah's parents found us out. I was hiding in the
closet. They didn't say anything, but it was clear they knew what
was going on. The next morning, I got a call from Sarah's mom,
but she didn't rip into me or anything. She was actually great
about it. She told me that I was always welcome in their home,
that she and her husband were mostly worried about me riding
my bicycle in the middle of the night, clear across town. She also
agreed not to tell my father, so I wouldn't get in trouble at home,
but somehow Dad found out about it and he was livid. He didn't
care so much that I'd snuck out; what set him off was that Sarah's
parents had conspired with me to keep something from him. Oh,
man . . . was he pissed! From a parental perspective, I can totally
understand his reaction. I get it . . . *now*. But back then . . . not so
much. My father ended up banning me from Sarah's house, which
I took as a kind of death sentence. I mean, this was my first real
romance. This was true love. I thought I was going to marry this
girl, so I was reeling.

I sank into a deep depression, spending hours and hours alone in my bedroom. Sarah, she took it more in stride. She was upset about it, but not too upset—and not for too long. She went back to her routines, and soon enough she started hanging out with other guys, and I looked on and sank into a darker place. That deep, black funk I wrote about earlier? I was all over it—or, I should say, *it* was all over *me*.

In the fallout after Sarah, I cast my father as the bad guy, the source of all my troubles. I hated him just then. He'd ruined my life. And it wasn't just this latest thing with Sarah. My mind wandered all the way back to him meeting my mother, him bringing her to the States to start their own little family. I hated that he'd set me up in this world in such an outside-looking-in way. I was different, and I hated that I was different, and I hated him for making it so.

I felt empty. I didn't think there was anything I could do to set things right, except maybe to disappear. So that's what I did: I stole my father's car one cold February night when I was sixteen, along with about $1,200. It was a beige 1999 Toyota Camry. It was in pretty decent shape—that is, until I was five minutes away from my house and I clipped a car parked on the side of a neighborhood street. Ripped my passenger-side mirror right off, which meant it probably did a bunch of damage to the other car as well, but I didn't stop to see. I just kept going—my first hit-and-run, and I'd been driving for only five minutes.

I took my father's car on a whim, but it was a calculated whim; I thought it through enough to know I could pull it off. I'd thought about it before, a bunch of times, only I never acted on it; it was more like a fantasy, one I sometimes shared with my friends. Weeks before I finally took off, I even turned one of those conversations into a deception; I told my friends I was running away to Canada. I suppose I did this to lay a bit of groundwork, to set it up in everyone's head so that when I finally did disappear the cops would start to question everyone and they would divert them to Canada, in the complete opposite direction.

Anyway, I didn't have a driver's license—hell, I didn't have more than two or three hours of driving experience, but that didn't keep me from my impulses. I pointed the car toward Philadelphia, pulled into a gas station, and bought a map. I hated the cold winter, so I decided I would drive down to Florida. I asked the guy behind the cash register how to get to Interstate 95 and he pointed me in the right direction and I was on my way.

I don't know how the hell I made it all the way to Florida, but I made it. Told myself to take it slow, to keep moving, to try not to freak out. Told myself I didn't really need a passenger -side mirror after all. Always, I'd been very good at compartmentalizing my emotions, my problems. I did the same thing here with any fears or concerns that came up along the way. I kept telling myself that fear would only make things worse. I half-expected to be pulled over by the cops, so I just gassed up and hit the road. No looking back. No thinking too long or too hard about any obstacles in my path.

It was 2003—way before someone like my father would have had GPS in his car. I did have a cell phone, though, but I didn't call home. Remember, I wanted to disappear, so calling home to let my father know I wasn't dead wasn't exactly high on my to-do list. It didn't even *occur* to me to call home, that's how checked out I was, how outside myself. If it had, I would have realized my father was probably going bat-shit crazy with worry, probably frantic, probably putting up "Have You Seen This Child?" posters all around town.

But I was gone. Just, gone.

I had it in my head that I would be a hobo, a drifter. I'd find a job in a restaurant kitchen and sleep out back. I'd be okay. But I wasn't okay; I think I cried for half the trip. At one point, "I Drove All Night" by Celine Dion popped on the radio and I remember laughing to myself and wiping away my tears—thinking, How appropriate.

The first call I made when I got to Florida was to Sarah. She still had my heart—so, yeah, definitely, she was the one I called. She told me the cops were interrogating her, said all of my friends were being questioned by the police. It was a giant mess. I hadn't thought about the mess I'd leave behind. I just wanted out, but when I left all these gears starting grinding. All these people were caught up in it. A distant relative of mine was a computer forensics detective, and he was on the case, looking for me. I didn't know it at the time, but whenever I used the cell phone he'd get a ping on my location, so they could track my comings and goings. And to top it off, there was a warrant out for my arrest. I was being charged with grand theft auto—not because my father was pressing charges, but because someone had told him the warrant would make it easier for the cops to track me down.

Sarah knew someone in the Tampa area—a friend of a friend of a friend—and she put me in touch, and this person put me in touch with another person who offered me a place to crash. It turned out this other person was a social worker who worked with at-risk teenagers, so it's like I was sent from central casting, like fate put me on this woman's doorstep, on her couch. This woman lived in a nice-enough trailer park just outside of town, and we'd sit around talking; she tried to get me to see my situation clearly, in a more objective way. She was very kind and sympathetic to my situation. She tried to get me to see my father's situation, too. Really, she did everything she could to help me set my demons aside and get back to the life I'd left behind, but I wasn't ready to hear it. All I could think was that I could maybe crash in her trailer until I got my shit together, but after a week she told me I'd have to think about leaving, said she couldn't harbor a runaway minor, said it was a felony. I knew as much, of course, but I was hoping it would take her a little while longer to kick me out.

From there, I had planned to double back to Ohio, where another friend of a friend offered to take me in, but before I got there the plan changed and I was headed back to Nazareth, Pennsylvania, about ten miles from where I lived in Easton. I was pissed, frustrated, to have made it so far only to be returned so close to home, but it's not like I had a whole lot of options. I'd blown through the money I'd taken from my father. I needed a place to stay, and I needed to stay gone, but I had to drive all the way to Florida and back just to hole up in a stranger's house I could have ridden to on my bicycle.

All told, I stayed gone for six months. No one in my family knew where I was, but I didn't do such a great job covering my tracks once I returned to Pennsylvania. I'd figured the cops would be tracking my phone, so I ditched it as soon as I got to Florida, only now that I was so close to home, I ditched the car, too. I left it in the parking lot of a convenience store in York, a nearby city known for its gang activity, so when the cops found the car people started to think I'd been killed or maybe joined a gang—anyway, that was the buzz among my left-behind friends. It was a selfish, hostile move, to disappear like that and to leave my father frantic with worry, to leave my friends to deal with the cops pressing them for information, but in my defense, I was desperate—also, I wasn't thinking very clearly. It was mostly about being gone, that's all, and I never stopped to think what that would mean for my father, who'd already had to deal with the trauma of losing a wife who'd disappeared on him—so, yeah, absolutely, it was self-ish, immature, thoughtless . . . all of that.

Oh, and there was also this: one of the first things I did when I arrived in Florida was buy a bag of oranges, and those oranges were still in the car when I got back to Pennsylvania. It was considerably warmer when I got back to town, so when I abandoned the car by that convenience store those oranges started to really stink. Remember, it was the middle of winter when I took off, but by now it was spring, and it got superhot inside that car, and those oranges were rank. Really, the inside of that car was *foul*, so when the car was returned to my father that's the one thing he filed away for later. Forget the side mir-ror, the other scratches and dings I collected on my travels. It was the smell that got him going—so much so that when we were finally reunited the first thing he said to me was "Why couldn't you have taken those oranges out of the car?" He said it as a joke, and it's become a kind of family punch line over the

Hanging out in our Rutherford, New Jersey, home. From left to right, Mom, Vanessa, me, and Dad—and check out Mom's Harvard sweatshirt.

Mom, holding newborn Vanessa as I look on. This was taken just a few weeks after we'd left Hasupuwe, where Vanessa was born. Those McDonald's french fries were one of her favorite Western foods. Twenty years later, when I returned to her, one of the first things she said to me was, "I want French Fries!"

Mom practicing her ABCs. English was a frustrating language for her, especially after us kids started to outpace her. After a great deal of practice, she managed to master her own signature— two squiggly circles.

With my little brother Daniel, to round out the picture— one big happy family.

There were many aspects of Western life that Mom enjoyed, including lounging by the pool and catching some rays. Here she is with Vanessa and baby Daniel. That's me, hiding behind the towel.

Making our way up the Orinoco River. Step by step we are getting closer to my village. A sudden sense of familiarity filled my ears, nose, eyes as I started to remember the trees, the water, the sultry air, the sound of the motor.

Setting my hammock in Hasupuwei, waiting for Mom to arrive. The women and children of the village flocked around me in order to "get to know me." I'd never had so many hands on my body at the same time. Everyone was touching my nose, ears, face, hair . . . It was a thrilling moment as I met my indigenous family for the first time in twenty years.

Moments after reconnecting with Mom. Though we are of two radically different cultures and we cannot speak each other's language except in fits and starts, the bond between mother and son could not be broken by the years or the vast spaces that separated us.

The first "family" photo taken with my Yanomami family. Me, Mom, and my brother, Ricky Martin. I love how Mom has her hand around my arm, like she's announcing to the village, "This is my son. He is back and I will claim him."

Ricky Martin listening to some punk rock on my MP3 player during my first trip to the territory. It's a safe bet that he's Taking Back Sunday's number one fan in Yanomami-land.

Here's Ricky Martin on my 2013 trip, talking to my father in the U.S. on my Iridium satellite phone. One of my uncles is in the background—no doubt wondering how in the world "Kenny's" voice is coming from this strange black brick.

Escaping the midday sun, relaxing in my hammock on my 2013 trip to the territory. This photo was taken minutes after I'd received my first Yanomami haircut in the traditional bowl style. Little by little, I was playing my part.

Doing my laundry with Mom in a nearby creek. Even though we were deep in the jungle, Mom found a way to make my clothes smell clean and fresh—nothing like a mother's touch when it comes to laundry.

Practicing archery with the boys during my 2013 trip. We used a small plantain tree as a target. After a few tries, I nailed a direct bulls-eye, which left the others in awe. Being able to hunt proficiently is one of many markers of what it means to be a man in Yanomami culture. Someday, I will kill my first tapir with a bow and arrow.

Occasionally, Mom would surprise me with a burst of English. Here, on my 2011 trip, she held out this segment of a gutted and cleaned boa constrictor and said, "Want some snake?"

Sharing a laugh with Layla—Wife #1. She was so kind and patient with me, teaching me much of the Yanomami ways.

A jungle selfie taken on my 2011 trip, with Lucy—Wife #2. We really got along, even though I wasn't exactly living up to my husbandly duties.

On our way to go fishing on my 2011 visit. Layla is carrying her daughter, Paula, in the traditional Yanomami way.

years, but at the time I remember thinking we could have used this moment in a more meaningful way.

In all fairness to my father, he did try to push me to talk about my disappearance, but he did it in his typical "hands-off" style. As I write this, I'm searching in my thesaurus for a word to describe how he handled emotionally charged situations like this one with me and my siblings, but I keep coming up empty. What's the opposite of "touchy-feely"? Whatever *that* is, that's a good description for my dad, and it fits here, because the closest he came to starting a *real* conversation with me was asking, "Does this have anything to do with Mom leaving?"

He really wanted to know what was up with me, what had caused me to take his car and disappear like that for six months, and all of this was somehow tied to this one simple question.

I said, "Yes." That's all, just one word, but there was nothing in my tone or demeanor to suggest I wanted to keep the conversation going, either, so we moved on to something else.

That's just how things were between us, how they'd always been, and the whole time I was away from home I imagined how this conversation would go. Of course, I knew—but *still*, I imagined. And remember, I didn't speak to my father once during those six months. I could only cry myself to sleep each night, pissed at my father for pushing my buttons in this way, pissed at myself for letting things go so far off the rails. Truth was, I missed my father desperately while I was gone—I would have given anything to unspool all those miles and climb into his arms for a hug, the way he used to pick me up when I was little. But my father couldn't find a way to reach back out to me, and I couldn't find a reason to head home.

And now that I finally had . . . well, it was as if I had never left.

LET'S BE CLEAR: MANY of the details surrounding my disappearance must be kept secret, even after all this time. Why? Because there were a lot of folks who helped me, harbored me, counseled me, and I don't want to serve them up in these pages. After all, some of them committed a felony, taking in a minor child, refusing to report my whereabouts to the police. I'm grateful to them, one and all, and the only way I can show my gratitude and repay their kindness is to keep the details out of this account and jump ahead to the moment I decided to check back in to the life I'd left behind.

I said goodbye to my "hosts" and made my way to the nearest police station. Inside, I approached the receptionist and told her I was a runaway minor and that there was a warrant out for my arrest. She took down my information and summoned an officer, and the next thing I know my father and I were reunited in the holding cell.

I could have cried . . . but I didn't. He could have cried . . . but he didn't. We awkwardly shook hands, though. And he did drop those grand theft auto charges, so at least I wouldn't be in the system as a juvenile delinquent. So, there was *that*.

While I was gone, I had a kind of emotional awakening. I had spent days upon days alone in a room, meditating, reading self-help books. I realized that whatever funk I was in, whatever uncertainty I was facing, it was on me to power through, so I decided to return to high school and clean up the mess I'd left behind. But not before I made another misstep or two. Things were a little weird between me and Dad when I got back. We were both kind of circling each other, afraid to say anything. Years later, when I read his book, it reminded me of the way he circled around Mom when he returned to the village after he'd been a way for an extended period. It took a while for them to get back to how they were, and that's a little like how things were with me and my father. In fact, I didn't move back into the house for a couple of months. I stayed with friends, camped out in the woods . . . generally, I tried to avoid him, I guess because of what was left unsaid between us.

The day before school was due to start, he called.(Oh, I'd gotten a new cell phone—paid for it myself with money I earned at my first job, as a clerk at a used sporting goods store called "Play It Again, Sports.")

He said, "David, it's your father. Do you have a place to sleep tonight?"

I said, "Not really, but I'll figure it out."

He said, "Do you have a place where you can study?"

I said, "Not really, but I'll figure it out."

He said, "Do you have food?"

I said, "I can usually find something."

Finally, he said, "Look, you're supposed to start school tomorrow. Why don't you just come home?"

And that was that. Looking back, I can't imagine what I'd put my father through, disappearing like that—and then turning myself in to the police and still finding a way to stay away.

But the pull of school and a return to some kind of normalcy was enough to get me to move back in with Dad, Vanessa, and Danny. The way it worked out, I'd missed the second half of my sophomore year, so when school started up that fall I enrolled as a junior, while making up all the classes I'd left hanging when I disappeared to Florida. My schedule was busy, but I was a good student so I had a handle on it. It was all the other stuff I couldn't quite grasp, despite my emotional awakening. I'd thought I had it all together, but now that I was back home it had quickly come apart, and that's when the drinking really started. It was just a weekend thing at first. But then I cranked it up a couple of notches. I started drinking during the week—during the school day, even. My grades went up and down, like a yo-yo.(Better: like a rollercoaster, because there was something dangerous and thrilling about all those highs and lows.)I'd always been a step or two ahead of the teachers and the other kids in class, but now I went off on these wild swings. I'd be the only kid in class who'd ace one test and fail the next one. I never knew how it would go, and I didn't really care.

Most of my friends were drinking just to have a good time. They were getting wasted, goofing off, blowing off steam, but I wasn't drinking to catch a buzz or make a little weekend noise. I was envious of the way my buddies could drink without a thought—to drink just to drink, to get shit-faced just to get shit-faced. With me there was an emotional piece to it as well. I was getting blackout drunk, almost like I was trying to push away whatever shit I was dealing with in my head, but I wasn't wired in any kind of introspective way back then. I didn't have the tools for it, I think. Or I did but didn't know to take them from the toolbox and put them to work in a *real* way. We all just kind of went about our days. I soon realized, the more I drank, the more I let in all these dark thoughts—thoughts I'd buried deep. But they were down there, somewhere, filed away for when I could deal with them. Only, I wasn't ready to deal with them just yet, so what happened was that the more I thought about my mother, who'd basically been out of my life since I was five years old, the more I sank into this deep, black funk. The more I thought about my father, keeping me from seeing Sarah, saddling me with this jungle back story, being *mostly* unavailable to me as I struggled to find my way, the more I tried to wash those thoughts away.

I ended up dropping out of high school. I went to work full-time at the local Verizon store, and somewhere in there I managed to take a bunch of classes and earn my GED around the same time my buddies were all graduating from high school, so it ended up being one of those *no harm, no foul* situations. Still, as I got older, my troubles seemed bigger—the space between the life I was living and the way I saw myself kept growing, too. I was out of control, drinking like a madman. Once I was out of that high school setting, my alcohol intake increased dramatically, not *just* because it was so suddenly, so readily available, but because it felt like it was expected of me. All around, my friends were drinking with abandon, but they seemed to have things under control. Me, I was all over the place, and nowhere, all at once. I was taking *abandon* to whole new levels.

Somewhere in there I met a girl I'll call Karen in this account. We started seeing each other soon after I returned from my Florida "road trip." In all, we were together nearly four years. I was madly in love with her, and it was an amazing thing, really, that

Karen stuck with me for so long, and tolerated my drinking, my emotional meltdowns—but even Karen had her limits. Once, after Karen had gone away to school at Susquehanna University, I got off work and hopped in the car to go see her. The school was about a three-hour drive from Easton, but I was back and forth so often the drive was like nothing. On this one drive, though, my inner demons hitched along, playing backseat driver. I stopped at the liquor store before leaving town and bought a bottle of my favorite rum. As soon as I hit the highway, I hit the bottle, and by the time I got to Karen's dorm, I was wasted. It's a wonder I drove all the way there without blacking out, and as Karen came out to greet me I spilled out of the car, face-first onto the asphalt.

I was gone . . . just *gone*.

Our routine, when I visited, was to check in to a crappy hotel near campus. I was pretty shy in those days, didn't like being around other people, and we also wanted a place to be together away from her roommates, so Karen peeled me off the ground and coaxed me into the passenger seat. When we got to the hotel she left me in the car as she went to the front desk to check us in, then she dragged me to our room. She turned on the shower, cold, stripped me out of my clothes, and shoved me underneath the cold spray, and I can still picture myself in that sad, low moment: drunk, shivering, naked, pathetic . . . It's a whole other wonder that Karen didn't leave me right then and there. She told me later that she thought about it, long and hard, but she hung in there.

I think Karen really loved me, really believed in me. Her mother, however, started to become deeply concerned. She was starting to realize that I might not be the best match for her daughter, and she invited me to lunch at the Olive Garden one afternoon.

Over the years, I'd become really close with Karen's mom. She was like a mother to me. At first I thought she was just inviting me out for some bottomless breadsticks. So that's how I approached it—free food! But halfway through the meal, our conversation turned serious. Karen's mom started tearing up. She looked hurt and scared. My mind raced. I braced myself for what was coming.

She said, "I love you like a son, David. And I know that Karen loves you. But I see how much you're drinking. Karen doesn't tell me everything, but I know enough to know you're in trouble. I fear for my daughter's life if she stays with you."

Her words were like a punch in the face—I'd say they surprised the hell out of me, but I'd be exaggerating. Truth was, I'd felt this way all along. On some level, I saw this coming. I sank low in my seat. I knew I was a danger to myself, the way I was drinking, and if I was a danger to myself then I was also a danger to Karen. I was on a destructive path, absolutely, and I didn't want to drag her down with me—but here I was, dragging.

I guess I could have gone to therapy and tried to change. I could have argued my case with Karen's mom, with Karen. The same way Karen had decided to hang in there with me, I could have found a way to hang in there and put on a good front for the next while, maybe find a way to set things right. But that's not how it played out. I was enough of a drunk to know I would not stop drinking. And I was enough of a romantic to know that I couldn't put Karen through these paces, so I just turned tail. Her mother was right, I was bad news, and I hated that I was bad news. Still, I had a hard time letting go. We'd been so close, for so long, it's like my identity was all tied up in the idea of being Karen's boyfriend. It's how I saw myself, even though deep down I never felt like I was good enough for her. I never felt like I was good enough for anyone, as long as I'm being honest—like I was disappointing life itself.

One day, in the middle of my despairing, trying to get my shit back together, I bought a case of beer and shut myself in my room. I was still living at home during all this time, becoming more and more distant from my father—my brother and sister, too. I'd been close to my siblings when we were little, but we were cut the same way as Dad; we didn't talk about our emotions a whole lot. We hung out, we had fun, but that was where it ended, and as we got older we each drifted into our own thing. My thing was dropping out of school, and drinking, and working, and feeling sorry for myself, and drinking some more, and here it just worked out that I had the place to myself one afternoon. My plan was to drink to oblivion and pass out, all alone. Halfway through the case, I stood with my back to my bedroom wall and sank to the floor. I sat that way for the longest time, with my legs splayed out in front of me. My thoughts were all over the place—everywhere and nowhere, all at once. Through my beer-soaked haze, I started looking at my fucked-up life. That's how I saw it at the time—how I look back on it, too. Nothing seemed to work; nothing seemed to fit. I couldn't understand why I moved about in such a sick, black funk, all the time; why I didn't feel alive; why I woke every morning with my teeth clenched; why everything seemed to fall apart all around me.

I was unhappy, depressed, desperate, confused.

I hated who I was, what I'd become.

I suppose on some level I always knew that the inner demons I was dealing with were tied in to my "mommy" issues—meaning, Mom's leaving left me a mess. I knew, but I didn't know how to explore these issues or get past them. I wasn't insightful or feeling enough to place my desperate unhappiness at my mother's bare feet—at least, not in any kind of conscious way. But then I started hearing from Karen, and then from other friends, that I had this weird habit of crying out for my mother just before I blacked out. It was all tied in. I'd never made the connection, but there it was—an emotional vomiting, an anguished cry for help. It was a leap, I realize now, and maybe it wasn't fair to blame all of this on my mother's leaving, but that's how I set it up in my head.

There were still some beers to be consumed, and as I got to the end of the case I was washed over by a complete and total sadness. Actually, *sad* doesn't quite get close to what I was feeling. There was way more to it than that. There was also *helpless* and *hopeless* and *terrified*. I started to think I didn't deserve to be alive—also, that maybe everything would be so much easier if I wasn't. Easier for me . . . *and* for my poor father, who didn't have the slightest idea of my inner turmoil. (Okay, so maybe he did have the *slightest* idea, but that's where it ended.)

I was in a state of desperation, and I decided that the thing to do was to get close to death. I don't think it occurred to me to try to kill myself. It wasn't like that. But I thought it would be helpful to just play with death a little bit, try it on, see how it felt.

And this was where I stopped thinking.

I grabbed a pair of Fiskars scissors, the ones with the classic orange handles. This was a serious instrument, equipped with high-grade, precision-ground, stainless-steel blades—a fine choice for the job at hand, especially since they were brand-new, razor-sharp. I spread the blades and pressed my wrist against one of the sharp edges. I started sobbing as I sank the blade into my skin—slowly, because I wanted to feel it, consider it.

The cuts I made were not too deep—not enough for me to sever a vein. In the end, I guess I didn't really want to die or else I would have done a better job of it. I wanted to take the decision whether I deserved to live or die out of my hands. It may not make sense, but it did to me at the time. It was all so crystal clear. I thought, Fuck, I'm so pathetic! I thought, Who the hell am I to decide if I belong in this world?

I did such a lousy job with this fine pair of scissors, I threw them down in disgust, and as I did my eyes fixed on a bottle cap I'd flung at my side, resting on the light beige carpet. It seemed to be calling to me. I imagined the damage I could do with the jagged edges of that bottle cap, so I reached for it and buried the twisted teeth into the bottom side of my left forearm, near the wrist. Oh, man . . . it hurt! I pressed harder and harder, and twisted the thing into my skin until I could feel the edges penetrating the epithelial layers, severing my superficial capillaries. I slumped over in intense pain, and imagined the rivers of blood that would come gushing from my wrist and spilling onto the carpet.

I wasn't done just yet. I took the cap and began to grind it even deeper into my skin, scraping it along the length of my forearm as I twisted it. With every mutilating turn, with every drop of blood and searing bite of pain, I felt an adrenaline shot of energy, almost like a resurgence. It was so weird! And yet I was in the vise grip of this intense weirdness, powerless against it. There was nothing to do but to keep going, so I pounded down the final few beers and kept grabbing whatever I could find in my room to cut myself in all these different ways. I slashed myself, scraped myself, sliced myself—just defaced the shit out of my arm.

And as I tore at myself in this primal way, I felt incredibly, wonderfully alive, and as I've worked to understand this moment over the years I've come to realize that it felt better to me just then to feel this intense pain than to feel nothing at all.

Eventually, I passed out—from the beer and crying. There wasn't enough blood loss to take me out like that, and I honestly don't think I was trying to kill myself. No. Like I said, it wasn't about *that*. It wasn't a cry for help, either. It was just a mindless attempt to dial back in to what it meant to be alive, and I never really stopped to consider the consequences, what it might mean.

I WAS DOWN SO low, for so long, I can't remember hitting bottom—but this was pretty damn close to it. Karen and I had been apart for a couple months. I was studying biology at Northampton Community College, still living at home. By outward appearances, it might have looked like I finally had my shit together, but that was hardly the case. Inwardly, where it counted, I was still raging, still searching, still out of control. I was twenty-one years old, and now that I was "legal," I was drinking more aggressively, more frequently.

I was at a house party on the Delaware River with a bunch of college friends. By now I was a full-throttle binge drinker, surrounded by a couple dozen party-hardy kids—a toxic combination. The night started out like any other party. I was a happy drunk, wild and playful. I flirted, did stupid things, entertained my peers. Toward the end of the night, my happy-go-lucky façade gave way to my darker side. The others continued to party—

laughing, singing, roughhousing—but me, the more I drank, the more I sank into one of my deep, black funks, like the one that found me a couple of months earlier in my bedroom.

I used to get wild panic attacks, only I'd never thought of them as panic attacks. I don't think it even occurred to me to name them or group them together or even to understand them. I just wanted to get past them. Whatever they were, I'd been getting them since middle school, all through high school, and lately, lubricated by all that beer, exacerbated by time and a growing disconnect with my father, a deepening concern for what the rest of my life might look like on my own, they became more intense, more terrifying. And the thing of it is, I could sense an impending attack. My heart rate would skyrocket. Then my breathing would become more shallow and labored. It would start to feel like I was losing control—although, frankly, I was never really in control of anything at that time in my life. I was just kind of going along for the ride, but during these moments I'd shake and sweat, rage and moan. I grew out of these panic attacks as I got older, but they still grabbed me from time to time, especially when I was drunk. There was no controlling them, no way to make them stop. It would feel to me for a period of several hours like I was having a complete mental breakdown, and then I'd pass out, or the black funk would lift, and I'd be left feeling just a little like I'd had the shit kicked of me, just a little depressed—not clinically depressed, I don't think, but down, down, down . . . on just about everything. I never knew when one of these episodes would hit—only that I would be helpless against it. It's like I moved about with a cloud over my head.

So there we were, at my friend's parents' house outside of Belvidere, New Jersey, drinking and drinking. It was a nice house, a vacation house, right on the river, and we were all having a great time, but my alcohol consumption was out of control. Reckless. Caustic. The night didn't start out that way for me. The night never started out that way. But somewhere in there it took a dark, dangerous turn.

The plan was for everyone to stay and crash, so no one was worried about overdoing it. We were dug in for the night. People were pairing off, hooking up, goofing around, passing out . . . and at some point in the early, predawn hours I found myself alone in the bathroom. Curled up in a fetal position. Crying for my mother.

I tried to understand what I was feeling. Wrecked—broken, actually. Also woefully, miserably sad. I couldn't put what I was feeling into words—not then, and even now I have a hard time articulating what was going on in my head. I can remember picking myself up from my spot around the fire because I felt myself slipping. I can't think how else to describe it. The night was getting away from me. My emotions were getting away from me. I didn't want to shame myself by breaking down crying in front of my friends, making a scene. So I ducked into a bathroom and shut the door.

This was me—coping, dealing.

After about forty-five minutes, I scraped myself off the floor, splashed some water on my face. I stared at myself in the mirror a good long while. My eyes were bloodshot from crying. My face had these crinkly lines pressed into it, in the fat of my cheeks, where I guess I'd passed out against a crumpled-up towel. I didn't recognize myself at first—and then I did, and didn't like what I saw.

The whole time I wondered how the hell I was going to explain myself to these people. But here's the thing: as far as I could tell, nobody really noticed I had gone. Mostly everyone was asleep, or into their own thing, and me and my little breakdown were just beside the point, you know, so I got it in my head that I didn't want to be at this party any longer. I was exhausted and just wanted to crawl into my bed, sink my head into a pillow, and pass out. These people were all my friends—*good* friends, a lot of them—but I felt somehow exposed. Vulnerable. I didn't want to be seen like *this*.

So I left.

I WAS IN NO condition to drive, but I wasn't thinking too clearly, and the argument against driving didn't exactly present itself. I could walk a halfway decent straight line and make my way to my car, so that was good enough for me. I could swing open the door and scramble-crawl inside. I could fumble for my keys and switch on the ignition. I was good to go. I told myself the car would tell me if I shouldn't be driving and the car didn't say shit.

In those days I was driving a ten-year-old Toyota Camry—dirt-beige. It was a solid, reliable ride, but it had a misalignment. When you held the wheel and pointed straight ahead the car leaned to the right, so you had to compensate. I kept meaning to have it fixed, but I never quite got around to it. There were a lot of things in my life I was meaning to fix, so this just took its place in line. It was nothing, really.

I didn't tell anybody I was leaving.

It must have been around three or four in the morning. I hadn't slept in twenty-four hours. The roads were quiet—the back roads, especially. I was headed north, trying to get to Route 22, which would have taken me home to my father's house in Easton—maybe a half-hour drive. I was exhausted. Nerve-racked. Spent. Or something. As soon as I got into the driver's seat, as soon as I got some road under my tires, I caught myself nodding off, but then I'd snap back awake and continue on. I was blowing past the speed limit, probably. Taking those turns like it was the bright of day, probably—like I was stone-cold sober and wide-eyed awake, like they were meant to be taken.

I say probably because I don't remember, though I wish I could.

And then I guess I nodded off and didn't snap back. I don't know how many seconds I was out, but I drifted off the road. This was where the misalignment kicked in. It saved me, I think, because I leaned into the shoulder instead of into oncoming traffic.

When I came to, I was bouncing, careening through a pasture, trees whipping by me at what felt like a million miles an hour. It's possible I'm exaggerating. But here's something: there was time in all that bouncing and careening for me to think, Oh, man, look at all those trees whipping by! It was dark, and I couldn't see for shit, but there was a terrifying rush of shadows. I don't think I had control of the car at that point—but I also don't think it even occurred to me to try to regain control of the car. I was just along for the ride, but then something told me to slam on the brakes, so I did. At around this same time, a ditch appeared in my path, and the Camry nose dived into it at full speed and came to a sudden, crashing stop.

The air bags deployed. A lot of people don't know this because they've never experienced it, but the sudden surge of air into those bags creates a sickening sound—like a wheezing vacuum cleaner. With a rattling something stuck in the hose. It's not terribly loud, but it's a creepy and unfamiliar noise, and I was conscious the whole time—enough to think, This doesn't sound good. Enough to think, Okay, this is what it sounds like when the air bags come out.

When the noise stopped, I noticed I was in pain. I'd let out a loud grunt, as if I'd been punched in the gut. Next, I recognized a strange burning sensation on my arms—a reaction to the exploding gas released by the airbags on deployment. It turned out I'd partially dislocated my sternoclavicular joint—which, like the name says, is the joint that connects the sternum to the clavicle. Just then, the pain wasn't much worse than noticeable but I dug myself out from the air bag, kicked the door open, crawled out of the car and walked around for a bit, trying to clear my head.

After a couple of minutes, a guy came by in a truck. For all of that bouncing and careening, I hadn't veered too far off the road, and this guy noticed my lights and pulled over to see what had happened. He said, "Dude, you okay?" Taking in the scene. Wondering how the hell I was walking around.

I said, "Yeah, man. I'm fine." Like saying I was fine was enough. Like I was anyone to judge.

He said, "Should probably get you to a hospital."

I said, "No, no. I'm fine. A friend of mine's coming. Already called. He'll take me."

This was bullshit, of course. I wasn't thinking clearly. I was concussed and in shock. As soon as this trucker was satisfied that I had things under control I fished out my phone and called my friend Jeff, back at the party.

He recognized my number—said, "Dave! What's up, man?"

I told him that I'd crashed my car.

This was confusing for poor Jeff, who by this point had likely had *way more* than enough to drink, judging by the state he was in when I had left. He'd thought I was still at the party, so he had a little trouble making sense of what happened, but he eventually corralled another buddy to come out and pick me up and take me back to the house.

My friends were worried for me. They were afraid I had broken my collarbone. Someone suggested we call 911. Another someone said I should go to the hospital. Another someone said maybe it wasn't cool for me to be at the house, like this. The general feeling was that somebody would see the car by the side of the road and come looking for me, and even though we weren't doing anything wrong—there were no drugs at the house, everyone was legal, the "host" had his parents' permission to use the house—you tend to get a little paranoid at three or four o'clock in the morning when you've had a little too much to drink and one of your friends crashes his car and busts up his shoulder.

Eventually, it was decided that we should call the cops to tell them about the accident, and that someone would drive me to the police station to make out a report. I went to the hospital to get cleaned up.

After I was released I wandered aimlessly around town on foot, feeling fairly helpless and hopeless. Eventually I sat down on a bench and stared off into the sky. I was in so much pain, inside and out. I couldn't think of a next move, so I just sat and sat, until I finally called a friend to come get me, and when he got there I broke down and cried.

Jesus, I was a mess.

When the dust cleared, as I played these low moments over and over in my mind, I kept coming back to how close I'd come to killing myself. How close I'd come to maybe killing someone else. I wondered if this had been rock bottom for me, or if it was possible for me to sink any further, if I could actually kill myself.

I kept hearing the voice of this one cop, who'd gone out to the scene to inspect the crash site and report to me over the phone. He said, "Kid, I don't know how you did it, but you managed to miss every tree, every telephone pole." He'd tracked the skid marks as I spun off the road, saw the path of my careening car, saw the dozen or so near-misses that could have, should have killed me.

I thought, Ah, yes, that would explain the terrifying rush of shadows.

This was my life back then. I'd drink to oblivion, embarrass myself in front of friends (and strangers!), dodge some type of bullet, get it together, and go about my days. Then I'd keep drinking and start in all over again on the same deal. So in this one respect, at least, this wasn't exactly an isolated incident. Only, this time around, everything was ratcheted up. Whatever red flags I was putting out into the world, they were now a little redder. Whatever warning signs I was choosing to ignore, they were now a little brighter, a little louder.

A COUPLE OF MONTHS before my terrible car crash, a couple of months after my split with Karen, I'd met a girl named Daisy. She was beautiful, shy, super-intelligent. Within minutes of getting to know her, I could tell she carried a pure heart, filled with compassion. She had this aura about her that made me think there was a soft kindness that couldn't help but follow her around.

It turned out Daisy was the first person in my life who truly understood how messed up I was inside, who helped me to embrace my identity, my family history. Basically, she helped me accept myself. I'd spent so much time denying any type of relationship with my mother—denying that she even existed!—it's like I was completely shut off from that side of my personality. I'd spent so much time trying to fit myself in, trying to appear happy and lighthearted and like every other American kid in the neighborhood, there's no way Dad could have seen how much pain I was in.

All along, there'd been no room in my thinking for another way of looking at the world, for an emerging sense of self, and it took a series of (admittedly) drunken conversations with Daisy for me to start thinking in a positive way about my past. To even *acknowledge* the Yanomami strain of my DNA. With Daisy, I did not feel ashamed to cry about my hard-to-fathom family, about my feelings of abandonment, about the confusing mess of emotions that had attached to me at this point in my life—all of them having to do in some way with my mother.

Really, Daisy was like a lifeline.

I started opening up to Daisy, more and more as we grew closer and closer. From the very beginning, she could tell that I needed a good friend who would simply listen to me. I needed a friend to validate me, to tell me my emotional instabilities and insecurities were worth dealing with. Over the next few months, she encouraged me to talk about the pain and anguish I'd been warehousing since childhood. She sat with me as we watched that National Geographic documentary about my family, as I reread my father's book—and whatever else we could find online about the Yanomami tribe.

Gradually, I started to feel comfortable in my own skin. And curious. I came to accept who I was, and how I'd come to be— and that feeling seemed to flow from this one terrible night, from looking long and hard in that bathroom mirror and not liking what came back at me.

Daisy made me realize that my breakdowns and all these other destructive behaviors were cries for help, cries for belonging. She taught me that it was okay to weep, to be vulnerable, to talk about what was missing in my life. She helped me to see that I'd been dealing with abandonment and identity-crisis issues for most of my life—to ignore them, she said, would only make my situation worse. She embraced me as a grieving young man who'd lost his mother—and seeing myself through her eyes, seeing my family through her eyes, I finally gave myself permission to heal.

Those inner demons . . . they went back to my relationship with my mother—although, in reality, I had no relationship with my mother. She'd been out of my life, out of the country, out of the picture since I was five years old. But it was my *connection* to my mother that needed to be set right. I needed to come to terms with her decision to separate from us all those years ago. I needed to understand that she had had no choice, really. I needed to accept that it was an act of self-preservation, returning to the jungle the way she did. With this not-so-gentle push from Daisy, I could see that now—with great clarity. In reconnecting to these bits and pieces of Yanomami culture, it was clear to me that Mom wasn't built for this Western world. She was wired in a whole different way, and she'd tried to make it work for a good long while—but the whole time it was like she could barely breathe, like a fish out of water.

And, so, I forgave her. She didn't need my forgiveness, hadn't thought to ask for it, wouldn't have known what to do with it if I found a way to offer it to her, but this was an important milestone for me—a milestone that helped to lift the millstone I'd carried all these years.

I wanted to reach out over all those miles, all those years, hold her close, and whisper, "It's okay, Mom. I understand."

As if I even had the first idea how to make that happen.

At around this same time, during my sophomore year in college, I was taking an anatomy and physiology course with a professor named Alan Spevak, and I used to go around to see him from time to time, during office hours. I was going through this phase of self-discovery, where I was learning more and more about my mother's tribe (about *my* tribe), coming more and more to a place of acceptance about who I was and my place in the world, and during one of my visits with Dr. Spevak we got to talking about anthropology. This wasn't exactly his field—he was a biologist by training—but he was a man of science, a student of human nature, and I knew from our classroom discussions that his interests ran in every direction. Somehow he'd mentioned an anthropology course he'd once taken—as an undergraduate, I guess—and next thing I knew I was spinning my story. I just came out with it. After all these years, keeping my "origin story" to myself, the thing fairly spilled out of me.

It's like I'd been tipped upside down.

I was a little outside myself as I talked. By that I mean that I was hyperaware of how I was coming across. At first I was tense, nervous, scared to expose my healing wounds. But as I spoke, I started to relax. I started to notice in the give-and-take between us that Dr. Spevak was interested in what I had to say—*really* interested—and I took this as a great, good thing. I don't know why I would have expected otherwise, but I remember being struck by this. I found myself giving voice to thoughts and memories I hadn't considered in years—all of it fueled by the wide-eyed interest of this man of science, this good and patient listener.

Somewhere in the middle of my rambling, I had professed that I wanted to go the rainforest to reconnect with my mother—a long-held dream I hadn't even realized I'd been holding on to. It just spilled out of me, along with everything else. As soon as I said it, I became aware of my vulnerability by stepping out of my zone of security and reclusion. As a matter of fact, I hadn't realized I'd been thinking in this way at all until I mentioned it, and now that I had, I wondered how to take it back. It made no sense—to head off for the middle of nowhere, with no money, no contacts, no context, no idea how to find my mother or even to know if she was still alive.

But then an amazing thing happened. Dr. Spevak didn't look at me like I was out of my mind. He didn't tell me that looking for my mother in the rainforest, after nearly twenty years, would be like looking for a needle in a haystack. No, he just said, "Wow!" That's all: "Wow!" And in this one little exclamation-pointed word there was tremendous power. There was boundless possibility. There was the feeling that I could put a thought like this one out into the world and somehow make it happen. I could will it so.

A lot happened on the back of that one word. *Wow.* Mainly, it set me off on a journey. I felt empowered. I laughed out loud. Then I cried. Then I had to restrain myself from running across the campus and hugging everyone in my path—that's how over-the-top I was about this one conversation and what it could mean. It put me in mind, a little bit, of how I used to feel roaming center field on a baseball diamond, with all that space to run and be alone with my thoughts and do my own thing. Free. Hopeful. Like anything was possible.

And so, that's where I date the beginning of my quest, to reunite, reconnect with my mom—that afternoon in Dr. Spevak's office. Who the hell knew if something like this was even possible? But at just that moment, it felt like my mother was close enough to touch.

I could make my way to her. Somehow. I could will it so.

UPPER ORINOCO, YANOMAMI TERRITORY

The storm came and went—only to suggest it came and went like nothing at all would not be fair to the storm. It was a good thing we were able to take shelter beneath those boulders. Along with the torrential rain, there were ripping winds and dark skies that seemed like something out of a horror movie.

As soon as the rain stopped, the skies brightened. The one followed from the other. The wind fell away. The heat of the morning swiftly returned. For most of those fifteen or so minutes, my mother had been peering out from the rock opening, looking up at the sky. She was calm, steady, unconcerned. She had taken the lead among our group. The others were looking to her for guidance, direction, and I remember looking on and thinking, Hey, that's my mom. She knows her stuff. When she was certain it was over she stepped confidently from our makeshift shelter and looked around. Then she signaled back to the group of us and made a kind of sweeping, continuing motion with her arm, like she was waving us along.

"Let's go," she said, her English once again startling me. It was a phrase she remembered from her time in the States, a phrase

137

she'd no doubt picked up from my father. She said it like one word—"lessgo."Like, giddyap. Like it was the next thing meant to happen, the one following from the other. And we could move only on her gentle command.

We headed back toward the abandoned shabono, presumably to join the others. We'd been out since first light—the way of the jungle, I was learning. The day starts when the day starts, so we'd begun our trek by five o'clock that morning—an arbitrary time marker that meant nothing in this part of the world. If I'd had to put a clock on it, I would have guessed it was now about ten thirty, and I was getting hungry. There were no prescribed meal times that I could determine; we ate when it was time to eat. We fished when it was time to fish. We gathered plantains when it was time to gather plantains.

Soon it would be time to eat, but now it was time to move. "Lessgo."

We walked silently for the next while, and as we moved I thought of the storm just passed. Steam rose from the ground, where the sun seemed to heat the puddles of left-behind rain to a boil. There was evidence of its might all around—a downed tree here, a fallen limb there. I instantly realized the danger we would have faced had we not found shelter. The others took out their machetes and hacked away at the downed limbs, clearing the way for the others. I helped, in what feeble ways I could, but underneath I could not shake thinking we had just avoided some major catastrophe. This too was the way of the jungle—you could be walking along, minding your own business, and a flash storm could develop, knocking down trees and branches big enough to crush you flat. Stepping over these fallen trees, it was a chilling reminder of the raw, beautiful power of the rainforest. The raw, beautiful power of the Yanomami people. My people.

We went out the way we'd come in. I was Yanomami enough to recognize the trail, American enough to worry over

*how close we'd come to getting injured in the storm. And as
we walked I thought back to my life in Pennsylvania, to how
I'd prepare for an impending storm. Back home, you listen
to the news, or check the weather online. If it calls for rain
you bring an umbrella or stay inside. But here in the jungle
there is no Weather Channel. You get up out of the hammock
at the crack of dawn and venture into the forest in search of
food. There's no way of ever knowing what the weather will
do, other than what the skies are telling you And when that
violent storm hits, you adapt. You seek shelter.*

   You do this without even thinking about it.

   You go about your day.

CHAPTER FIVE

Home

OKAY, SO IT WAS ONE thing to put it out there that I wanted to find my mother. It was a whole other thing to actually make it happen, but this was a start. I was energized, just by entrusting my story to someone. And Dr. Spevak, he was generous and encouraging. We met several times to talk things through and he started reaching out to anthropologists he knew . . . whatever he thought he could do to help.

I was incredibly nervous, as I set off on this quest, because I didn't know how people would respond. For so long, I'd been running from my story, denying my mother her rightful place in my life, rejecting my Yanomami roots, so to make this grand pronouncement, from out of nowhere, from a place of ignorance . . . it set me up for rejection. I kept thinking I'd hear, "Oh, you can't do that." Or, "Who the hell are you, to want to find your mother, after all this time?" I'd have been the first to admit it was a crazy notion, but I didn't want to hear from anyone that it was crazy.

Eventually, I realized it didn't much matter what other people thought. It only mattered that the people closest to me, the people in a position to help, were able to buy into it, so that's where I placed my focus. Incredibly, everyone embraced the idea—it was totally the opposite of what my stupid little mind was fearing. People were into it, and eager to help, in what ways they could. Daisy encouraged me, big-time. Dr. Spevak, big-time. My friends . . . big-time.

For whatever reason, I didn't reach out to my father for a couple of weeks. I guess I wanted to get some traction, some momentum, before bouncing the idea off him. I finally approached him on it one night at his house, late. I was still living at home, still treading water in my relationship with my father. After I disappeared to Florida, after I spent those extra few weeks crashing with friends or camping out in the woods, things were a little tense between us for a while, but those edges were smoothed over in time, and now it was like that whole episode never happened.

We were in the kitchen, cleaning up after dinner. It was just the two of us. I put it to him plain. I said, "Dad, I'm thinking about going to find Mom."

Just like that. No big thing.

He was surprised, certainly. A little flustered, probably. I was sitting at the table, and he was standing, and I can remember him facing the kitchen cabinets, away from me. I thought maybe he didn't want me to see his face—or maybe he didn't want to look at mine. His break with my mother had been ugly, painful, and here I was asking him to relive all of that again. He couldn't have known how messed up I'd been over my mother's leaving. I'd done a great job of hiding it from him, of bottling up my emotions and slick-packaging them, so publicly no one could tell I was hurting, so here again, I can't put this on him. He didn't know about my breakdowns. He knew I'd crashed my car that night of the party, but he didn't know what led up to it. And for whatever reason, we never really talked about it—the same way we never really talked about that time I ran away from home. Yeah, he knew the details. He knew I'd stolen his car and disappeared with it to Florida, but he didn't know what led up to *that*, either, other than that clipped conversation we had when he asked me if it had anything to do with Mom. On a very basic level, he knew all the little fuckups I'd had that required his attention, but he never knew the anguish behind any of them. I'd somehow managed to keep up the charade of being the all-American, clean-cut kid. I was an all-star baseball player. I mowed the lawn. I had a paper route, on average got decent grades, spent time having tea and cookies with the elderly. My father had no reason to think that there was anything wrong with me. So when he heard me put it out there that I wanted to find my mother, he didn't really get the emotional piece behind it. Perhaps he just heard it as me wanting in on some type of adventure, like I was just going through some phase.

I realize now that I kind of blindsided him with this. There's no way he could have seen it coming; after all, I was the one who'd spent all that time and energy rejecting my mother and my heritage. How could he have known what was really going on with me?

After a while, he turned to me with a confused look on his face—like, *really* confused. Like, he had no idea where I was coming from. He said, "Why? You were the one who hated being Yanomami. You wanted no part of that."

I could only shrug. I didn't have a good answer, but he didn't have it in him to wait for one. Right away, he started in on all these different considerations I'd have to factor and consider, if I meant to go through with this.

My father had been slogging through a bunch of his own shit, all those years. Financial troubles. Academic troubles. Ongoing troubles with the Venezuelan government. Some of this I'd picked up on, but I didn't know the details. I didn't stop to consider how his world must have appeared to him. And yet to his great credit he wasn't at all discouraging, that first night. I don't know that he was *encouraging*, but at least he didn't dismiss me out of hand.

We ended up talking all night. For the first time, my father and I openly talked about my mother. He told me the story about Mom being kidnapped, being held hostage in that crappy apartment in Caracas, being forced to go on national media to talk shit about my dad. I'd never known any of that as a kid, not even bits and pieces, and it shook me up. It's like he flipped open the cover of a whole new book, a whole new chapter in our life as a family, and between the lines a new story took shape. I began to see that my mother *did* try to reach out to us kids. She *did* make an effort. But she was so traumatized by these events, so terrified for her safety and ours, that eventually she slinked back into village life and set our family aside.

If anything, this new angle on Mom's story only deepened my resolve to make my way to her, and as this long night wore on in my father's kitchen our talk eventually turned to logistical matters. My father had a bunch of questions for me—questions I couldn't possibly answer. It's not like he was trying to trip me up, but he wanted to know if I'd thought of this or that contingency, if I'd given the whole thing some serious thought. He was worried for my safety.

But the only way he could find to talk about it was to reach for that old family stand-by, the dis that pretty much said it all about how un-Yanomami I was . . . to the core. He said, "You're afraid of bugs, David."

I saw that one coming—said, "Yes, I'm afraid of bugs. I'll have to get over that, I guess."

He wasn't being dismissive, I don't think, just practical. But his practicality could only leave me second-guessing myself. And yet I was determined. The yearning was too strong to ignore. I would see this through. I would make my way to the rainforest. I would find my mother.

Somehow.

MY FATHER WANTED TO help, but he no longer had any contacts in Venezuela. This was a frustration for him—but after all, it had been twenty years. Still, he knew a lot more than I did about the region, and the logistics of mounting an expedition. Together, he and I decided after that all-nighter that a good place to start would be to call Dr. Robert Carneiro, curator of the American Museum of Natural History, in New York. Dr. Carneiro was a prominent and well-respected American anthropologist. He and my father spent time together among the Yanomami many years ago. He was a longtime family friend and knew my family history—including all the highlights (or, I should say, *lowlights*) of some of my struggles—so in a lot of ways it was like calling on a favorite uncle for a professional assist.

Actually, I didn't call—I sent an e-mail, which might have been a passive move on my part but I wanted to choose my words carefully. "I am simply a son in search of his mother," I wrote. "However, I am having a tough time figuring out where to start. I've brought up the idea to my father. We sometimes spent many hours talking about all the events leading up to my mother's leaving. I've concluded that my father is still living with the hurtful and painful accusations made against him. I do not want him to relive any of that. I love my father and do not wish any further aggravation."

Even as I was typing the e-mail, and hitting SEND, it felt a little funny, reaching out to Dr. Carneiro in such an impersonal way, but I guess I wanted to avoid a confrontational conversation right out of the gate, and maybe find a way to gauge his interest before putting myself out there. With an e-mail, at least, he'd have time to reflect, reconsider, in case his initial reaction wasn't all that positive. And I'd have time to measure my response. With a meeting or a phone call, if Dr. Carneiro had challenged me or questioned my motives, I don't think I would have handled it all that well.

It turned out there was no reason to worry. Dr. Carneiro responded almost immediately with a big show of support and enthusiasm. "What a challenging and exciting odyssey it will be, searching for your mother!" he wrote back. "I'm very sympathetic to your desire to find your mother in her rainforest home in southern Venezuela. I'm sure it will be a most emotional moment when you see each other. It won't be easy to reach her, as I'm sure you're fully aware, but I know you won't be put off by such impediments."

From his e-mail, he seemed absolutely ecstatic, so I was eager to sit down with him and come up with a plan of action.

Dr. Carneiro hadn't been to the region for decades, so *plan of action* was a relative term, I'm afraid. As it was, he'd only visited the *Hasupuwe-teri* for a period of months; most of his research in the region was with another tribe. Still, he had a lot of contacts in the Amazonas, and his name opened a lot of doors and lent a certain legitimacy to my planned trip, so he went to work immediately trying to hook me up. He wasn't moving around so well when I went to see him at his office at the museum, but his mind was still razor-sharp. He seemed to chew on my every word, consider every eventuality, in a meticulous, thorough way. He saw the positives and negatives of my proposed trip straightaway, and thought on balance that it could be a great, good thing.

One of the first calls he made on my behalf was to the Instituto Venezolano de Investigaciones Cientificas—the Venezuelan Institute for Scientific Research, or IVIC. That one call triggered a chain reaction of calls that eventually led to Dr. Hortensia Caballero, a Caracas-based anthropologist who had met my family on one of our early trips, back when she was still a student and I was just an infant. I had no memory of our meeting, but Hortensia did—and, happily, she agreed to hear what I had in mind.

More than anyone else, Hortensia would become the single most influential person in opening the canopy of the rainforest to an *inside* outsider like me, but what was amazing in the days and weeks following that first e-mail to Dr. Carneiro was how excited the anthropological community in general seemed to be about my quest. These were just my general impressions, of course, based solely on conversations and communications I'd had directly with various individuals and organizations. Everyone I contacted on this was warm, accommodating, and endlessly optimistic.

This was a welcome and unexpected thing. My father hadn't said as much, but I have to think he was a little gun-shy about me picking up the thread of our family story in such a public way. After all, that thread had nearly been his undoing, all those years ago, so he didn't know how things might unravel once we started pulling on it. He offered to help, in what ways he could, but I think we both came to the realization that the heavy lifting would fall to me. He would make introductions where he felt they would be helpful; he would advise me in a behind-the-scenes sort of way; but for the most part I would cut my own path back to the jungle.

This wasn't just a way to motivate me as I set off on this great journey. No, it was also a strategy—a defensive strategy. You see, there were many individuals within the Venezuelan government who hated the fact that Dad had married a Yanomami woman— he'd been painted as a kind of pariah, and for several years after returning to the United States he'd had to deal with all kinds of accusations about how he'd taken advantage of my mother and her people. This was the groupthink behind those charges he was facing in Caracas, back before I was born—charges that never really went away and took on different shapes as my father's Yanomami family grew. For years, he'd been under attack in the government-backed Venezuelan press for acting against the best interests of the indigenous peoples of the rainforest—to the point where there was now a network of lies and misconceptions about my family's story that seemed to stand as truth among certain Venezuelans who knew no better.

Plus, I'm sure, he missed my mother terribly. Even then.

For me to surface after so much time, looking for a path back to the region, a way back to my mother, reopening all of these old wounds, it set my father's mind racing. He no doubt worried there'd be a hue and cry of protest, and that he would once again be portrayed as the villain of this piece, and I can't say I blamed him; I would have felt the same way.

And, even worse than a new onslaught of negative publicity, there was the chance that my intentions could reignite the legal troubles stemming from my family's initial departure in 1986. I started to feel like I was kicking up all this dust, when the dust had finally settled.

I didn't want to put my father through any of that, of course—

and in fact had sought to go through these motions as quietly as possible, but there was no way to launch an expedition like this one without making a little bit of noise. People were just too pumped about the feel-good aspects of my story to keep quiet, and it turns out the anthropological community is relatively small and tight-knit; everyone knows each other's business, so once word got out that Kenneth Good's kid was looking to trek back to the jungle in search of his mother . . . well, people paid attention. Relief workers, missionaries, anthropologists . . . everyone was eager to see how this new chapter in our oft-told family story might play out. Even people who had challenged my father in the past seemed inclined to put their feelings aside and embrace the positive—almost like they were waiting for me to slap a happy ending on our family saga, so everyone could move on.

In some cases, the response was overwhelming. Early on, we got a call from a National Geographic producer, offering to fund my entire trip, in exchange for documentary rights—which would have naturally included complete access and editorial control. They wanted to film the reunion between me and my mother. They wanted to repurpose some of the archival footage they'd taken twenty years earlier. It was an important story, they said. Initially, I was thrilled; not for the media attention but for their offer to fund the trip. Already, money was looming as a major issue—basically, I didn't have any, and I was beginning to realize that this would be a problem. But the National Geographic name would mean more than money; just as Dr. Carneiro's blessing legitimized what I was trying to do, it would lend a certain seal of approval to my mission and help to shine some positive light on the Yanomami—so I counted this, too, as an encouraging development.

What I hadn't counted on, however, was my father's reaction to National Geographic's expression of interest. He was livid. He'd had a major falling-out with his contacts there soon after the release of the *Yanomami Homecoming* documentary. He felt that, during the filming, he was mistreated, and that some of the producers' interviewing methods (especially when they interviewed my mother) were unethical. Also, I believe he blamed them in some way for inviting the treacherous Armando into our midst—even though it was Dad who brought this man back into our lives after the filming.

It had been twenty years, and those wounds had yet to heal.

Sure enough, some of the very same people involved in the original documentary wanted in on this homecoming project, and my father bristled at the thought of my having anything to do with them. It would have meant the world to me to have National Geographic underwrite this trip, but I wasn't about to go against my father. He was my father, after all. In fact, out of respect for him, I decided that there wouldn't be any media attached to this trip at all. It would be for just me and my family. Strike that—it would be for me and my mother.

I told my sister, Vanessa, about my plans as they were taking shape in order to make sure she knew what I was up to and to see if there was any message she wanted me to bring to Mom in the jungle. She was very excited for me and maybe even a bit jealous of the adventure. This was the first time I brought up my conflicted emotions about Mom with one of my siblings. We'd never talked about how I'd felt abandoned by our mother, how I'd struggled with my identity—and now, as this trip was taking shape, we didn't *really* talk about these things, either. Vanessa had enough going on in her life—she was married, with a young child of her own, and another on the way.

Still, it was a chance for us to talk in a sidelong way about our unique family history, and I asked her if there was any message or keepsake she wanted me to share with our mother. She gave it some thought and then said, "I don't really have anything to say to Mom. Don't get me wrong, David. I don't harbor any ill will against her. I wish you the best and I hope you find her."

She wasn't angry, wasn't holding any grudges, but the trip did not have the same meaning for Vanessa as it did for me.

As for Danny . . . I put it to him over breakfast one morning at my father's house. He'd just finished high school and was still living at home, same as me. We'd each been into our own things lately, with school and work, so we hadn't been spending that much time together, except for some stolen moments in the house, between our comings and goings. Like Vanessa, his head was someplace else, where my mother was concerned. He was too young to remember her firsthand, too young to connect any real memories to the few pictures he'd come across over the years, to the documentary I'm sure he'd watched at some point.

He was in the kitchen making eggs. We lived in the same house, so of course he'd heard all of our talk about preparations and supplies for my trip, but he never weighed in on it until just this moment. He put his arm around my shoulder and said, "So I hear you're going down to the Amazon to get in touch with your roots."

"Something like that," I said. "I'm trying to find Mom."

He squeezed me tighter for a warm "bro" hug and wished me luck. He said, "Whatever you're looking for, Dave, I hope you find it."

Then, as we broke our hug, he gave me a gentle shove, smiled and said, "You're one crazy bastard."

Yes, I guess I was—but I caught myself wondering how it was that my sister and brother had been born into the same circumstances and as far as I knew they didn't feel this kind of siren pull to the jungle. Or maybe they did and hadn't expressed it yet . . . at least, not to me. We were on different paths, and they could only live their lives the way they were sculpting them. I had dealt with Mom's absence in my own way, and here I was looking to deal with it in a whole new way going forward, but it wasn't up to me to call the shots for Vanessa and Danny. I could only set an example, and in order to do that I could only continue on my discovery journey and hope that someday they might follow. Or not—but that would be up to them.

Until then, it was enough that I had their blessings, their encouragement.

HORTENSIA CABALLERO SENT ME a very sweet e-mail shortly after our first conversation, pledging her full support and offering to do as much work on the ground as she could ahead of my visit. She wasn't able to tap into any grant or research money, but she would be an enormous help slogging through all the red tape and paperwork I'd likely face returning to Venezuela—basically, she'd take me under her wing, making all-important introductions for me throughout the region. It somehow worked out that Hortensia was scheduled to attend the next annual meeting of the American Anthropological Association in Philadelphia, so we made plans to meet. I was nervous, excited, because even in this early going I had the sense that the trip wouldn't come off without Hortensia's help, so I didn't want to do or say anything to set her off. I didn't want to miss this opportunity to reconnect with her, face-to-face.

We met at a Starbucks in Center City, at the hotel where she was staying. I ordered a Caffè Americano. Normally I just order coffee, without pretense, but I thought this would make me appear like a world traveler. That's how nervous I was about this first meeting, but it went great. We swapped long-lost-relative stories—she told me she'd been searching for a relative in the western United States and felt a powerful connection to my own quest to find my mother. We ended up hanging out for the rest of the afternoon, and the whole time I was thinking, Holy shit, this could actually happen! It was almost as if it took meeting Hortensia for me to believe this was real.

And across the table, Hortensia was thinking her version of the same thought—like it took meeting me, the child she'd met *twenty-something* years earlier, a multicultural son of the rainforest, to grasp the significance of this adventure.

This was the beginning of a remarkable friendship—and an invaluable professional relationship. I couldn't have set off on such

a ridiculously ambitious adventure without Hortensia's generous
assist—she's an exceptionally beautiful soul, deeply committed to
the Yanomami people and their way of life. On a purely practical
level, she would play a key role; she spoke fluent English, with a
lilting Venezuelan accent that sometimes slowed her down. She
had many friends and contacts in and out of Yanomami territory.
Most important, I trusted her. On an emotional level her true
spirit came into play; she would go on to fight for me so diligently,
so tirelessly, so selflessly in my efforts to enter the territory that
I came to believe that my mission to reunite with my mother and
reconnect with my Yanomami heritage was as important to her as
it was to me.

Following our meeting in Philadelphia, Hortensia was true
to her word. She kept sending me updates—paperwork I'd need
to be allowed into the country; the itinerary we'd follow once I
landed in Caracas and we made our way to Puerto Ayacucho;
supplies I'd do well to bring along. She had it all worked out. She
even made a kind of exploratory trip into the jungle, to see if she
could get a lead on my mother's whereabouts. She started asking around—first, among the missionaries in the region, and soon
enough among the tribespeople she met along the Orinoco River,
as she attempted to retrace my mother's last known movements.

It turned out everyone knew Yarima. In her home village, her
neighboring villages, up and down the river and deep into the
jungle, my mother's story was well-known. She wasn't exactly a
celebrity—I don't think there was room in Yanomami culture for
such a concept, but her marriage to my father, the *nabuh*, had
been much discussed; her travels to his part of the world and the
stories she'd brought back had become the stuff of village legend;
so it wasn't too hard for Hortensia to track her down.

Eventually Hortensia followed my mother's footsteps to Koripi-
wei, a village much closer downriver. How she came to be living
among the *Koripi-wei-teri*, it was never made clear, but there she
was.

Hortensia e-mailed as soon as she could. She was thrilled to be able to tell me my mother was alive and well—which, of course, we could not have known without this extra piece of due diligence. We could have only hoped, and here the odds suggested we would have been hoping against hope. For one thing, I'd had no good reason to think we could even locate my mother. The Yanomami are a seminomadic people; my mother's tribe—*my* tribe!—moved with the seasons, and it's not like they'd leave any kind of forwarding address. The ebb and flow of jungle life would place them in one part of the territory for a period of time, and then another, and another. Once an area was farmed out, its resources picked clean, they'd move elsewhere in the jungle.

Geography was only part of the problem I would have had in finding my mother, on my own; chronology was another. It's difficult to calculate life expectancy among the more remote Yanomami, where there is no concept of an annual calendar, no way to quantify or mark the passage of time beyond life-cycle events and the approaching rainy season. However, it has been generally assumed that the average life expectancy in my mother's village was somewhere in the mid-forties—an age my mother would have certainly reached. It had been twenty years since my father had been in contact. A lot could have happened.

I was overjoyed with this bit of news—moved to tears, even. It surprised me a little that I was so emotional. I'd spent all of that time telling everyone that my mother had died in a car crash. She had been dead to me, all those years. This part of my soul, my connection to the rainforest and its people, had been dead to me as well. And now, all of a sudden, when it finally occurred to me to care about who I was and where I'd come from, when I'd brought her back to life and held out this idea of reuniting with her as a way to get my life back on track and regain my focus, her health and well-being suddenly mattered to me most of all.

All along, I'd been operating under the assumption that Mom was right where she'd left us, doing her thing, but it was an ignorant assumption. And coming from me, of all people—me, who'd written my mother off all those years ago; me, who wasted the core of my childhood forcing her from her rightful place in my head, in my heart; me, who'd taken my heritage for granted and then pretty much set it aside—it was a little arrogant as well. It took hearing this good news from Hortensia for me to know Mom was okay—although, frankly, I'd refused to believe that she *wasn't* okay. My father, Dr. Carneiro, Hortensia . . . every anthropologist I'd consulted about this trip, every ethnography I'd read in preparation, told me to be prepared to find out that my mother could be forever out of reach, either dead or disappeared into the heart of the rainforest. But I tuned them all out. I'd done a complete one-eighty in my mind, to where nothing less than a full-on, epic, emotional reunion could make up for all of that lost time.

Hortensia reported back that my mother smiled when she heard that I wanted to see her. She asked after each of us, in turn; she was thrilled to hear I wanted to see her, thrilled to hear Danny had grown to be big and strong, thrilled to hear that Vanessa was now a young mother, and thrilled to hear that Dad was still teaching and doing okay. According to the missionary who'd acted as go-between, my mother was suddenly impatient for my arrival. Through a translator, she said, "Tell him to get on a boat and come down."

Of course it wasn't that simple. Not anyone can simply walk into Yanomami territory. There was a mess of paperwork, and vaccinations, and government bureaucracy to get past and special permission to obtain. While I am half-Yanomami, it is no secret that the American side of me was going to be confronted with suspicion and scrutiny. Apparently, Mom had forgotten all that hassle, all that headache—or maybe she wasn't capable of fully understanding it. There was also an issue of funding. Airfare alone would cost more than a thousand dollars. Additionally, I would need to buy trade goods for the Yanomami that included machetes, pots, pans, fishhooks, and many more steel goods. I would need to purchase food, lifesaving medicines and supplies, like a hammock, mosquito nets, and insect repellant. In all, the journey was going to cost thousands of dollars—money I did not have, now that National Geographic was out of the picture; money my mother could not comprehend or measure.

Working with that same translator, Hortensia had the foresight to get a letter of invitation from my mother, which Hortensia thought might be helpful to include among my papers, as a kind of supporting document to add legitimacy to my visit. The letter was written in Yanomami, and then translated into Spanish. Here's what it said:

> Davi, we want you to visit us, to the Koripi-wei village. I am your mother. You must visit your family, your grandfather, your grandmother, and your brother-in-law. We surely want you to come and visit us, and bring things. We need machetes, bowls, fishhooks, materials and fabric, and beads. Those are the things you have to bring as gifts for us. Davi, you can bring your brother and your sister. We want to see their faces. I am your mother, Yarima. I am sending this letter to you. Surely, I will wait for you in the Koripi-wei village. Surely, you must come to visit your family. Davi, surely you can come in August and you can bring your nephew. I want to see the face of my grandson.

It was a remarkable thing, this letter. I was thrilled to receive it—although *thrilled* probably doesn't get close to the rush of emotions that washed over me as I read my mother's words. Yes, it was a twice-removed translation—and the English was so broken it could only strike me as sweet and funny. It was the first piece of communication I'd had with her in twenty years. That's a lifetime, really, and as I read the letter a second time, and a third, I tried to imagine what my mother's voice sounded like as she spoke these words. It killed me that I couldn't remember the sound of her voice, and I strained to hear it. Then I closed my eyes and pictured how she might look, and thought ahead to what we might say to each other when I was finally at her side.

When I thought about it (and, believe me, I thought about it *a lot* as my trip took shape), I realized this letter was the first and only indication that my mother had even thought of me and my siblings since returning to her village—no small thing, since a part of me worried she might have put us out of her mind as she returned to her ways.

That letter was like a validation. I kept thinking, These are my mother's words. And as I kept reading and rereading those words, it was like the past twenty years had never happened.

IRONICALLY, THE WHOLE TIME this trip was coming together, I never once asked my father if he wanted to come along. It would have meant as much to him as it meant to me. He wouldn't have come, but that's not the point. He was convinced the Venezuelan government would lock him up, that there'd be big trouble waiting for him once our plane touched down in Caracas. Still, I could have asked. I could have made room in this sea-changing moment for him. But I wasn't thinking this way. I was thinking of just me and my mom. I needed this trip to happen . . . for *me*.

My father did support me in any way that he could. I sprang for my own plane ticket—which cost about twelve hundred dollars. But he lent me one of his expensive Pelican cases—a hard-backed, watertight case for all of my electronic equipment. He bought me a lot of the gear he knew I'd need in the jungle, like a framed Kelty Redwing backpack, and mosquito-proof river shirts. He took me to Wal-Mart and loaded me up with a mess of gear. And, with the right kind of fishhooks, the right kind of fishing line, basically the things he knew the villagers would need (and probably expect) as gifts upon my arrival. He knew the type of yarn the Yanomami women loved to use to help them make skirts, so he hooked me up with that as well.

His expert knowledge and the benefit of his hard-won experiences meant so much to me, but he supported me emotionally as well. We spent hours laying in supplies and talking through logistics. He shared so much wisdom and advice. The whole time,

I was hoping that he would put his arm around me and say, "Son, I'm proud of what you're doing." But as I believe I have made clear, he wasn't *that* guy, so he did these things instead. And I knew he was proud.

On July 24, 2011, I left for Newark International Airport. I had a bit of a clumsy exchange as I wished my father farewell. He gave me his blessings and I thanked him for all of his help. A part of me wanted to pull him in for a hug, even though we hadn't hugged in twenty years. But we were just two awkward men, circling each other in the middle of this moment of moments—one sending his firstborn son to the wilds of the Amazon rainforest, to possibly/hopefully reconnect with his long lost mother; the other, longing to make repairs and rediscover a piece of himself in a place he could only imagine.

IN THE TRADITIONAL YANOMAMI culture , conflicts, often surface when a village population gets too large within the confined area of a shabono. That's usually what's behind the village fissions I described earlier. It's not something that's even discussed or negotiated, the way we might work through an impasse in the Western world. It happens organically, almost like it's understood. It just *is*. If the population gets too large, it'll splinter. One group will stay and the other will move to another part of the jungle and build a new home there.

That's kind of what happened in the twenty years since I'd seen my mother—like, a bunch of times over—so when I went looking for her in July 2011, after a short plane ride from Caracas to Puerto Ayacucho, and continuing by boat from Samariapo to Mavaca, and from there by another boat to Platanal, arriving finally at my mother's village in Hasupuwe, I should have been prepared to hear that she'd moved on.

And yet it was about the last thing I was expecting. Why? Because my mother knew I was coming. She didn't know when, exactly, but she knew. She knew I'd been working with an anthropologist at the Venezuelan Institute for Scientific Research. She might not have known the specifics, the institution, but she knew I had found some local authorities to help me. And Hortensia, as I have written, knew the region. She knew the Yanomami. She knew the local missionaries. She knew my mother, from her various expeditions. She knew me from when I was a baby, and she couldn't have been more generous, more helpful as my plans took shape.

It wasn't exactly smooth sailing. There were military checkpoints to be gotten past, scheduling mix-ups, and other snags that threatened to keep me away . . . but in each case, we found a way to power forward. Father Arroldo, one of the Catholic missionaries who'd signed on to escort me into the territory, offered an important piece of advice the first time we were stopped by an armed guard who seemed to want to make trouble for us. He said, "You are Venezuelan, protected under the constitution. You look Venezuelan enough, David. You have every right to be here so you'll be fine. Just don't say anything."

So I kept my mouth shut as we made our way into the interior.

Hortensia joined me in Caracas for the Venezuelan leg of my journey, of course, and after nearly two weeks we made it all the way to the Guajaribo Rapids, after discovering that my mother was no longer with the *Koripi-wei-teri* and had returned to her home village. For centuries early European explorers had thought these rapids were the headwaters of the Orinoco, which explains why for so long the river was never really explored beyond this point, why the Yanomami of this region had lived for so long in isolation. I knew this, of course, but to set my own feet in these waters and experience the isolation in such a full-on way brought all the histories and ethnographies I'd been reading to life.

These rapids were a symbolic marker. I'd been to this very spot twenty years earlier, on a return visit with my family. I *knew* this, even though I could not remember it. Ten years before *that*, my father's boat capsized in these waters, while he was sick with malaria, and he lost everything but his life. And now here I was,

preparing to shoot these treacherous rapids in an aluminum outboard motorboat piloted by a local named Jacinto, whose only
qualification, best as I could tell, was that he'd navigated these
waters before.

But he knew his stuff, Jacinto. He knew exactly when to turn,
when to throttle, when to kill the motor. He knew the currents.

We were joined on the river by several missionaries, and we
all sat low in our seats, braced for some kind of impact—but there
was no impact. There was only a series of lurches and fits and
starts. As we throttled closer to the base of the rapids, I scanned
the width of the river, making mental note of the swimming route
I would have to take if we capsized—always a possibility in these
treacherous waters.

At one point, we approached a fairly large rock in the middle
of the river that created a hydraulic pull. Jacinto's demeanor did
not change, as he contemplated the rock, as we drifted toward
it, and the missionaries did not show any fear or concern, but I
began to worry. On the other side of the rock the water seemed
to drop, and it felt to me like the bottom was about to fall out on
us—literally. I wondered when Jacinto would punch the throttle,
because we were drifting, at the mercy of the current. It felt to me
like he should be more aggressive, more proactive—and finally, at
what seemed to me the last possible moment, when we were about
to crash broadside against the rock, I heard the roar of the motor
and watched in white-knuckle amazement as we shot past.

Once we cleared the Guajaribo, we all cheered in triumph.
There were high-fives all around, and I was outside myself enough
to realize what an odd picture we must have made—a Catholic
priest, a nun, a Yanomami-American, a Venezuelan anthropologist, a local guide . . . all of us joined on this one emotional quest.

I looked on at Jacinto and wondered how he had become so
proficient, navigating these waters. He was fearless, calm, laser-
focused. I wondered, too, how I could ever move about in these
same ways, how I could even attempt to shoot these rapids on
my own. Where could I find such confidence? How could I learn

these skills? How could I survive in this remote corner of the world, on my own?

I wanted to know everything the Yanomami knew. I wanted to be just like them. But I worried there was too much to learn.

As we crept deeper into the jungle, there were flocks of beautiful parrots soaring overhead, as if in greeting. It was a magical thing to see. The foliage began to appear greener, denser, more welcoming. The trees loomed high above us. I played the theme song to *Jurassic Park* in my head as we plowed deeper into the Amazon. Soon I could see the Yanomami standing along the riverbank, clustered for our arrival. As eager as I was to reconnect with my mother, as much as I longed to embrace her and wash away the years that had separated us, it was a jarring sight, to see all of these hardly dressed, native-looking people lining the shores of the river. I'd been here as a child, of course, and I'd spent months studying up on the region, but I wasn't prepared to see myself in these people. It was hard to imagine that I was one of them. They seemed so different, so foreign, so *unlike* me—and yet, if I looked closely, I could see that we were more alike than different.

As Jacinto cut the motor and we leaned toward the shore I realized it was one thing to look at pictures, it was one thing to see a documentary or read a book, but it was quite another to approach a large crowd of such strange-seeming people. I'd visualized this moment a thousand times, but to have it materialize was shocking, and I couldn't shake thinking, Could I really be one of them?

The *Hasupuwe-teri* had come out to greet us because they could hear the sound of our motor for miles—the sound of progress. The sound of the world encroaching. Missionaries, anthropologists, government workers . . . by now these good people had been on the map of our civilized world for centuries. But each visit was as the first, I would learn. Each roar of the motor whipping through the trees was like new music, sounding for the first time, so the villagers clustered along the muddy shores of the river as we pulled close, desperate to see what they could see.

I scanned the crowd of people—the crowd of *my* people. The women were topless; many wore skirts that appeared to be fashioned from vines, or stitched together from discarded Western clothing. The men wore T-shirts and shorts, some of them with logos and slogans I recognized from back home—the end result, no doubt, of any number of relief efforts in the region. Or maybe they'd received them in trade. Everyone was barefoot. Children ran up and down the riverbank naked, squealing with delight.

These were the *Hasapuwei-teri*—the people my father had lived among for so long. The people of my mother, Yarima.

My people.

Jacinto spoke first. I'd studied up on the Yanomami language, but I couldn't understand a word he said or a word said in return. Still, I could tell from the tone and the body language and the corresponding hand gestures that my mother was no longer living with the *Hasupuwe-teri*. This was a dispiriting turn—nothing like I expected, but as I was learning, nothing was like I expected in this part of the world.

I will wait for you, she had said.

Surely, you must come, she had said.

But she was not here.

I could have cried—really. All my life, I'd been telling people my mother was dead. It was my go-to line, all through grade school, middle school, high school. But here I had a brief, fleeting thought that maybe something had happened to her. Hortensia's last contact with her had been some months earlier, when she was inexplicably living among the *Koripi-wei-teri*—a long, long way from her home village in the Upper Orinoco. When we arrived in the region, we'd heard she was once again among her people, but we couldn't be sure the information was reliable. This deep in the jungle, on the edges of nowhere, we couldn't know if my mother was here or there, alive or dead.

Now, it *should* have occurred to me that my mother might have been someplace else, given what I knew of the Yanomami culture, but the news nonetheless took the wind out of me a little bit. It had taken me nearly two years to prepare for this expedition. And now there I was, deep in the jungle, at a kind of crossroads. To have come all this way and oh so close . . . only to have her slip away from me once more . . . I did not think I could bear the thought of losing her all over again.

She hadn't slipped far, it turned out. She was living with a smaller group in another village that was now known as Irokai—about a half-hour trek. It was the same village she had lived in many years earlier, after her lineage first split with the *Hasupuwe-teri*.

I huddled with Jacinto and Hortensia to consider our options, and as we moved to pull away and continue on to Irokai by motorboat, the villagers started waving their arms and trilling, as if to get my attention.

"What's going on?" I asked Hortensia.

"They want to see you and touch you," she said. "They have been wanting very much to meet you."

Even though Yarima had moved on, these two villages were connected. Intertwined. They were family. In fact, I had a great many aunts and uncles and cousins waving to me from the muddy riverbank—a half brother, too, as I'd soon learn. Anyway, it isn't every day that a stranger alights on these parts, so word of my impending arrival beat me down the river, and here I was, no stranger.

"What do I do?" I asked Hortensia. Really, I had no idea.

"Get off the boat," she said.

So I did, and as I stepped to the shore I was swallowed up by these happy, welcoming people. This was no tribe of savage warriors. It was more like that scene at the end of *Close Encounters of the Third Kind* where Richard Dreyfuss is collected by all those happy, welcoming alien creatures and escorted onto their ship, into their world. I was nervous as hell—super-crazy-excited, too. And, happy to be led from the alien life I'd been leading back home.

I must have looked otherworldly to these Yanomami, dressed in my Western-style clothing—khakis, tucked-in shirt, belt, shoes. The women and children all clambered toward me and put their hands on me. They giggled and oohed and aahed. They tugged at my hair, at my ears, at my clothes. They touched my nose and the scruff of my beard—something they had rarely seen because Yanomami men don't have a lot of facial hair.

I was a living, breathing novelty, and in just that moment I wasn't quite sure how I felt about being the center of all that attention. Back home, I would have hated it. As a kid, I'd spent all that time shrinking from whatever spotlight was shone on my father's work and our exotic family. But here in the jungle, I was relishing it, because I took it to mean they knew who I was; I took it to mean I belonged.

It was decided that we would wait here for my mother. One of her sons (my half brother!) would race off to fetch her, so we gathered our gear from the boat and began to walk the short trail to the village, where I would wait for them to return.

Before he raced off, Hortensia introduced me to my half brother, who by my math had to be at least seven years younger than I—about eighteen or so. He was good-looking, with a thick head of dark hair buzzed short at the sides—a classic barbershop "fade." I couldn't imagine what a haircut like that was doing out here in the jungle, on the head of my Yanomami half brother, and then I looked him over a bit more and saw that he was wearing a red-green Unimed soccer shirt, black shorts, and several necklaces of brightly colored beads. He was barefoot, just like everyone else.

It was an odd mix of *here* and *there*.

I did not know the appropriate form of Yanomami greeting when meeting a half brother for the first time, so I extended my arm for a handshake, which was just the first of many stupid, bone-headed moves I'd make on this visit. Such a meaningless gesture! What was I thinking? The Yanomami don't do handshakes; I should have known; I might as well have asked him to kiss my ankles, that's how bizarre my behavior must have seemed.

Hortensia introduced him as *Micashi*, so I pulled my hand back in a lame attempt to recover and repeated the name.

"Micashi," I said.

My half brother put his hand on my shoulder. He said, "No, no." Like he was racing to correct me. Then he pointed to himself and said, "Ricky." He spoke in a thick Spanish accent.

"Ricky?" I repeated, making sure.

He jumped up and down a little—a small show of enthusiasm, appreciation. He seemed to like that I *got* him.

"Ricky," he said again. "Ricky Martin."

It was the strangest thing. To have traveled all this way to meet my long-lost mother in the Amazon jungle, and to encounter a young man introduced to me as my half brother, calling himself Ricky Martin . . . absolutely, I was living *la vida loca*!

I later learned that "Ricky Martin" had recently been down-river to Esmeralda. It was the trip of a lifetime for him. That's where he picked up those clothes, I reasoned, those bits and pieces of Spanish, that haircut. It's probably where he heard a Ricky Martin song, or maybe seen a video. Our popular culture knows no boundaries, I was realizing. And it turns out, the Yanomami love adopting Spanish names, so it made sense that this was Ricky Martin—my half brother, Ricky Martin. These things would all become clear to me over time.

"Ricky Martin," I repeated.

He smiled, then he pointed to me and announced that he would call me "Herman," as in *hermano*—Spanish for "brother."

I smiled back. I had a nickname—a half brother *and* a nickname. Already it was a good day. My heart was full. I hadn't met my mother yet, but Ricky Martin was heading into the jungle to find her and bring her back to me. It felt to me like I'd arrived.

I WAS BURSTING WITH anticipation but I tried to keep my excitement in check. In her letter, my mother had said she very much wanted to see me.(*Surely, you must come.*)But what if she didn't recognize me? What if I didn't recognize her? We didn't speak the same language, so it's not like there was anything we could say to each other.

I started to obsess, a little bit, over how the encounter would go. I was nervous, anxious, agitated. Mostly I was eager to get on with it. I'd come all this way and yet the moment was still just out of reach.

As we walked, an older woman approached me, half-naked, speaking to me in a rapid-fire way. I couldn't make out a single word, of course, but what was most troubling was that I couldn't tell from her agitated state if she spoke words of welcome or words of aggression. Clearly there was a lot of emotion in what she was saying, but there was no way to match that emotion to the expressions on her face. One moment, she appeared stern and judgmental; the next, warm and pleasant. She scowled; she smiled. She yelled; she whispered. It was weird—and a little unsettling. But then this woman did the most surprising, most wonderful thing. She grabbed my face and pulled me in close as if she wanted to whisper something in my ear. Then she pressed her nose against the side of my head and rubbed it vigorously across my cheek— back and forth, the way a small animal might nuzzle its mother. This, I learned, was a traditional gesture of love and friendship, and I would have been transported by it, and lost in the spirit of welcome, were it not for the thick traces of saliva and tobacco juice now sluicing across my face.

(Everyone in the village chews tobacco—not the way we might here in the United States, but with a tobacco leaf rolled and wedged between the cheeks and gums. It's actually relatively healthy, I'm told, if you can get past the constant soft spray of tobacco juice everybody seems to spit from their lips as they speak.)

We reached the entrance of the *shabono*. All around me were images and touchstones I recognized from my father's photographs. It was as if I had been here before—only, my memories were tied to the pictures I had seen and studied, and not to the time I had actually spent in a structure just like this one, many years before. They were my father's memories, not mine.

I noticed something new: a hut breaking up the continuity of the *shabono*. And in the middle of the structure there were patches of grass. I saw many items of clothing—some Western, some homespun—hung on crossbeams. There was also a collection of pots and pans. Clearly there had been many visitors to this village over the years.

I began to set up my hammock and unpack my gear, and as I settled in I was surrounded once again by women and children. They sat on the ground at my feet, their heads tilted up, watching my every move. They smiled. As soon as my hammock was strung, some of the children jumped into it. There was a lot of laughter. The men of the village stood on the perimeter, silently taking in the scene. Perhaps they did not know what to make of me. Perhaps they were just waiting to see what would happen next.

The women and children spoke to me in their rapid-fire way, and I could only smile back and repeat a word or a phrase. Going in, reaching back over layers of childhood memory, I could only remember two Yanomami phrases: *ya-ohi* ("I am hungry") and *ya-posi-shiiti*("my butt itches"). The first certainly applied, because we hadn't eaten since we reached the rapids. The second . . . not really. But I said nothing—I was too excited to speak. I was about to see my mother, after all this time. There was nothing to say.

Finally, she arrived, a little out of breath. I could only imagine what her expression was when Ricky Martin informed her that I had finally arrived. Surely she must've been excited, abruptly stopping whatever it was that she was doing and hurrying down the path to her son, her long-lost son. Her arrival was announced by a rush of quiet. All the laughter, all the chattering, the rapid-fire talking . . . it fell away the moment my mother entered the *shabono*. All eyes turned to her, and then back to me. I could hear people whispering, and I could make out my mother's name in the whispering: "*Yarima.*"

I looked up and instantly recognized my mother.

My mother was carrying a traditional Yanomami basket on her back as she approached, anchored with a strap pulled taut across her forehead. I'd seen pictures of these baskets—this one was filled to overflowing with manioc. She was dressed in the native fashion, which basically meant she was dressed hardly at all. She was barefoot, topless, and wore a red skirt. She also wore a set of *hii-hi* sticks through her nose and lower lip—the decorative needles favored by the women of the rainforest. Around her neck were necklaces made of blue beads, and adorned in her ears were tropical flowers. Her hair was cut short, in a typical bowl cut. Her face was painted with red decorative lines.

I knew this was how my mother would appear before me. Intellectually, I knew. But I was still a little taken aback. I mean, this was my mother. For the short time she'd lived with us in the States, the time I best remembered, she dressed like a typical American. She wore jeans, had her hair done up like every other mother in the neighborhood—although, even then, she wasn't crazy about shoes. She went barefoot, whenever possible. But to see her here, now, looking the part of an exotic Amazonian jungle woman . . . I was paralyzed in awe and admiration.

She unstrapped the basket from around her head and set it on the ground. I stood from my hammock and crossed to her, and as I did I started thinking, Oh crap, what do I do now? I was conscious of my every movement—probably because there were all these sets of eyes on us. I thought back to everything I'd read about the region, about the people. How do you greet a Yanomami woman? How do you greet a Yanomami woman who happens to be your mother? Already, I'd screwed things up when I tried to shake my half brother's hand. But this was my mother; we hadn't seen each other in over twenty years; I *desperately* wanted to get this one right.

But there was no template for this moment. We stood just a couple of feet apart, and I longed to reach out to her, to wrap my arms around her, but the Yanomami don't bear-hug. It's not a part of their culture. They don't kiss—or, as I now knew, shake hands. Compared to the fuss us Westerners make with our coming and going, the Yanomami appear to not do much of anything—in greeting, in parting. At least, they don't *usually* do any of these things. She crossed those few feet toward me and placed a hand on my shoulder, and I could feel that her hands were trembling. Then she started to cry. They were soft tears at first, but they quickly grew into deep, heaving sobs, together with moans of grief and happiness.

I was immediately flooded with childhood memories of my mother . . . images of us wrestling on the living room floor, dancing together on the bed, going on roller coasters, eating french fries. I lost it. I broke down and cried right along with her. The women who'd been watching us—Yanomami, as well as Hortensia and some of the missionaries—they cried, too. For a few moments, we were all overcome. After a while I placed my arm on my mother's shoulder and stared into her dark brown eyes, and for a beat or two I marveled at how beautiful they were. At how beautiful *she* was. She left her hand on my shoulder and continued to touch me, but she was careful not to grab me or hold me close. Her fingers only brushed up against me, like she was reaching out to see if I was real. Like maybe I was a ghost.

I could not think what to say. Finally, I came out with "Mom, it's me. It's David."

It was just something to say, I guess, and in the middle of all that fussing and crying and trembling I wasn't sure she'd heard or understood, so I spoke again. This time I said, "Mom, it's me. It's David. I'm home."

UPPER ORINOCO, YANOMAMI TERRITORY

The Yanomami women, they gossip as they walk. These treks, they're not just about collecting food and other resources needed to survive. They're also social. The women take the time away from the pulse of the village and its daily routines to chatter and laugh. A lot.

The whole way back to the abandoned shabono, my mother was lost in singsong conversation with the other women. Even while we were huddled under those boulders, waiting out the storm, they were talking, talking, talking. I could only imagine what they were saying, so I tried to do just that. I listened to the lilt of my mother's voice and in my head she was talking about how pleased she was that I had returned to her, how much she admired the way I was trying so hard to fit myself in. I was still a work in progress, as far as my Yanomami transformation was concerned, still fumbling through the many customs and rituals I was trying to learn. It was far more likely that she was giggling with the young woman who was meant to be my wife, and telling her some embarrassing story from when I was little; or even more likely, something that had nothing to do with me. But there's a certain freedom in not knowing

169

the language. You can tell yourself what you want to hear.

It had been difficult for me, as I had been preparing for this homecoming journey, not knowing how I might fit myself in to village life. Assuming I could even find my mother, I wondered, would she be excited to see me? Would she even remember me? Yes, I had a letter from her, encouraging me to visit. Yes, I could read her wistful affection between the lines of translation. But in moments of doubt I allowed myself to think that she'd been coached on what to say, that she had to be reminded who I was, reaching back to her from so long ago.

Happily, my worries were unfounded, and when I finally reunited with my mother it was as joyful as I could have imagined—with happy tears all around. Really, it could not have meant more or gone any better. But here as we returned to the rest of our group, following a flash storm that might have left a Westerner worrying about our safety, no one looked up from what they were doing. No one raced to greet us, or even to help us unload the plantains and fish we carried. And for our part, we didn't shout with happiness at the sight of the others, right where we'd left them, safe and whole, for surely they had been in just as much danger, waiting out the very same tropical storm.

Everyone just went about their business, did their thing, so I tried to follow along. It was late morning by this point, and there was some activity by the hearth. I laid down the plantains I'd been carrying and wandered over to the fire to see if I could be of some help. There was fish, rice, some meats. I looked for an empty pot, and then I remembered I had brought some spaghetti in my pack. I no longer recall why I'd thought to cart it along on this short trip, but there it was, calling to me, so I decided to cook it up, as a kind of surprise for the others. I was still finding my way with this group, trying to fit myself in, and this seemed as good a way as any to make a contribution.

The Yanomami, I felt sure, had tasted spaghetti before—from some of the missionaries who'd visited the village, perhaps even from my father, but they certainly weren't expecting spaghetti, so I busted it out. Two packages—enough for everyone.

I could only imagine what the Yanomami thought about this kind of food. I wondered how they thought the nabuhs obtain pasta. Did they think we had spaghetti trees or that we plant spaghetti seeds? Whatever they thought, they absolutely loved it. We cooked it plain with a little salt. It was a nice little treat, and after a while I wandered over to my hammock, which was strung up next to my mother's, to clean my plate. It was the heat of the day, and my belly was full, and my plan was to rest for a bit before taking up the chores of the afternoon. But soon another group of chattering, giggling young girls wandered over. They wanted to talk, only I couldn't understand them. They were talking so fast, talking over each other. Mom was nowhere around, so I couldn't look to her for assistance.

Soon it became apparent that these girls wanted me to join in on their chanting and to dance with them—or to dance like them. One of them fairly pulled me from my hammock and motioned for me to do as she did, only I couldn't quite replicate the traditional Yanomami dance style she put on display. I was game, but ungainly. The others were chanting, clapping, offering some version of accompaniment, and they seemed to take a great deal of pleasure in my confusion—and in my inability to move as the others were moving. Whatever the Yanomami expression is for having two left feet, that's most likely what they were saying about me. Two left feet and all thumbs for toes.

After a while of this, I grew tired of being the target of all that laughter. Already I'd made a fool of myself, chanting and stomping around like the village shaman, ridiculously trying to blow away the storm. Already I'd been on the receiv-

ing end of a whole lot of snickering and pointing—because I didn't understand the language or the customs or what was expected of me.

The spaghetti might have helped, but it didn't change anything, so I decided to turn things around and show my Yanomami family how we dance and celebrate back home. I moonwalked. Really. I went into my best Michael Jackson impression, hard, and what I lacked in grace and subtlety I made up for in grit and determination. Here again, I was all thumbs and two left feet, but these good people didn't know any better. They looked at me with complete astonishment— they'd never seen anything like it!—their faces frozen somewhere between confusion and horror.

And then, one by one, they started laughing.

I really got into it—and, soon I was able to convince some of the others to join me, and for the next hour and more we must have made a weird, curious site: one or two of us at first, and then three and four and more, traipsing around a cooking fire deep in the Amazon rainforest, dancing our little heads off like we were onstage at Madison Square Garden.

I know, I know . . . I'd gone from making one kind of fool of myself to another kind of fool of myself, but I counted it a good trade, because in this moment, for the first time, I allowed myself to move about with utter, joyful abandon. I danced without a single, blessed care, like I was at the edge of the universe, with no place to go but up.

I danced like I belonged no place else.

CHAPTER SIX

My Yanomami Ways

I WAS WEARY FROM THE journey, spent, moving on fumes. The reunion with my mother had gone as well as I could have hoped, and yet a thing like this, reaching back across all these many years, over all these many miles, reconnecting with my family—it takes an emotional toll.

It was still so brand-new to me, being in the jungle, a world away from any world I had known. To call it surreal would be a big-time cliché, and the Yanomami don't do clichés, so let's just say my mind was racing a million miles a minute—also a cliché, I know, but it gets close to it. My heart was racing, too. Mom was hovering nearby, and it felt like the entire village was pressed close to my hammock, wanting to soak in the drama and excitement of the moment just past, the moments still to come. Mom was giddy, like she was drunk from the swirl of emotions, from having her Davi back. Me, I was more thrashed than pumped, relieved that all had gone well, yes, but mostly looking ahead to whatever might come next.

As I tried to settle myself and adjust to my new surroundings, I kept coming back to something my father told me about *observing* the

Yanomami. He wrote about this in his book, at length, musing about his shifting role in the community and the tug-and-pull he felt between being a participant and a social scientist. To him this was a big deal. It weighed on him most of all as he considered his betrothal to my mother, and it was at the heart of that harrowing story he shared about his friend from a neighboring village who was dragged into the bushes and gang-raped by a group of teen-age boys. It's what kept him on the sidelines, unable (or unwilling) to interfere . . . at first.

And he didn't just *write* about it. It's a dilemma he talked to me about before I left, also at length. He said, "Dave, you might not like some of the things you'll see."

Sure enough, it's a dilemma that found me straightaway, fresh off the boat. I'd hardly had time to catch my breath, let alone figure out what role I might play in this community, observer or participant. I'd walked through a bunch of different scenarios heading in, but as I arrived I could see my role had already been cast. Here's what happened: As I was sitting in my hammock next to my mom, I noticed two Yanomami boys roughhousing across the *shabono*. They looked to be about eight or nine years old. One boy pushed the other, who started to cry and then pushed back—no big thing, except for here among the *Hasupuweteri*, where it's way bigger than I would have thought. The situation quickly escalated. Soon it seemed like the entire village had descended on the scene. A woman took one of the boys aside and handed him a club. Next a woman appearing to be the second boy's mother or aunt handed *him* a club. The boys were given instructions on what to do with their clubs, which were about the size of a policeman's nightstick, made out of solid wood—definitely *not* an implement you'd want to get hit with, even if you were being struck by a small boy.

The boys, coerced by their parents, began trading blows to the head with the clubs. They were both crying by this point. Neither one wanted to be on the giving or receiving end of these blows, but this was what their older relatives expected. It was like a rite of passage—a cringe-worthy, stomach-turning rite of passage—and it struck me as chilling, brutal.

My father was right; I would not like some of the things I'd see, and here I was, not even unpacked, enraged.

One of the boys was much bigger and stronger than the other, only he seemed more upset than his opposite number, but I don't think anybody watching this display was more upset than me. The boys were bloodied, sobbing, staggering from the force and effort of trading these blows. It was horrifying, too painful to watch, and at one point, around the time one of the boys' heads looked like it had been split open from one of the blows, I stood in anger. I almost didn't recognize myself, I was so angry. Really, I was pissed!

But as I stood, I stopped myself. I told myself I was meant to respond like an anthropologist; I should not interfere; it was not my role; I was there to observe, not participate. All these bullshit thoughts started racing through my head, and for a moment I thought I should listen to them. But then I saw the bullshit for what it was. This battle between these two boys, it wasn't about winning or prevailing, I was realizing—it was about putting them through these adult-type paces, and preparing them for the possibility of being in a real fight. I suppose the Western equivalent would be a father telling his son that if somebody hits him he should hit back—an eye-for-an-eye sort of message. But in the jungle, played out with clubs, it seemed a little more vicious than that—to *me*, anyway. But it was the Yanomami way, and if I was to remain in the territory for any stretch of time and adapt to the local customs, it would have to be *my* way as well. I worked the situation through in my head and thought, Okay, so there's been a little-kid dispute, probably over nothing much at all, and this was how the elders would have the little kids settle it. To the elders it was a teachable moment, a point of honor; and yet to me it was just plain brutal, almost like a form of child abuse, to force these two kids to pummel each other in the head with wooden sticks.

I didn't know what the hell to do—what was expected of me,

or what I could get away with. A part of me knew full well that this was an aspect of the culture—a culture to which I belonged only in a tenuous way. To step into the middle of this exchange would set me up as an outsider when, really, what I wanted to do was fit myself in . . . just like I'd wanted to fit myself in when I was growing up in New Jersey. (Funny how our wants and needs tend to circle back and tie together.) I didn't want to call any attention to myself, but I couldn't stand by and watch these two boys beat the crap out of each other. I was in culture shock. I couldn't stop myself from injecting my Western morals and standards into this situation.

I must have stood there for a good long moment, frozen, unsure what to do next, if I was meant to do anything at all, and in that long moment the boys seemed to lose some of their fight. One struck the other, the other stumbled back and righted himself, and then after another few beats the second boy took his swing at the first. It's like it was happening in slow motion—almost like they were trying *not* to hurt each other, because of course they knew that whatever punishment they meted out would be returned in kind.

Finally, I couldn't stand it anymore, even at this gentler pace, so I grabbed a T-shirt from a bag, a bright orange one I'd brought down to donate to the villagers, and crossed with it to one of the boys—the one who'd gotten the worst of the beating. Keep in mind, I didn't break up the fight; it was already over. But this one kid was in bad shape. His head was split open at the scalp, and there were splotches of blood running down the side of his face, mixed with tears. The poor kid was a mess—his wounds probably looked way worse than they were, but it was bad. I moved without thinking, going through the motions I'd learned in an emergency medicine class I'd taken back home—and nobody moved to stop me. My mother, my brother, my uncles . . . they left me alone to do my thing.

As I approached the boy, I ripped the shirt along its length, the way they show you to do when you want to stanch a wound to the head. It was a brand-new shirt, and it made a clean, crisp tear, and I could almost hear this gasp emerging from the crowd that had gathered to watch the battle. Suddenly people started yelling at me, and I could tell they were incensed and confused by my behavior. As a group, they were wondering what the hell I was doing, but it seemed to be even more troubling to them that I had just ruined a perfectly good T-shirt.

It occurred to me that the rubbernecking villagers cared more about the T-shirt than these two little kids . . . but they saw the whole thing from a different perspective. I couldn't spend a lot of time worrying about this, though, because I went into triage mode. I took some water and poured it over the boy's head, to quickly clean the wound. I sat him down—to calm him, I thought at first, until I realized it was me who needed to be calmed down. Then I wrapped a torn-off rope of T-shirt around his head, to stop the bleeding. The whole time, the people just watched. It's like they were curious to see what I would do—even the boy with the bloodied head was confused by my behavior. They all knew who I was at this point, so it's not like I was a complete stranger. My arrival had been anticipated for months, and Yarima was like a rock star among her people—she was the girl who'd gone to live with the *nabuh* with the big forehead off in his faraway village and come back to tell the tale. They didn't care that I was interfering, but it was beyond their understanding. The way I'd bandaged this boy, it was like no dressing they'd ever seen applied to a head wound; the poor kid looked like a cross between a pumpkin and a pirate, with that orange swatch draped tight across his brow.

Soon the moment passed, and the boys returned to their families, to their sections of the *shabono*, and in the whispering that flowed from this exchange there was talk of this strange young man with his strange new ways, unaccustomed to the customs of the jungle . . . namely, *me*. Hortensia translated for me, told me what the people were saying, and the gist of it was that I should have known that these blows to the head were good for the children. I should have known that it makes them strong, hardens their heads. In all, their fight was seen as a positive thing. And I was seen as this odd *nabuh* interloper, willing to ruin a perfectly good shirt that could have been put to much more meaningful use.

I went back to my unpacking, but the moment stayed with me. Mostly, the *dilemma* stayed with me. I went back and forth between telling myself that I was there to observe and learn, not to interfere, and telling myself that this was my family, my village, my people. I'd been in the jungle for all of one afternoon, and already I'd stepped from the anthropologist's ideal. Already I'd crossed some kind of line. But I was not an anthropologist. I could not sit by and take notes while two boys clubbed and bloodied each other; I was not here to *just* study these people, I was here to *connect* with them, so I came away feeling good about how I'd intervened. I thought, Fuck it. I thought, To hell with what was expected of me. I was Yanomami—same as these good people—and my time in the village would pass in my own way.

There was a strange footnote to this story, and it came about just twenty minutes later and continued to haunt me throughout my stay in the village. Well, maybe *haunt* is too strong a word for how it went down, but it did follow me around. The boy who'd gotten the worst of the beating, the one with the bright orange tourniquet, it was almost like I'd embarrassed him by my show of concern. Like the lesson that was meant for him was now somehow lost. He shed the bandage after about two minutes, like it was this great nuisance.

So after this great fiasco, I was the fool—a role I would get a bunch of chances to play in the days and weeks to come.

I'D BEEN IN THE village only a few hours and already a lot had happened. I'd been reunited with my mother, met my half brother Ricky Martin, my uncle Shoape, a mess of aunts and cousins I couldn't possibly keep track of. I'd strung my hammock in a place of honor in the *shabono* and gladly accepted the stares of the

Yanomami children, who looked at me like I was an alien from outer space. I'd "interfered" with this mini clubbing ritual, which left me looking even more alien to the people of the village.

But we were just getting started.

Next, my mother brought around someone else for me to meet. This was unexpected, but I should have seen it coming. Already a large group had gathered around us, because the village had not seen such excitement in just about forever, but as my mother approached the people kind of parted and made a path for her. If there was such a thing as a Yanomami drum roll, this would have been the spot for it, because this was my *Welcome to the Jungle!* moment. This was where the skies should have parted to announce my arrival—the big reveal! Absolutely, Mom was bursting to make this introduction, almost like she'd been planning it for a long, long time. Like she'd been waiting for just this opportunity to present me with a gift of welcome, a giant surprise.

The gift? A beautiful young woman who looked to be in her late teens—if I had to project my Western judgment and consider her age. She had the typical bowl haircut of the Yanomami woman, with the slender *hii-hi* sticks through her lower lips and septum. She was topless, adorned with a multicolored necklace of beads, a red skirt, and a strap made of vines draped diagonally across her shoulders—looking, oddly, like the sash worn by beauty pageant contestants back home. She was stunning, this girl, and I was pretty much speechless as she approached. I couldn't think what to say, what to do, couldn't imagine who she might be in my family's lineage. She approached me and put her arm around my torso—a gesture of familiarity that struck me as extraordinary for this part of the world, where this type of physical display was uncommon, particularly between men and women. Then she giggled and smiled, exposing a thick, wet tobacco wad resting on her lower lip.

I gave a nervous laugh and smiled back and did what any Yanomami wannabe would do in this situation—I placed my arm around this girl and patted her on the head.

You have to realize, at this point I had no idea if this girl was my half sister, or a cousin, or maybe even an aunt . . . so I wasn't thinking about her in anything other than familial terms. But that didn't stop me from checking her out.(Come on, she was half-naked!)She was exotically beautiful, even with the wad of tobacco on her lip and the sticks through her nose; however, her body was marked with cuts, mosquito bites, inflamed bumps from the biting gnats and other signs of the harsh jungle life. As she pressed close, I could smell the ceremonial *onoto* paint decorating her cheeks.

I said, "Hey." This wasn't exactly the most appropriate response to such a warm greeting, but it was about the best I could manage.

The whole time, my mother was smiling—beaming, almost—and then she said something to me I couldn't understand. I crinkled up my face in confusion, so she said it again. Still nothing. Finally, Hortensia leaned in to clear things up. She'd been standing just off to the side, recording this encounter, and she could see I was lost.

"This girl," Hortensia said. "She is your wife."

Well, you could have knocked me down with a parrot feather. In the back of my mind, I was prepared for something like this to come up during my time in the jungle—only I thought it would come up in theory. My father had told me this would happen—and so did the other anthropologists and missionaries I'd consulted ahead of my visit—so I wasn't completely surprised. Still, I thought that after a couple of weeks, if all was going well, one of the headmen would take me aside and suggest I take a wife, the same way it happened for my father. It would either mean something, or it wouldn't, but by that point I would have eased my way into the life of the village.

I never knew her name—it was not the Yanomami way—but in my head I called her Layla. I was instructed to call her by the Yanomami word for woman, which was *Sua*, and that's how I referred to her whenever we spoke directly, but there was something about her that just screamed "Layla"—like in that great Clapton song.

Then, before I could even begin to think what this relationship with "Layla" might mean, all eyes seemed to turn to another young girl, who had approached in the first girl's wake. She was also beautiful, although she appeared to be a bit younger. Also, she was a little less forward. She didn't call as much attention to herself, or move about with the same confidence and purpose. She wore what looked to be a pair of yellow Capri pants and a multicolored necklace of her own, and as I checked *her* out, I wondered where these girls got their hands on these clothes, these necklace beads. My mind raced to consider who might have come this way before, bearing this items. Doctors? Government officials? Missionaries?

But there was no time for me to think too long along these lines—because this girl, too, was meant to be my wife. She did not approach me with the familiarity of my "first" wife. She was shy, wary—and I can't say I blamed her. If I were in her shoes (okay, no shoes, but if was walking around in her bare feet), I would have taken one look at me with my goofy clothes and my goofy ways and made for the river, but Wife No. 2 hung in there—I had to give her that.

Wife No. 2 would be known to me as *Sua* as well—only I decided to think of her as Lucy. Here again, I don't know why, but the name seemed to fit—like Lucy in the Sky with Diamonds.

It turned out my two wives were sisters, so the whole thing started to take on the feel of a *Saturday Night Live* Jerry Springer parody, but I was careful to extend the same warm greeting to Wife No. 2, so I turned to "Lucy" and said, "Hey." Because, hey, I didn't want to offend anybody.

It turned out too that each of my wives already had a husband— one of them even had a kid! So the whole Jerry Springer analogy started to seem more and more appropriate—and more and more unsettling. One of the husbands was there at this impromptu "ceremony"—but I didn't make the connection just yet. Still, this one dude stood out—a rough-and-tumble-looking man who appeared to be in his mid-twenties, maybe even a little older. He looked like he could kick the shit out of me if he wanted to—and here I'd given him plenty of reason. He was clearly stronger than I—more brutish-looking than most of the men of the village—and thick around the middle. I recognized him from the boat ride I'd just taken with Jacinto and Hortensia. He'd taken my Penn State ball cap and started wearing it—playfully, I thought at the time, but now I wondered if he was taunting me in some way, because he refused to give it back.

Mom was elated to be pairing me off with these two women; in her mind, I would consummate these marriages and start making Yanomami babies, cementing my ties to the village and ensuring that I would never go back to my father's "village" in New Jersey. It was a way to keep me close—but, also, it was a way to make me more Yanomami, like an initiation right.

To the village elders, I gathered that these matches were meant to bring honor on the *Irokai-teri* and to bestow honor in return. Who the hell was I to get in the way of that?

Another word or two on the jealous husband front. Later that afternoon, a group of us were relaxing in our hammocks while the missionaries prepared a fine welcome meal of rice and fish. Coffee, too—we'd brought our own, but I was surprised at the richness of it. I was soaking in the sights, the smells, the sounds . . . trying to absorb my new surroundings all at once. There was a lot of talk, but I couldn't understand any of it, other than a few words or phrases. Luckily, Hortensia was nearby to translate, as she had pledged to be throughout this first leg of my journey.

It was a gentle, peaceful scene—again, everything I could have imagined for my first afternoon and evening. But then, suddenly, that same man I recognized from the boat and from the moment I'd met my two wives jumped from his hammock and walked over to me. His tone, his posture, his demeanor . . . everything about him was aggressive, menacing.

His approach gave me pause, so I turned quickly to Hortensia and said, "Who's that?"

She said, "That is the woman's husband."

I said, "Which woman."

She pointed to Wife No. 2—said, "That woman."

I thought, WTF!?!

Wife No. 2—the younger one, the shy one. Somehow she'd married this brute, a guy I didn't want to mess with. He looked like he was good with a bow, good with a machete, quick with his hands. Strong enough to snap me in two and then maybe cook me over an open fire. The last thing I wanted was to step in the middle of this guy's marriage and claim his wife.

He shouted something at me as he drew near. Then he stood just a few inches from me and shouted some more. After a while of this, he paused, like he was thinking if there was anything else he wanted to say. Then he returned to his hammock. He went from threatening to passive-aggressive in the space of a few steps.

All around, the people were lightheartedly laughing, as if they'd just gotten the punch line to a confusing joke. All eyes had been on this strange and sudden display—and now all eyes remained on me, to see how I might respond.

My mother, she was sitting next to me the whole time. She had not moved to intervene, or to defend me in any way. She was simply by my side.

I turned again to Hortensia, for explanation. I said, "Okay, so what was *that*?"

She said, "He wanted you to know that he is husband to your wife. He wanted you to be careful because he will get very jealous."

I said, "So why was everyone laughing?"

She said, "Because at the end he changed his mind and said not to worry, he won't get jealous."

Still, I made a mental note: *don't mess with this dude's wife.*

LATER THAT FIRST DAY, the headman let me know through an interpreter that the men of the village wanted to help me build a hut—

something they had helped *my* father to do thirty-something years earlier. I thought that was kind of cool, a sweet little through-line from how things were now to how they were then.

In the meantime, I was to sleep in a hammock in the *shabono*. I didn't sleep too well that first night. Right away, Mom expected me to be a full-blooded Yanomami. This was her thing, at every turn—she wanted me to move, sleep, breath, eat, *act* Yanomami. Down to the bone. I was her son, returned to her after a *wayumi* of many, many years, and I would move among her people, *our* people, as one of them. She was determined. This meant I would sleep by the fire without a mosquito net. This meant I would eat grub worms and monkey meat and whatever else she put in front of me. This meant I would move about in my underwear— because, hey, I might have been willing to drink the Yanomami Kool-Aid, but I wasn't quite prepared to prance around naked, or in one of those traditional penis-strings the men of the village seemed to all wear.(Have you *seen* one of these things? It's pretty much self-explanatory—you tie the foreskin to a string wrapped around the waist. Not the most flattering look—and not the most comfortable, either.)

It also meant I would shed my shoes—although I had some trouble with this one. My mother pointed to my Reeboks and said, *"Zapatos, shami!"* Shoes, bad!

I tried to go barefoot that first afternoon and evening, because I really, really wanted to please my mother, but the soles of my feet weren't tough enough to withstand the jungle floor, so whenever I returned to my hammock I slipped my sneakers back on, until my mother would start pointing at me again.

Zapatos, shami!

I had forgotten that my father had passed his first couple of nights in the jungle with a flashlight and a knife in his hammock, but I ended up doing the same thing. I didn't make the connection until I was back in the States, rereading his book, but there I was, clutching a flashlight and a knife to my chest, listening to the sounds of the night, chasing away the bugs, trying to get comfortable, wondering how I'd adjust to this wild, wonderful place. It turned out I would wield those two survival weapons many times that first night, and many times more in the nights to follow.

I was too excited to sleep, but I was also scared. You have to realize, I was deep in the rainforest, unable to speak the language, unfamiliar with the flora and fauna, terrified of bugs, completely cut off from the only world I'd ever known. As excited as I was to see my mother and connect with my Yanomami roots, I was worried I was in over my head, out of my element. And I was! It started to mess with my head, more and more as darkness fell and the night dragged. I must confess, as I lay there not sleeping, I couldn't shake thinking of all those stories of violence and tribal warfare that for years had been the default image of these Yanomami villagers. Forget the wild animals that may or may not have been lurking in the forest; forget the gnats and the creepy-crawlers and the no-see-ums. I was more worried about the wild Yanomami of neighboring villages. Chagnon's words hung in the night air above my hammock and scared the crap out of me, filling my head with gruesome, spooky pictures. Stories of rape, revenge raids, gang attacks . . . they kept playing over and over, on an endless loop, and I couldn't tune them out for trying.

Let me tell you, in the middle of the night, when you're surrounded by dozens of sleeping, snoring strangers who don't quite know what to make of you, beneath a canopy of unseen jungle terrors you can't begin to fathom . . . your imagination runs a little wild. Especially when there is a jealous husband, leery of your motives, only several hammocks away. So there I was, completely spooked. With nothing else to distract me, the sounds of the rainforest were amplified in the middle of the night, and I lay there wondering what the hell I could have been thinking, setting out on this adventure. Also, wondering what was lurking in the jungle, ready to pounce and do me in. It was pretty extreme. The fact that I was here, so far from the comforts of home, so far from anything I could recognize as civilization. Me, of all people. Me, who was deathly afraid of spiders. Back home, I'd freak out at the sight of a ladybug, for fuck's sake. If a bee found its way through an open window, I'd lose it, so all that first night (and the next one, and the next one), I listened in silent panic to the sounds of sticks crackling, insects chirping, wild nocturnal animals rustling in the brush beyond the *shabono* clearing. I wished like crazy there was a volume button I could reach for, to turn down the killing white noise of the jungle . . . but these creatures would not shut up!

I'd hear a twig snap somewhere in the distance, and I'd lift my head and point my beam of flashlight in the direction of the noise. *What was that? A raider from a neighboring village? A jaguar?* The flashlight revealed nothing, and I wondered why no one else was hearing these same noises.

At one point in the middle of that first night—it could have been an hour after everyone else had drifted off to sleep, it could have been three or four—I had the sense that the air around me was being displaced by some warm-blooded animal slowly making its way toward my hammock. Prowling. Getting ready to attack.

Shit!

I jumped from my hammock, knife in hand. "Who's there?" I whisper-shouted. I didn't want to wake anybody, but at the same time I wondered why I was the only one hearing these noises. Stupidly, I kept my voice down while trying to be heard.

I switched on my flashlight and scanned the area around my hammock, but could see no signs of strange movement. I half-expected to see the jealous husband of Wife No. 2—after all, the dude had basically threatened me in front of the entire village just a couple of hours earlier. It made perfect sense to me, just then, that he'd come to get me in my sleep, when no one else was looking, to preserve the honor of his marriage.

"Who's there?" I said again.

As soon as I said it, I beat myself up about it. It was another stupid thing to say, really. I mean, if there was an intruder lurking somewhere in the night, he'd have no idea what I was saying. If it was an animal . . . also, stupid. It would have made as much sense to burst into song.

But there was nothing, no one. After a while, I realized that none of my Yanomami relatives had been awakened, so I told myself it was all in my mind. Mom was sleeping soundly in her hammock, just off to the side. My brother Ricky Martin was across the *shabono*, snoring peacefully. And I was just some dumb-ass from Easton, Pennsylvania, jumping around in his underwear, pissing off the crickets and frogs that were probably laughing their cricket and frog asses off, chirping and croaking, *Hey, look at that idiot! Go back to sleep, you fucking pansy!*

THAT WHOLE FIRST NIGHT, my mind was all over the place. In between all of that tossing and turning and thinking I was going to be eaten alive by snakes or jaguars, or beaten to death by jealous husbands, I worried how Mom and I would fill our days. It was one thing to come all this way to reunite with her, but it was another thing entirely for us to find a way to truly interact—for me to insert myself into village life, for Mom and I to find some meaningful points of connection.

Just to be clear, just then, I had no idea how long I'd remain in Mom's village. I'd come to Venezuela on a one-way ticket, so my return was open-ended. If I continued to struggle through these long sleepless nights, it would be a short stay. But if I got comfortable and adjusted . . . who knows? Best-case scenario, I was thinking, I would stay with Mom for several months—just enough time to get the full flavor of jungle life and lay a strong foundation for a return visit.

As I lay there, absurdly awake, I started to realize for the first time that I definitely hadn't thought this trip through in all the ways I should have. I'd acted impulsively, irrationally, and it felt to me like these next couple of weeks would pass slowly, miserably. I hadn't been worried about this, it hadn't even occurred to me, but now it was all I could think about. However, before I could beat myself up about it, before I could worry over how I'd ever sleep in the wilds of the jungle, how I'd get along, the sun began to smile on our little clearing, and as the *shabono* brightened with a pre-dawn glow there was haste and movement all about. My mother was one of the first ones up and out of her hammock, and she moved about in a blur of activity. She was back and forth, here and there, making ready . . . for *something*. It had not been clear to me when the group drifted off to sleep what would happen the next morning or for the remainder of my trip. We never got that far in our planning—for months, the only concern we had was to arrive at this place, at this moment, and now that we were here the rest was kind of up for grabs, only here was Mom, flitting about like a little windup toy.

The one thing I knew for certain was that our boatman Jacinto would be with us for the rest of the day with his outboard motor-boat, ready to transport us to my mother's new village of Irokai, about a ten-minute ride upriver. We had not realized, setting out, that Mom no longer lived here in Hasupuwe, but this was now clear—and since my plan was to spend as much time with her as possible, to immerse myself as significantly as possible in the daily life of the village, to bond with her people, *my* people, it made sense to decamp to where she truly belonged, where she was most comfortable.

But before I could slip from my hammock and see about plans, Mom and Sor Antonietta had made some arrangements of their own. We were going fishing, I was told—and we would only be gone a short while.

Like Hortensia Caballero, Sor Antonietta played a key role in my odyssey. Like Hortensia, she'd known my family back in the day—only I hadn't thought to reach out to her ahead of my trip. Still, she turned out to be one kick-ass nun. She'd been serving the mission in Yanomami territory for decades. If I had to guess, I'd say she was about sixty years old at the time, only you wouldn't have known it to watch her do her thing. She was healthy, active, strong—good with a machete and a piece of wise, warmhearted advice. Also, she could gut an animal, fish for piranha, and steer a motorboat. Once, she treated an infection in my foot with a bucket of hot water mixed with salt and mango leaves—so, clearly, she knew her way around the rainforest.

I came to think of Sor Antonietta as our "jungle nun," but I never lost sight of her spiritual connection to this place. She had an endlessly sweet disposition, and she was quick to smile. Her heartwarming laugh, which I'd hear often, was something to cherish, and here on this impromptu fishing expedition with my mother it filled the air like a song.

I quickly got dressed and got excited for my first fishing experience in the Amazon. The last time I fished was about fifteen years earlier when I was just a young boy. I didn't even have time to ask any questions—we just went. Once in the boat, we didn't travel very far—just a few minutes upriver, to a small estuary where the feeder stream met the main river. Jacinto eased the boat toward shore, and Mom hopped out into the water without saying a word.

Her actions became clear soon enough, as she started digging on the banks of the stream with her machete—clear enough, that is, to everyone but me.

"*Qué está haciendo?*" I asked Sor Antonietta. *What is she doing?*

"*Está sacando gusanos,*" Sor Antonietta replied. *She is getting worms.*

Of course. Worms. I was no outdoorsman, but this made perfect sense even to an idiot like me, and just then it also made perfect sense for me to hop out of the boat and help. So I did. Only, the thing was, I couldn't really communicate with Mom, other than to do as she did, and smile, and keep close. So I jumped into the water, sneakers and all, grabbed a machete, and started digging. I wasn't very good at it, but Mom was having great success, scooping the blade into the wet mud and unearthing dozens and dozens of slithering worms, so I tried to follow her lead. Whenever she turned to face me, I made sure to smile. I squatted along the shore directly alongside my mother, and there we were, side by side, doing our work—woman's work, I was later told, and this was a cause of some concern back in the boat. Jacinto turned to Sor Antonietta and said, *Why is he doing this? Davi, he is a man. He should not be digging for worms.*

Sor Antonietta replied, *He is doing it for the love of his mother.*

I could hear them speaking, but I could not make out what they were saying—my Spanish was strong enough, but they were too far away. Hortensia filled me in on the details later. For the moment, I was too busy copying my mother's every move, smiling like a desperate lunatic, trying to keep up. Also, I was distracted by my mother's actions, because as soon as I sloshed toward her and squatted alongside I noticed she was crying. I could not think what to do, how to comfort her, or if I should even try. So we continued to dig in silence.

For a while, things went on in this way, and Mom cried the whole time.

It was the most helpless feeling, to be so close to her and at the same time to be so far away. We were by ourselves, with no one around to interpret for us, so we could only be there for each other. I was caught between thinking it was a nice, sweet moment between a long-lost mother and her long-lost son, and that it was an incredibly awkward moment between strangers.

Whatever it was, the moment lasted just a couple of minutes, and after that we took our worms and fished for another while. When we got back to camp a short time later I caught up with Hortensia and went to fill her in. Sor Antonietta had gotten to her first, though, so Hortensia already knew about the worms and the fishing and the crying. She said, "You know why your mother was crying, don't you?"

I said, "Not really, no."

She said, "She was crying because she was spending time with her son."

I said, "What did she say? Did she say something to Antonietta? Tell me."

Here Hortensia repeated what my mother had told Sor Antonietta: *It will always be a mark on my memory.*

And as she spoke these words I vowed that I would remember them, always.

WE FELL RIGHT AWAY into a mini-routine. We were up with the sun, off on some kind of task or trek. The time fairly flew—even at night. There was so much work to be done in and around the *shabono* that I was too tired at the end of a long day to do anything but crash. There wasn't time to toss and turn in my hammock and worry about the night terrors—that was all so Day One.

A couple of days in, I decided to share some pictures with my mother. She had been asking, through a translator, for news about my brother and sister, for news about my father, and I thought it would be helpful to show her what they looked like. Actually, I'd been waiting for the right moment to share a bunch of family photos with Mom, thought it would be a great way for us to reconnect and maybe get past the language barrier and the long distance between us. I'd loaded up my laptop with recent photos as well as years-ago shots from our time in the jungle as a family. I'd even created a timeline slide show of the whole family, covering the time from when Mom left up until the present, so when the moment was right we sat down together and I opened the file.

There were two wonders at play for my mother—the first, that these brilliant color images kept appearing on this bizarre machine I held on my lap; the second, that she was looking at pictures of her faraway *nabuh* family, that her children were now adults, that her husband was now an older man. I couldn't begin to imagine what was going through her head, but it pleased me to see her eyes brighten with each new shot as it scrolled across the screen, her wide smile grow wider still. There was Danny, who was just an infant when she left, now a full-grown adult. There was Vanessa, now a mother. There was Dad, with a lot less hair.

Next, I showed her some older family photos from Mom's time in the States. Each image of her younger self, with her younger family, brought back a sweet memory, and we found a way to laugh and reminisce at the life we all shared. It's funny, but Mom got comfortable with the technology right away. It started out, she was eyeing my laptop warily, but after a while it was like she'd been working with a computer her entire life.

We were having so much fun, I opened up a folder that contained photos of the *Hasupuwe-teri* from twenty years ago, thinking it would be a great way to keep this party going. Big mistake—and I should have known better. Actually, I *did* know better, but I was caught up in the swirl of memories and got a little careless with Yanomami beliefs. You see, the Yanomami have a whole bunch of superstitions and rituals concerning death and burial. At the heart of all of these is the belief that there shall be no traces of the dead once they are gone. They burn all the possessions of the deceased; they burn the body; they leave no remembrance or trace of any kind. I knew all of this, from the research I'd done ahead of my trip, from talking things through with my father, but I got caught up in the excitement and completely forgot where I was, what I was doing, and as I was paging through the pictures we came across a picture of one of my uncles. He was an uncle I remembered as kind and patient. He made me my first bow and arrow when I was just a young boy. I was eager to hear of any news of him—and, for the life of me, I couldn't remember his name.

So I asked.

Another big mistake.

While my uncle's picture was still on the screen, I turned and noticed my mother's face. Her wide smile was gone. Her expression was one of overwhelming sadness, profound grief. Right away, I knew what I had done. I took her hand and started apologizing, but I didn't have the words. All I could say was, "I'm so sorry."

Over and over. She grabbed my head and gently pulled me in to whisper my uncle's name into my ear. I turned and faced her and was about to repeat it to make sure I had heard her right. Before I could, Mom cut me off and raised her index finger to her lips and made a *sssshhh* sound, a shushing gesture. Then she started to cry— softly, sweetly.

I cried, too—because Mom was crying; because my beloved, kind uncle was dead; because I was such an ass that I made her confront his image and his memory on my magic little machine.

We sat together like this grieving for a long while—me, with my computer resting on my knees; each of us waiting for the tears to pass. And in that moment, just a couple of days in to my return visit, I was able to fully appreciate the vast space between the two sides of my family. Yes, my mother might have been a housewife in Rutherford, New Jersey . . . for a time. Yes, that might have been the lasting image I'd carried of her, all those years we'd been apart. Yes, those might have been the images I carried with me on my laptop. But at heart, at bottom, she was an Amazonian jungle woman.

AS I LOOK BACK on my first visit to the jungle, it feels like I'm sorting through a lifetime of memories—a lifetime of memories compressed into just these few weeks. I kept a journal, of course, but my notes are a hodgepodge, mostly useful as prompts to help me place these memories in context.

Many of these moments have bunched themselves together, leaving me with a feeling, a mood, a sense of belonging, an observation about some aspect of Yanomami culture as it might relate to my own experiences. But a few stand out . . .

There was a real Flintstones-Jetsons moment on this trip, a culture clash between the Stone Age and the Space Age, and it occurred at the Catholic mission in Mavaca. It came about in an impromptu way, but I might have planned on it. What happened was that after a couple of nights in Hasupuwe and a short visit to Irokai we doubled back to the mission. Hortensia needed to get back to Caracas, so it was decided we would travel to the mission together and make our goodbyes there.

Mom came along on this short trip; we'd only just reunited, after a lifetime, so she wasn't ready to leave my side just yet.

We'd been to Mavaca just a week or so earlier, on our way into the territory. I hated to leave Mom's village so soon after our arrival, but this was the plan. The missionaries thought it would be smart for me to kind of ease my way into Yanomami life—and as my journey was taking shape I could only agree with them. But now that we were back in Mavaca, it felt to me like I was cheating myself out of the full-on Yanomami experience. Already I could see dramatic differences in the outlook and demeanor of the "mission" Yanomami, who'd been exposed to Western culture for decades, and the Yanomami of my mother's village, who in comparison hardly see outsiders.

Still, there were advantages to mission life that I hadn't considered—chief among these was the satellite dish the Catholic missionaries had installed since my father's time in the territory. There was electricity, too—powered by a diesel generator.

What did all this mean to a tech-savvy Yanomami-American? Skype!

This alone was no revelation. I'd already had a few Skype conversations with my father on our way into the territory. No, the revelation came in thinking to put my parents back in touch in this way, so I took my mother by the hand and led her to a small room where I kept some of my gear. It was just a little cubicle with a tin roof and a cement floor. At first Mom had no idea where I was taking her, but once we were inside I pointed to my laptop, which I'd set out on a makeshift table.

Remember, I'd showed her this laptop back in her village—that's how we looked at those family pictures. So, whatever it was, she knew this machine had these unexplained, supernatural powers. It was charmed, in some way.

I pointed to the laptop and said my father's name. I said, "Kenny."

She looked at the laptop and then back at me, confused as hell. She repeated my father's name, turned up like a question: "Kenny?"

I was making no sense to her, I was realizing, so I held out my hand and patted the air—a Western gesture meant to put the conversation on pause. I said, "*Waiha.*"

Wait.

"*Waiha,*" Mom said back.

I sat down at the computer and logged in. It felt like forever, as the Skype call went through, together with the annoying singsong jingle that accompanied the call. It jingled and jingled, and Mom looked on in fascination, bewilderment. On the other end, I knew, Dad's computer would chime and chime until he responded, and it occurred to me that I should have probably scheduled this call, because there was a good chance he wouldn't be online.

Finally, he answered. His face filled the small screen of my laptop. There was the face of my father, her Kenny—a little older, of course.

I said, "Dad, I have Mom here. Do you want to talk to her?"

Of course he wanted to talk to her. He jumped right into it. It took him a couple of beats to slip back into Yanomami, but soon the two of them were talking back and forth, like it hadn't been twenty years since the last time they'd spoken. Like it was the most natural thing in the world to be speaking in this way.

One of the peculiar things about this Skype call was the way my mother appeared to *get* the technology in a way my father did not. He couldn't seem to look at the camera on his computer, couldn't seem to remember that there was a video component to the call . . . but that's how it is with dads, right? They can be a little clueless about this stuff.

Mom, though, she couldn't look away from the screen— although she was a little freaked out by my father's appearance at first. He'd lost most of his hair since the last time she'd seen him, and baldness doesn't really exist among the Yanomami, so I think it frightened her to see him this way. She'd already seen those pictures of him on the timeline slide show I'd put together, so his appearance wasn't a *total* surprise—but still, it must have been jarring, disconcerting, to see him moving around, looking like this. She made him put on a hat—a Penn State ball cap he happened to have near his desk—and after that she was okay.

It was a touching, rousing, astonishing event all around. Also, a little weird—I mean, to hear Mom and Dad, talking back and forth like they'd just seen each other last week, like we were all together back in New Jersey . . . it's like we'd stepped into a time machine. The way they interacted, even through Skype, was just so natural and fluid. And Dad, once he got going, his command of the language was perfect—or at least it *sounded* perfect to my untrained ears, but what the hell did I know? Despite the miles, the years, the many distances that separated them, it was clear to me that my parents still loved each other. They were still very much connected—and here they were, for the first time in twenty years, together again in the same room. Kind of, sort of.

Like I said, it was a weird moment, but it was also wonderful— really, really, wonderful. And then, when the call came to an end and the screen went blank, Mom approached the laptop tentatively. She touched it carefully, reverently . . . like it was some sort of talisman from our *nabuh* world.

A world she had once known.

THERE'S A WHOLE LOT that gets lost in translation when I communicate with my Yanomami family. It's not just the language—it's the customs, the concepts, the frames of reference. In the developed world, there are certain universal truths we all seem to grasp, no matter where or how we grow up. We understand the idea of commerce, the getting and spending that defines our days. We understand the idea of traveling long distances—a basic map of the planet and our place upon it. We understand the idea of compartmentalizing time, of building for the future.

Most of my Yanomami family cannot fully grasp what lies beyond their jungle borders. The rainforest is what they know, so it's become their worldview. To an outsider, this might seem like a limiting notion, but if you're in the deepest, most remote part of the jungle, what else is there to know? When my father spent time there, when he came and went over a period of months and years, the *Hasupuwe-teri* seemed to understand only that he was from some other Yanomami village, far away. They saw that he arrived with all these items from outside their experience—clothes, machetes, fishhooks, tools, food, medicines—but it was as if he'd simply come across these items in some other village and gathered them in trade. My half brother sees me with these things and makes the same leap in his thinking. I have arrived on the shores of the Orinoco with these same useful foreign objects. Surely, I must have bartered for them up river, or in some unknown part of the forest. He wants to come with me to my village in America so he can obtain some of these items and return home with them, maybe pick up some things he has not yet considered.

It's a tough concept. Even a somewhat "worldly" Yanomami like Ricky Martin, with his little bit of Spanish and his little bit of exposure to the missionary outpost of Esmeralda, has trouble thinking beyond the typical trade transaction. How can I explain to him that our exchange involves currency? The idea that we earn "money" so that we can "buy" things . . . it's way beyond his thinking. Wages, jobs, taxes . . . it's a whole other language, a whole other mind-set, and when I lay it all out for him he can only get close to it. Here's what I mean: Once, I thought I was making great progress, explaining to him that I work very hard back in my home village in America. I told him that I must do a great many things in order to buy the plane tickets I need to travel in that great big bird in the sky, to buy the pots and pans and fishing wire and other items his village so desperately needs. Even as I went into my long-winded explanation—*plane tickets?*—I wondered how I could possibly make myself understood. And, of course, I could not. At the end of my long, roundabout description, he nodded his head, as if all was clear. And I guess it was, in a way—only, this was what he said in response: *Ah, yes. You must work very, very hard in your garden. Your garden, it must be very big. I will go with you to your America and I will help you in your very big garden.*

Sigh.

I DON'T WANT TO generalize and suggest that the Yanomami are a nonriver people, because there are villages scattered across the Amazon that have lived on and around the river for many years, but the Yanomami of *my* experience are mostly foot people. They live in the jungle, inland, and whenever they need to approach the river or travel along it they do so with great care and worry. Historically, *my* Yanomami have lived deep in the jungle, away from the big river, which until recently was never treated as an important waterway or an essential resource. It was simply something to get past, through, up, or around.

Most of our fishing was done in the creeks, and here there was a surprising bit of ingenuity to the enterprise. The Yanomami do a fair amount of line fishing—that's why my father spent all that money bringing hooks and fishing line on his many trips into the territory to use as trade goods; for bait, they use good old-fashioned worms, as previously described. But when time permits, they also fish in a clever, sophisticated way. What they do is dam a flooded creek that's known to have abundant fish. Once they create a small catch basin, they drop a special liana vine, which apparently has these weird properties. After leaving the vine to soak in the water for a while, the fish are momentarily stunned and float to the surface, belly-up, where the Yanomami can simply grab them and drop them into their baskets. It hardly seems fair—and yet I can't help but marvel that these people have somehow figured this out. Of course, they cannot scientifically know that the toxins in the vine, while harmless to humans, were interfering with the gill function of the fish, but they have learned over generations that a liana vine soaked in a pool of water will yield a bumper crop of fresh fish, there for the picking.

There is cause and effect, on full display.

HERE'S ANOTHER MEMORY THAT has attached itself to the "scrapbook" I keep in my head of my time in the rainforest. And, like a lot of my memories, it comes with a cultural observation—this one about a traditional piece of woman's work among the *Irokai-teri*, collecting firewood.

When I first arrived in Mom's village, it was a great puzzle to me that the Yanomami women were typically assigned this task, because it was brutal, backbreaking work. I had no idea. I went out with Mom and some of the other women one morning a few days after returning to Irokai from Mavaca, just to chill and observe. I was still getting used to this new environment, so I was mostly expecting to hang back and watch my mother do her thing.

I was blown away—really, just a couple of minutes in, I was completely shocked at the strength and endurance of these Amazonian women. My mother is tiny—and by Yanomami standards, she's getting up there in years, but there she was, hacking away at these trees, hauling ass. She was tireless, like the Energizer Bunny; strong, like a weight lifter. There was also something ingenious about the way she set about this task. The way the Yanomami women carried the chopped firewood was a lot like how they carried plantains, only with bigger baskets. The baskets are attached to a strap, which is placed around the forehead as a way to distribute the weight, and then the basket is carried along the back as you move forward in a hunched-over way.

I felt useless, watching Mom and my aunts and my wives doing all that work, so I decided to get off my ass and help out. Wife

No. 2—"Lucy"—was closest to me as I approached the work area, and I reached for her basket, which she had placed on the ground and started loading up with wood.

I said, "I got this." In English. As if my young wife would have the first idea what I meant—not just the words, but the gesture, because most of these women hardly ever see a man do this type of work.

Still, Wife No. 2 backed away and watched as I tried to lift the basket. She stood with the others and giggled as I placed the strap around my forehead, bent my knees like a sumo wrestler, and tried to straighten up with the loaded basket in tow. Holy crap, that thing was heavy! It took every ounce of strength, every drop of dignity I had to keep from toppling over—and then I had to ferry the load to the communal fire by the *shabono*, which under the best of circumstances was about a twenty-minute trek. The women were making repeated trips, back and forth, and here I was lightening their load for just one of these trips, and it just about did me in.

I fell in line behind a group of three women headed back to the *shabono* and noticed that they managed to walk in a very graceful way, even with this heavy burden strapped to their backs. They stood slightly pigeon-toed, almost like they were tiptoeing across the forest floor—and me, I could only lumber behind, panting for breath, tripping over vines and roots, and slipping on the muddy banks of the creek. At one point I actually tripped and fell, sending Wife No. 2's cache of firewood every which way, and this of course brought about another round of giggling.

I waved away Mom's offer to help me reload the scattered wood. I thought, Shit, if these women can do this, then I can do this. I was stronger than them, tougher than them . . . but, in truth, I wasn't even close.

In fact, I was holding up the entire operation. Without the large basket I was carrying, Mom and the others could have chopped another load and made a second return trip, but they slowed to accommodate me, and even when I was able to stay on my feet and make a little progress, I was terrorized by the low-hanging branches and loose vines I'd brush up against on the path back to the village. Every branch, every vine was covered with fire ants— hundreds of them—so every time I brushed up against one the ants would fall onto my neck and I'd start screaming in pain and surprise. These little ants, they were tiny, almost imperceptible, but they hurt like crazy, especially when they attacked you in bunches, so the whole way back I was slapping at my neck and forehead, trying to chase them off me, and the constant slapping caused me to lose my balance a time or two, sending me and my basket of firewood clumsily to the ground.

Somehow I made it back to the village and dumped my load of wood by the fire. All told, I'd only been "helping out" in this way for an hour or so, and in addition to being no help at all I was also embarrassed, spent, upset with myself for not being able to perform such a simple task.

I thought, Okay, Dave, you're a long way from home, but you're also a long way from Yanomami.

COMMUNICATION WAS TOUGH AT first. I don't just mean I had a tough time picking up on Yanomami words and phrases—actually, that was the easy part. Where it got weird or strange was in *how* things got said, and in what was left *unsaid*. There were a lot of subtleties that took some getting used to. For example, I noticed that the Yanomami don't nod their heads to indicate *yes* or shake them to indicate *no*, and you don't really realize how much we nod and shake in the Western world. I had a hard time breaking myself of the habit.

Yes, in simple Yanomami, is *awei*. It's said in answer to just about everything, as long as you're in agreement with whatever is being discussed. Often, it seems to be used as a way to string along a one-sided conversation, the way we might keep saying "uh-huh" whenever someone pauses in the middle of a long-winded story, so when it's used in this way it can be more of a grunt than an ascent—a placeholder comment that can mean nothing much at all.

Even as a kid, I recognized this—and even as a kid, it was a source of confusion. I half-remembered this story, throughout my growing up, but it came back to me front and center when I was living among the *Hasupuwe-teri*. I was five years old, splashing around in the creek with other little kids. I'd seen some home-movie-type pictures of this scene as I prepared to make my way back to the jungle, and some of the footage was included in the National Geographic documentary of our family, so it all had a familiar feel. I remembered those little kids. I remembered their faces, the way they smiled, the way they laughed. To me, they were no different from the little kids I played with back home in kindergarten, except that I was mostly dressed and they were mostly not. We did not speak to each other directly, except in the universal language of children playing. We followed each other's lead, mimicked each other's movements, ran around like the carefree children we were. It didn't matter who we were or where we'd come from. Our lineage didn't matter. It only mattered that we were four and five and six years old and that the jungle was our playground.

Anyway, my grasp of the Yanomami language was paper-thin in those days—it still is!—but I did understand a few simple words and phrases. Some of these I'd picked up from Mom back in New Jersey, and some I'd collected here in the jungle, just from paying attention. I could follow along, at least.

So there I was, playing and splashing and having a grand old time with a little girl about the same age as me. At some point during the day, we splintered off from the rest of the group and headed back toward the *shabono*. We were like cousins, running through the rainforest—and who knows, maybe we *were* cousins. After a while, this little Yanomami girl started talking, talking, talking, so fast that my paper-thin grasp of the language couldn't keep up. I could no longer keep up and I wasn't all that interested in listening to her. For a few moments I was hopelessly lost, but I knew enough to make some kind of response, so I did in this knee-jerk way.

"Awei."

Over and over, this happened—and I don't think I was fooling this girl into thinking I was fully understanding what she was saying. But my cluelessness did not seem to matter, because she kept at it. She wanted what she wanted; I understood what I understood—which was, basically, nothing. We strolled down a trail and she talked and talked, and I answered *yes* and *yes*. Over and over.

This went on for a while, probably twenty minutes or so, and at some point we decided to stop for a rest. This happened without discussion, which worked out pretty well since any discussion would have been pointless. The whole time leading up to this moment, I was offering up an *awei* or two, whenever I thought it was appropriate. (It's like we were singing a call-and-response song and neither one of us knew the words!) Once we stopped, the little girl reached for me in a playfully aggressive way. She got too close for comfort so I pushed her back. She pulled at my shirt; I pulled it back. She said something I didn't understand; I responded in the only way I knew.

Awei.

Apparently, I was putting out some serious mixed signals, because all along the little girl had been asking for my shirt. That's all. She liked the color, I think. And, all along, without me even realizing it, I'd been telling her she could have it. That's what she was talking about; she wanted my damn shirt. And I kept telling her I would give it to her, but when it came time for me to complete the transaction, I inadvertently reneged on the deal.

She got close to me again.

I pushed her back.

She pulled at the shirt again.

I pulled it back.

Finally, I shoved the little girl to the ground and left her on the dirt, crying, and when I made my way back to my father I told him what happened. Somehow, news of the incident had reached him before I could—another hard truth about Yanomami village life, where there are no secrets, where everything that happens is pretty much known to all. But in all fairness to me, just then I did not know the language. Listening would not have helped. It was all just a bunch of nonsense syllables to me, except the nonsense syllables I'd learned at home from my mother were familiar. Like the word for *yes*.

By the way, as long as I'm on it, *ma* is Yanomami for *no*. Apparently it takes more than a single *ma* to negate an afternoon's worth of *awei*s, because in all that tugging and pulling I kept saying *ma* and *ma* and whatever happens to be the little kid equivalent of *No fucking ma!*

So in the end I got to keep my shirt and the little girl got a couple of skinned knees and together we could charge the transaction to a language lesson.

WHEN I RETURNED TO the jungle nearly twenty years later, there was still a communication gap with the Yanomami women. This business with my two wives was kind of funny at first, and kind of nervous-making after that. I didn't want to offend anyone in the village, and I certainly didn't want to disappoint my mother, but I had no interest in "marrying" either one of these beautiful girls. Maybe, back home, I would have been interested in "dating" them—but here in the jungle there was no Italian restaurant down the road where I could wine them and dine them and get to know them a little better. As it was, I couldn't imagine why they had any interest in me.

My first thought was to finesse my way out of each relationship—or at least to skate past each confounding moment that came my way. One morning, just a couple of days after my arrival, we were all bathing in the Orinoco River—my two wives and several others, including Hortensia, who was able to translate for me.

After we'd been splashing around in the river for a while, I collected Hortensia and waded over to Wife No. 1. I had something I wanted to say and I needed Hortensia's help, so here's what I asked her to translate for me: "I already have a wife, in my home village. Where I am from, we can only take one wife. I cannot have another."

Here again, I was projecting my ethnocentric Western mentality onto a local custom that had nothing to do with that mentality. I thought that if I simply explained that I was already "taken," the whole discussion of marriage would abruptly end. It was kind of like being at a bar and asking a girl for her number, only to be put off by talk of her boyfriend or husband. In my head, I thought this was how I'd avoid the issue. I'd just tell her I was already married. Done. Problem solved.

But that's not exactly how the scene played out.

Wife No. 1—"Layla"—replied quite angrily, *You are Yanomami. I am your Yanomami wife. Now you are here, in my village. Now we are going to have many children together!*

So much for that.

The truth was, my two wives were good companions. I came to rely on them—and I always enjoyed our time together. Really, they were enormously helpful as I tried to cope with the demands and peculiarities of jungle life. For example, they always made sure I had enough food and water, that my hammock was tied right, that the right-size worm was on my hook, that I had fresh wads of tobacco. They carefully pointed out slippery rocks or any other dangers as we walked the trails. They became good and trusted friends, and I admit that I started to develop a bond with them—but not in a romantic or sexual way. It was more of a deeply felt friendship, but in the back of my mind I knew that they were courting me, lining things up so that we might be together as *husband* and *wife*.

I knew this, but I didn't quite know what to do about it—and so, I did nothing.

One of the most intimate moments I shared with Wife No. 2 was when she sat close behind me with her legs straddled around my hips. She'd begun to slowly comb through my hair with her fingers, carefully inspecting my scalp. At first I couldn't think what she was doing back there, but then it became clear: she was looking for fleas! Among the Yanomami, this is a common ritual, a gesture of friendship, of kinship. It goes beyond the simple act of hygiene. It has more to do with a sense of closeness, of doing for each other, supporting each other. I suppose the closest we might get to this type of behavior in our Western culture is when we ask a close friend to scratch our back, or comb our hair, or give us a shoulder rub.

After a while, we switched positions and I returned the favor—*you scratch my back and I'll scratch yours*—and Wife No. 2 trilled with laughter as I imitated her movements and pretended to pick out fleas. And as we went through these oddly intimate motions I realized this was the Yanomami version of two young lovers holding hands, flirting. I hadn't meant to put out this kind of signal, but there it was.

Very quickly, I became a little closer to Wife No. 2. Wife No. 1—"Layla"—was constantly baiting me, pressuring me, reminding me of my duties as husband because I wouldn't have sex with her. She was a little more aggressive in her approach. Wife No. 2—"Lucy"—was more relaxed, laid-back. I believe she understood that I wasn't keen on getting married and she seemed to accept that. We became good friends, and Mom seemed to take special pleasure in this relationship because she really, really wanted me to make a Yanomami family. But I could not get there in my thinking. I was no Yanomami warrior, hunter, gatherer, fisherman, or shaman. I was just a punk American kid who, in a pinch, could make a decent peanut butter and jelly sandwich.

After a week or so, it was made clear to me that I was meant to impregnate one of these young women. This was my role, my fate, my duty. This was the message I kept getting from my mother and from my aunts. It was the only way to seal my position in the community. But like I said, I couldn't quite get there.

Still, my two wives were playfully relentless in their pursuit of me. One afternoon, early on, I pulled open the mosquito netting in my hammock and cocooned myself inside. It was the heat of the day, and everyone was taking a rest from the day's labors. As soon as I'd gotten comfortable and wrapped myself tight with the sides of my hammock, I noticed Wife No. 2 ambling toward me. She grabbed the rope that held my hammock and smiled at me. She really was beautiful. I returned the smile, and tried to imagine what kind of girl Wife No. 2 would be back home. Probably she'd be this badass, down-to-earth chick who listened to punk and wore Hurley clothes. She wouldn't give a shit about the material things that some of the girls I dated seemed to covet, like fancy clothes, expensive jewelry, and makeup. She'd shop at the thrift store, wear hemp bracelets, listen to Bob Marley. She'd play with bugs, climb trees, and fight to save the rainforest.

Then I thought about her role in my life here in the jungle. There was pressure from my mother, from the tribal leaders for me to consummate these marriages, and here I could only imagine Mom had put Wife No. 2 up to this latest approach. I looked over to Mom's hammock and could see her peeking over. And here's the thing: I really wanted to please my mother, to be a good son to her, to fit myself in to village life. I wanted to live up to the expectations she had for me, to fulfill her dreams for me. Mostly I didn't want to disappoint her, so I did what I thought I was supposed to do: I allowed Wife No. 2 to sit down on my hammock as I scooted over and made room. Soon we went from sitting to lying down, cuddled close, the way gravity kind of forces you to do when you're sharing a hammock built for one. Her arm was draped across my chest, and she began to brush her fingers down my arm—the same way a girl might do back home. I could feel her breasts pressed against my side.

It was actually really nice, lying there together like this. I have to admit, I was pretty turned on. I mean, how often do you get to lie in a hammock with a gorgeous, topless Amazon babe? But the cross-cultural barrier was too much to overcome. I panicked, and played the lame-ass *I'm so tired!* card. I pretended to drift off to sleep, and hoped she'd get bored and move on.

But Wife No. 2 wasn't moving on anytime soon. She had something else in mind, and she kept at it. She began to press her lips against my arm, making her way to my shoulder. She was like one of the biting gnats the netting was meant to keep away, except she was *inside* the netting, and naked, and gorgeous, and seriously flirting. She started nibbling at my shoulders, and I didn't think I could contain myself any longer. But like I said, I couldn't quite get *there*, so I jumped out of the hammock and offered up one of the few Yanomami phrases I'd committed to memory:

"Peheki yarimou!" Come, let's go swimming.

Now, I should have known from reading my father's book that this was precisely the wrong way to put off Wife No. 2. Remember, *let's go swimming* was a kind of local euphemism, offered up by horny Yanomami husbands suggesting to their wives that they disappear for the nearest creek or riverbed so they could mess around in relative privacy. But I didn't make the connection just then—and Wife No. 2, bless her horny Yanomami heart, she picked up on my confusion, or my disinterest, or my general state of cluelessness, and she let this one slide.

So we went swimming—no need to read between the lines, just swimming. After all, Wife No. 2 was a cool, tree-climbing, badass chick. She was up for anything. So we crawled from the hammock and off we went on our next adventure—"chaperoned" by a couple of other women and children, so at least I knew there'd be safety in numbers.

As we made for the river I thought, Bullet dodged.

But for how long?

THE YANOMAMI I CAME to know and love have a very basic, very intuitive way of looking at the world. They're genuine, with no room in the culture for disingenuousness. They problem-solve, without realizing they're working a puzzle. Somehow the answers come to them, even when they're not being sought.

For example, there's no distinct word for every different type

of leaf, every different type of tree the Yanomami might encounter, but they'll know what the leaf is good for, what it's not good
for, what berries to eat, and what berries to avoid. They know
these things innately, it seems. The thing itself might not have a
specific name, but what the thing is good for, what it can provide
. . . it will be known to them in some way.

I understood some of this as I set off for the jungle, but it takes
living among these good people to get close to their thinking.
Some of that comes through in the language—what they choose to
express and what is simply understood. I came to think there was
something very clean, very elegant about the way the Yanomami
communicate with each other. Their interactions are stripped
down, elemental, honest, and genuine. Nuance? Tone? That kind
of stuff just doesn't enter into it. If someone is angry, he will let
you know he is angry, in simple terms. If he's sad, he'll be sad
. . . and you'll know he is sad. There are hardly any reasons that
would inhibit a Yanomami's expression of emotions. Nothing is
held back, nothing is private. The social script we seem to follow
in our Western, developed world has no equivalent in the jungle.

Something to think about: how many conversations with
strangers have you started while in a packed elevator? The Yanomami would find it quite odd that we Westerners could be together
in the same room, or in the same metal box for that matter, and
not even say a word to each other. We live in such an impersonal
way. In the developed world, we're conditioned to shield our
emotions from others; men are often taught not to cry in public,
for example. In the rainforest, if a man is upset and misses his son,
he'll openly express his sadness; he'll cry, without shame or concern for how his crying might make him appear to others. It's not
an issue, the way it might be back in the United States.

The quality of vulnerability, the feeling that you're being
judged or second-guessed . . . these things have no place in Yanomami life, and I started to think this was a great good thing.
Why? Well, the Yanomami are extremely healthy, well-adjusted,
forward-looking. Their demeanor is almost like the absence of

demeanor—everything is as it appears. I found a pure, absolute sense of purpose that permeates the culture, free from woes and strife of our so-called civilized world. There's no hypertension, no post-traumatic stress syndrome, no ADHD, no suicidal thoughts. Depression? Chronic fatigue? These are Western-type afflictions, and they simply don't exist in the mind and psyche of the Yanomami.

The Yanomami just *are* . . . without thinking about it.

It took a couple of days, maybe even a week or more, but I began to see why my father had felt so at home in the rainforest, why he was so attracted to these people, to this elemental lifestyle. It's a life based on reciprocity. You give and you get, and each side of the transaction is understood. It's an amazing thing, really—you have this interrelated group of seventy or eighty people, living under the same *shabono* roof, and they're all, for the most part, getting along. There's a sweet harmony to village life that I'd never seen back home. Imagine sharing a house with seventy or eighty of your close and distant relatives . . . not just for a night, or a weekend, but for generations. It's not gonna happen, right?

As an outsider looking in, the differences between the culture of the developed world and the culture of the undeveloped world are immediately apparent. It's not like the Yanomami are sitting back, observing their own behavior and marveling at the simple elegance of their lives, but it's plain to see. There's nothing synthetic about the Yanomami lifestyle. There's no stark dichotomous separation between nature and people—they are connected, one and the same. There was nothing "fierce" about the people of my village—at least, nothing that I could see. Even the apparent ferocity of those two boys being made to beat each other with clubs soon after my arrival was nothing like the warrior mentality I was half-expecting to find. Yeah, it looked brutal, but it was a tradition meant to prepare these boys for manhood and to teach them a lesson in settling disputes without resorting to lethal violence—a lesson their fathers had experienced before them, and their fathers before them.

My Yanomami village appears to be a mostly egalitarian society, although there is a form of leadership, and it's fairly fluid
compared to the way we govern ourselves in the Western world.
Decisions are not made unilaterally, but collectively. Individuals
act with an authority granted to them by age, by wisdom, by lineage. The headman will decide it's time to go on a *wayumi*—an
extended trek through the jungle—and if the village agrees a
group will naturally form and make ready for the journey.

It will just be so.

And even the so-called leaders of Yanomami society are not
placed on any kind of pedestal. They don't live at a different level,
in a different way from the other men of the village. They still
have to hunt. They still have to fish. You can be the best shaman
in the village, but you'll still have your daily tasks.

There are strict gender roles, but they're bent a little bit from
what you'd expect. For some reason, only the women go crabbing—an excursion that allows the women to gossip and socialize.
Only the men go hunting—in all my time in the jungle, I never
once saw a woman pick up a bow and arrow, so there's a clear line
here. Both men and women will fish, but the women do most of
the cooking. It's not like the men won't fend for themselves in this
area—you know, put another few plantains on the fire—but it's
considered women's work to prepare the food. Very often I'd see
my mother resting in her hammock and then she'd get up with
a start when she realized the exhausted men were coming back
to the *shabono* after a trek, and hurry to get some food ready for
them.

Shaman work is almost exclusively men's work. (There are rare
accounts of female shamans—and it worked out that I got to see
one in action!)But the male shamans are typically the only ones
who use the hallucinogenic *epena* plant—again, with rare excep-
tions. To the Yanomami, the inhaling of hallucinogenic plants is
part of a sacred spiritual ritual. To my Western sensibility, it's a
complete mind trip, but it serves a higher purpose in the jungle.
As such, it's considered a male activity, because women aren't

thought to be connected to the spirits in this way—it's like they don't have enough bars on their spiritual cell phone signal.

The ritual comes with elaborate preparation. The way it works is you collect seeds derived from the *epena* tree. You can find the seeds in clusters of six or eight in a long, slender pod. The seeds are sticky to the touch when you remove them from the pod, almost like they've been coated in a kind of paste, so they're left to dry in the sun. Next, the dried seeds are mixed with spit and the ash from the bark of a *hisiomi* tree and ground to make a fine, grey powder, which is dried in a small pot and then inserted into a hollow bamboo pole about a meter in length—called *mokohiro mo*. The shamans pack about a teaspoon worth of the powder at one end, and the other end is placed in the nostril of the recipient—it's a two-man job. One man at the loaded end then blows the powder into the nasal cavity of the guy on the receiving end . . . and boom! The mind trip begins.

I watched this ritual unfold almost every day during my first trip to the rainforest—usually played out with the same group of village elders, usually at the same time of day, in the same way. I don't mean to diminish or disrespect the practice in any way, but it reminded me of a group of barflies hanging around the local pub, in the middle of the afternoon, getting their drink on while the women kept house and prepared their meals. There was something shiftless about it, something decadent. But to the Yanomami, nothing was more sacred, and I came to respect that, and I confess it was a little bit thrilling to watch these men react to their hits of *epena* and start dancing and chanting. They'd lapse into these ritualistic shaman chants, using a different kind of Yanomami language—almost like a turbo language. Even my father and some of the missionaries in the area who spoke fluently had trouble understanding some of what the shamans were saying when they were in the throes of one of their *epena* chants—or *henimou*.

I was invited to join in the ritual at some point early on in my visit, but I kept declining. I took it as an honor, but maintained

This photo was taken during my 2011 trip, as I huddled with Mom and several others beneath the shelter of two boulders during that strong tropical storm. Those boulders turned out to be a lifesaver, because there were trees and branches falling all around us.

On that first trip to the territory, I went fishing with my favorite niece—the little spitfire. I had to lend her my shirt, to give her relief from the pestering gnats.

With one of my nephews on my 2013 trip to Mom's village.
We'd just passed a long, rainy night beneath the leaky roof of the shabono,
so we spent the next day making repairs. Home improvement—Yanomami-style.
(And the Amazon rainforest was our Home Depot!)

Here's a shot of one of my aunts, hauling a load of firewood during my 2013 trip.
I was amazed at how strong these women are. They're graceful, too, because they're
able to carry these loads over vines, roots, and muddy banks without missing a step.

This is the uncle who christened me with my Yanomami name: Ayopowe, or "detour."
He'd been a good friend of my father's, during his time in the village. Even in his
old age, my uncle was strong, agile, and full of life.

An aunt stopped to collect some mushrooms one afternoon when we were out hiking.
She brought them back to the shabono and we ate them hungrily with a bunch
of crab meat—an impromptu feast!

A night shot of the shabono in Irokai. I showed the picture to my mother after I'd taken it and the image seemed to frighten her. She must have been wondering how I could capture such an image in pitch darkness. How could I ever describe the basics of photography and aperture?

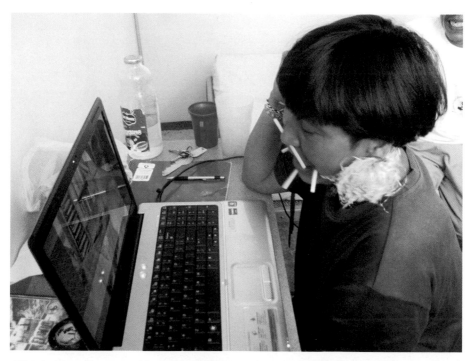

Here's Mom Skyping with Dad in 2011, on a visit to Mavaca, a Catholic mission. This was the first time my parents had seen or spoken to each other in twenty years. Mom handled Skype like she'd been using it for years.

Take a look at the expression of pure joy on Mom's
face as she speaks to my father, all the way in
Easton, Pennsylvania, during my 2013 trip.
She was so happy to be able to speak with her
"Kenny" from her home.

After our 2011 reunion at Hasupuwei, we traveled to Mom's new home village
of Irokai, where this photo was taken. From left to right, that's one of my nieces;
Hortensia Caballero, the anthropologist from Caracas who was so incredibly
helpful to me on my journey; Mom; Lucy (Wife #2); me; Layla (Wife #1);
a cousin; and Lucy's "real" husband—the dude who told me
he had his eye on me on my first night in the village.

A moment of pause and laughter from my 2013 trip. On the left is a Yanomami man named Ruben, from the faraway village of Cosh. Next to him is my friend Andrew Lee —another incredible resource. Don't let Andrew's light skin and gringo looks fool you: he is a warrior of the Amazon who was raised in Yanomami territory. He speaks fluent Spanish, English, and Yanomami. He's also married to a Yanomami woman and has several children. He has a rich, kind heart and he loves the Yanomami deeply.

A Yanomami hut in one of the more Westernized villages in the territory.
Note the separation of the "living quarters," power lines, metal roofs and lights.
Though the village is clearly more contemporary than those I spent time in,
it is still known as a shabono.

An aerial shot of Puerto Ayacucho.

Posing by the Guajaribo Rapids on my 2013 trip. I'm on my way to see Mom
for the first time in two years. It's amazing to think that decades before,
my father was shooting these same rapids, making these same return visits
to see his beloved Yarima after a long time away.

My very first jungle selfie of me and Mom—taken on my 2011 trip as we were about to go fishing with some Yanomami near Mavaca. This is one of my favorite pictures from my time in the jungle. I can see my face in my mother's and her face in mine. We were from two vastly different worlds, and yet we were able to look on as one.

my skepticism. I'm not afraid of recreational drugs but this ritual seemed so exotic, so uncertain, so out-there that I resisted at first. Still, I found the practice so fascinating that whenever I was in the *shabono* at *epena* time, I was drawn to it—as an anthropologist, say. I looked on with great admiration and wonder as the elders of the village snorted this jungle powder, as they went through these motions with great respect for the spirits. Each man seemed to react a little differently. Some danced and chanted with abandon; some would appear dazed and lost in their own spiritual journey; and some would be so zonked out by the soporific effects of the plant, I wanted to walk over and poke them with a stick just to make sure they were still alive.

One afternoon I happened by with my mother as the men were doing their *epena* thing. We stopped to watch, and I took the time to ask her about it.

I said, *Epena, you?*

Mom said, *Ma, you!*

I KNEW MY TIME in the jungle would come to an end, but there was a beautiful stretch of days in there when I didn't think at all about the calendar or my responsibilities back home. I wouldn't say my body clock had switched *completely* to Yanomami time, but I was getting there. Another beautiful stretch of days and the passage of time wouldn't have meant much at all.

But soon—too soon!—it came time for me to leave. The day of my departure had been lurking behind every new sunrise, and here it was. Father Nelson, another Catholic missionary, showed up in the village one evening to collect me, together with a nun, Sor Yarmila. I knew they were coming for me, but only in general terms. It could have been on this day, or the next; this week, or the next. It was already dark when they arrived, so they made camp and planned to head back out with me in the morning.

The moment I saw them, my heart sank. I sat down in my hammock for the longest time. I hadn't even left yet, and already I was homesick for this place, for these people. I didn't do anything, say anything—it's like I was paralyzed by sadness. All around I could hear the whisper-murmurs of my friends and family members as word seemed to buzz around the *shabono* that Ayopowe, as they called me, was making ready to leave, and the sniffling and the swallowed-up tears of the small children who seemed to have a never-ending list of reasons to approach my hammock.

After a long while, I started to gather my things, just to have something to do—busywork. As I packed, Wife No. 1 quickly came over to my hammock and climbed in. We sat together for a sweet, long moment. Her daughter Paula was with her, and I remember thinking it was interesting that my wife had named her daughter Paula; it was a Spanish name.

As we sat together, I could see my mother looking over at us from her own hammock. Some of the sniffling and the swallowed-up tears I'd been hearing were hers, I knew. I also believed she was behind this urgent goodbye visit with Wife No. 1. She's clever and intuitive, and wise to the ways of the Western world, and here I believed Mom wanted the missionaries to witness this bittersweet visit from my wife and her child, to let them know that I had a family here in Irokai—that I was *Irokai-teri*, in the end.

Of course, it wasn't up to Father Nelson or Sor Yarmila to determine whether I should stay or go. I had made these arrangements weeks earlier; I had a life back home in Pennsylvania; I wanted to continue my education and go on to graduate school—perhaps to study anthropology, or biology. Most important, there were financial obligations that needed to be met—I'd charged a lot of the costs for this trip to my credit card, so I had to get back home and start paying it off. As much as I might have wanted to, I could not stay in the territory and disappear forever. This was understood, all around, but at the same time it wasn't really considered.

The "real" world beckoned. M*y* world beckoned. But at the same time, *my* world had opened up to include this special place, these special people.

There wasn't a whole lot I could say to Wife No. 1, but we sat and swayed back and forth for a while. I put my arm around her shoulder and gave a goodbye squeeze. It was a bit awkward. I could feel the eyes of the village on us . . . on *me*. The silence, too. It's like I was on death row, slowly organizing my affairs, waiting for dawn so my sentence could be carried out.

Mom came by after a while and took Wife No. 1's place in the hammock, and now the two of *us* sat and swayed in silence. There was nothing to say, really. We both knew what this moment meant. After a while, I drifted off to sleep—the packing could wait until morning. The goodbyes, too.

Looking back, I can't imagine what my mother was thinking at just this moment. I don't think she understood that I had only come to the rainforest for a short visit. In her mind, she must have thought it was now her turn, her time with me. I had been with my father for all that time in his *nabuh* village, and now I would be with her for all of that time in Irokai. This was probably the way she worked it out—like the way she'd assumed that that five-day National Geographic trip all those years ago would somehow balance out all those years in New Jersey. It must have been a great disappointment for her, to have been away from her son for so long, and to be so soon in parting.

In the morning, I woke with the sun and continued with my packing. I moved about the *shabono* with a heavy heart. The village was uncommonly quiet. Some of the children began to cry.

Finally, all of my gear had been packed and stowed. The only thing left was my hammock. Father Nelson came over to me and announced it was time to leave, so I grabbed the rope of my hammock. It was tied in a slipknot and I gave it a gentle tug. As it fell to the ground, it felt to me like I was the conductor of a great orchestra. I lifted my arm, my wand, and suddenly the *shabono* filled with the music of crying. The children, the women . . . everyone was crying. There were even some men choking back tears, but the only grown man I saw crying unabashedly was my brother Ricky Martin. He was really broken up about my leaving—and the moment I saw him hurting like this, I was hurting, too.

I crossed to where he stood and took the baseball cap off my head and placed it on his—it was just a white cap, given to me earlier on this trip by one of the missionaries. Ricky Martin—Micashi—was honored to have it.

He smiled. I smiled, too—then I smacked the bill of his cap in a playful way and said, "I'll see you, brother. I'll come back. I promise" In English.

Father Nelson noticed I was having trouble separating from the villagers, so he walked over and offered some advice. He said, "It's best to do this quickly. The longer you are here, the more difficult this will be for everyone."

He was right, of course.

I turned to face the small crowd that had gathered by my area in the *shabono*. I extended my hand in a wave. I said, "*Ya-ko.*" I am going.

I started walking toward the river, and the small crowd followed. As we walked, my favorite niece ran up to me and started tugging at my shirt. I reached out my hand for her to hold. I loved this little girl—she had a spitfire personality, a lot of spunk. She stood out among the other little girls of the village. She held my hand all the way to the river, crying and sniffling. I tried to keep my composure but it was futile. I could not hold back any longer and began to cry with her.

When we reached the bank of the river, I turned to my mother. I really wanted to give her a giant hug, but as I've written, the Yanomami don't *do* hugs like we do in the Western world. Still, I wanted to hold her, touch her, collect her in my arms, so I ended up giving her a half hug.

Then I said goodbye to Wife No. 1 and Wife No. 2, and when I looked up Mom had slinked back among the crowd—it's almost like she wanted to take this one final opportunity to demonstrate that I was now bound to this village by my two wives. In my mother's mind, I imagine she saw my time in the village in this way: I had come as a child, to reconnect with my mother; I would return as a man, to make a family with my Yanomami wives.

I turned and faced my rainforest family a final time and said, "*Ya-ko!*"

CHAPTER SEVEN

Returning

CAMERAS WERE A FIXTURE OF my childhood—both in the jungle and in the wilds of New Jersey and Pennsylvania. During the time my mother was in the States, my father did a lot of media interviews, and there was enough noise to keep those cameras pointed at us for several years. This was a good thing and a not-so-good thing. It was good for my father because it shined some light on his work, and helped to deflect some of the scrutiny he'd been facing regarding his relationship with my mother. It was not so good for me, especially after Mom left, because it left me with no place to hide, at a time in my life when all I wanted to do was hide. People couldn't get enough of our story—an American anthropologist, returning from the Amazon rainforest with his Yano-mami bride to raise a family in the suburbs. It was like something out of a movie, so we lived in the thin spotlight of celebrity for a couple of years. In fact, just before my father's book came out, the story of my family nearly *was* made into a movie. It appeared for a while that Alan Alda was going to star as my father in a movie based on my parents' story—that's the kind of noise we were making.

At some point, Dad was interviewed by a feature reporter at WABC-

TV, the local ABC affiliate in the New York—a young broadcast journalist named Steve Hartman. My father hit it off with Steve. He met and interviewed us kids. He met Mom. He hung out with us. Dad told me years later that, more than any other reporter who covered our story during that time, Steve seemed to *get* our family. There was a connection there. Steve treated us fairly, with respect and good cheer. The stories he filed were truthful and touching, bighearted and personal. For a while, Steve was hoping to grow these interviews into a documentary or a miniseries of some kind—although, like the Alan Alda movie, that project never materialized. Part of the reason was that my father bailed, because this was around the time those National Geographic producers came calling, and Dad basically backed out on the project with Steve to pursue what he thought was a more prestigious opportunity.

Twenty years later, on my return home from reuniting with my mother in the rainforest, Steve reached back out to me. He'd never forgotten my family, he said. Yeah, he was frustrated with my father for bailing on him all those years ago, but he also said he understood my father's thinking. He said he might have done the same thing if he'd been in my father's position—after all, a National Geographic documentary is hard to pass up.

Understand, I had no specific memory of Steve from those early interviews—I was just a kid. But he remembered us Goods; mostly, he once told me, he remembered the huge cultural disconnect that should have divided my parents but had brought them closer instead. By this point Steve was working as a producer at CBS News. He'd seen a story written about me in the *Pocono Record*, which had been picked up by the Associated Press, chronicling my trip to my mother's village. It wasn't a major article or anything, but it caught Steve's attention. The unusual thing about this was that Steve happened to be searching for me online when he came across the story. He was just sitting around, thinking about my family, realizing that Vanessa, Danny and I would be young adults by now, when he asked his assistant to google the three of us and see what was going on, and it was this *what-the-hell* type search that just happened to take him to this newspaper account—a world-class coincidence, and since I was just back from the jungle, where my Yanomami family believed in the spirits and the fates and all that good stuff, I was inclined to believe that Steve and I were meant to connect on this.

On the back of this coincidence, we got to talking. There was a story here, Steve said, maybe even a story for *60 Minutes*. I didn't watch a whole lot of television, but even I knew *60 Minutes* was like the Super Bowl of television news shows. Steve pitched it to the executive producers and was given a green light, and from there we started talking about a second expedition to my mother's village. I'd always planned on returning, sooner rather than later, but money was tight. I was in my second year of grad school and struggling to stay ahead of my bills, my rent, my tuition.(Also, from time to time, I thought I should probably eat a little something—you know, keep my strength.)So it took this jump-start from *60 Minutes* to put this next trip on an accelerated schedule.

One of Steve's strengths as a journalist was that he asked great questions—the kinds of questions that seem obvious and natural but just out of reach when you try to turn the conversation on yourself. Talking with Steve, and some of the other journalists who interviewed me on my return home, it forced me to consider the transformation I'd made just on the back of this one trip. On the one hand, I'd reconnected with my mother and reignited an interest in my unique family history. On the other, I'd ventured way out of my comfort zone and confronted some of the negatives of my growing up and turned them into these giant positives, so on these two very basic levels the trip was a game-changer for me. It forced me to look at myself—my past, my present, my future—in entirely new ways.

I have to tell you, it took me some time to readjust to my American lifestyle. Compared to my father's first few expeditions to the rainforest, I hadn't been gone too long, just a few months, but during that time I'd undergone a kind of sea change—a *jungle* change, really. Physically, I was a different person; I'd lost twenty-two pounds. Though I looked gaunt and frail, I felt strong and healthy. For months my diet consisted of the purest foods, pulled straight from the earth, free of any preservatives, chemicals or additives. I ate mostly plantains and fish, with fresh meats and fruits when they were available. Other than the spaghetti I packed along with me, I didn't eat any pasta. It wasn't a long stretch of time, but it was time enough for my digestive system to adapt, so when I got back to the States I had a tough time holding down the old staples of my diet—burgers, fries, chips, soda . . . whatever crap I was used to scarfing down on the fly, on the cheap. I could only eat salmon and plantains, which I washed down with beer. (For some reason, my beer-drinking ability was unaffected by my time in the jungle.)

But the change was more than just physical: I no longer saw myself or looked out at the world in the same way, only I didn't really take the time to process this change. I returned to my life—to school, to friends, to having no money and no clear idea what I wanted do with myself—but underneath my familiar routines I was restless, searching. Hanging with Mom and my Yanomami family left me thinking I was meant to do something more, something *bigger* with my life. Really, the whole wide world was out there just waiting for me, but underneath all that there was all this media stuff lining up to distract me from my thinking. There were interviews, lecture appearances, meetings with Steve at CBS News and people at the Discovery Channel, who also wanted to document my experiences in some way.

What I should have been doing during that period just after I returned was kicking back, reimagining myself in this strange, new light. There was a lot to process, a lot to consider. For years I'd struggled with my identity, with feeling like I didn't belong, like I'd been abandoned by my mother. I'd messed up in school, messed up in my relationships . . . oh, man, I was messed up. All of that was what had driven me to the rainforest in the first place. And here, finally, I had a more certain sense of self than I had ever carried, a renewed appreciation for the life of my mother, for the relationship she shared with my father, for the iron will and resilience of our people.

I still didn't know where I belonged, but at least I came home from that trip knowing I belonged . . . *somewhere.*

It sounds corny, I know, but I felt alive in the jungle—truly and absolutely and wholeheartedly alive. My senses were heightened to this superattentive place, and my sense of self was also lifted. I'd never felt more in tune with the world around me and my place within it than I'd felt in Mom's village, so right away I started thinking about how to get back there and continue to explore this new heightened state. I remember thinking it was kind of ironic, the way the lives of the *Irokai-teri* can seem so small up against the frantic wonders of the modern world, but it was that very smallness that opened up all these other possibilities for me.

And here's another thing: my relationship with my father was completely remade on the back of this trip. We went from that low point after I'd run away from home for six months during high school, to an uncertain standoff as we tried to put that episode behind us, to a place of mutual respect as I set my first trip to the rainforest in motion. And now that I'd returned, it was like a whole new door opened up for us. All of a sudden, we had this vast swath of common ground—experiences we could share, points of connection we could explore together. I had a whole new appreciation for the work he did in the jungle, for the difficulties he faced when he fell in love with Mom, for the pain he must have felt when the siren pull of the jungle split our family apart. And, in turn, I think he had a whole new appreciation for *me*—I went from being a fucked-up kid to an accomplished world traveler and apprentice anthropologist, all on the back of this one journey.

I'd gone to the jungle to find my mother, to find myself, and somewhere in there I developed a bond with my father as well.

And so I had all these thoughts bouncing around my head, big thoughts and small, and it just happened to work out that this renewed relationship with Steve Hartman kicked in at just the right time, and got me thinking more immediately about returning to the rainforest—perhaps for another short stay, or maybe this time for an extended visit. What was great about meeting with Steve and sorting through my thoughts was the way it forced me to think of what was possible instead of what was impossible. Once, during a kind of pre-interview, I actually heard myself suggest I could live in the jungle—*live*, as in stay there, make a permanent home there, *become* Yanomami. I don't think I'd ever thought along these lines before, and here I was, saying these things out loud, opening up, to someone I was just meeting. It's almost like I was putting it out there just to hear how the idea sounded—how *I* sounded, talking about it. Maybe a part of me wanted to see Steve's reaction—you know, if he looked at me funny, in an indulgent or patronizing way, or if his eyes brightened at the cool possibilities. But as soon as I said it, I was all over it, and this became my focus, my purpose.

Of course, it's one thing to *say* these things and another thing to set them in motion. On that front, I was still a shiftless, rootless, directionless kid, still moving about the planet with tentative steps, and about the only thing I thought I could control was making plans for a follow-up expedition, and it's because of all of these feelings, because of the timing, because of the adrenaline rush of excitement that had stuck to me since I'd returned home from Venezuela, that I began making serious plans with Steve about a second expedition.

That's how it goes, right? You stumble on a plan, and it takes you to another plan, and another . . .

AND SPEAKING OF PLANS . . . sometimes life throws you a wonderful curve and you have to change things up on the fly. This part needs a little setup, so here goes: In the months since my first trip to the rainforest, I started seeing a girl named Chrissy. We hit it off, and for a while things were good between us. I liked Chrissy's spirit, her thirst for life, and she seemed drawn to my sense of adventure. Chrissy loved hearing stories of my time in the jungle, and I loved sharing them, and we had a kind of instant connection, an instant attraction. But then I pulled one of my usual moves and found a way to screw things up. That's how it goes with me and relationships—when things are good, they're great, but then something happens. And, almost always, it's on me. I used to think the way I sucked at relationships had something to do with the way I sucked at being Yanomami, the way I moved about not feeling like I belonged. That was one of the reasons I'd set out for the jungle in the first place. I thought if I didn't know or trust myself I couldn't really let myself be known or trusted. It was all tied in to the way I'd rejected my mother, my Yanomami roots, my story. Or maybe it had something to do with the feelings of rejection and abandonment I'd had as a kid, when Mom up and left—you know, maybe it was a preemptive strike, a chance to reject and abandon others before they had a chance to reject and abandon me.

But now that I *knew* my story, now that I'd embraced my heritage and reconnected with my mother and set things right, that was all supposed to go away, and along came this great girl and all I could offer was the same old me.

Old habits die hard, I guess, so Chrissy and I agreed to just be friends and go our separate ways—that is, until we found out Chrissy was pregnant. (This piece of news was the wonderful curveball, in case you haven't figured it out.) Chrissy really wanted to have the baby, and I was totally up for it—totally unprepared, too. She was about twenty weeks along when I was finalizing my plans to return to the jungle with *60 Minutes*, and I'd worked it out in my head that a good chunk of my precious battery life on my Iridium satellite phone would be devoted to checking in on her, to see how Chrissy was doing. No, I wouldn't be there for her in a physical sense—I'd be half a world away, in fact—but I'd be there for her in this high-tech way, and it would have to be enough.

I had a hard time believing I was about to be a father. It was a terrifying thought, really. Exciting, too—but mostly terrifying. The thought of our baby—a little girl, we learned!—was front and center the whole time I was making ready to leave. A part of me hated that I was going, but I was still on a quest to reclaim the Yanomami part of my life. I didn't think I could be a good father to my baby daughter if I never returned to the jungle, so I stuck to Plan A even as Plan B was taking shape.

THE WAY IT WORKS at CBS News, like it does at every other major news organization, is they don't "pay" for stories—meaning, the network couldn't underwrite my trip. The reason for this, Steve Hartman explained, was that the network news division was in the business of covering news, not making it. They couldn't facilitate the story in any way. I understood all of that, in a broadcast journalism code of ethics sort of way, but as Steve walked me through it, it reminded me of the tug-and-pull my father wrote about in his book, the conflict I felt between being a participant and an observer during my first hours in the jungle. It was the same with journalists: they could observe; they couldn't participate. However, there was nothing in the broadcast journalism code to prevent me from tagging along on the inland transports *60 Minutes* might arrange for its crew, provided I could make my way to Caracas on my own. From there they would need to film me throughout the rest of my journey, and they would need to ferry their camera crew into the interior, and their cameras needed to be pointed at me—so it was legit for me to hitch a ride with them.

Another key preliminary discussion I'd had with Steve was about the importance of treating my Yanomami family with respect. I told him he and his crew would need to bring along a mess of trade goods—pots and pans, machetes, beads, yarn . . . whatever I might have brought on my own—and in this way I was able to trim the costs of *those* items from my budget.

(No sense doubling up on these calling-card-type items for Mom's village—although as I write this, it feels a little like I was planning to sign my name to the gift card at a friend's wedding without really contributing anything.)

Steve's interest put a kind of clock to my loose plans for a second trip—not least because the involvement of CBS News would make it easier for me to raise the funds I needed, which I guessed to be about $6,000. That's not a whole lot of money, I know, especially when you stack it up against the $250,000 Penn State grant that funded my father's first expedition to the territory more than thirty-five years earlier. Still, it was an enormous sum to me; I was a graduate student, with no visible (or even *invisible*) means of support, no way to connect the trip to my field of study and hope to win some grant or research funding, so it might as well have been a quarter million dollars.

Meanwhile, I'd been able to build on some of the press attention that attached to my first trip; there'd been coverage from NPR, the BBC World Service, Outlook Radio, and tons of local press—all of it positive. Plus, there were lots of e-mails from documentary filmmakers looking to follow me on my next trip, and other inquiries from relief agencies, nonprofits, and advocacy groups with ties to the region—all of it encouraging me to build on what I'd started. The sliver of spotlight encouraged me to jump-start the nonprofit organization I hoped to launch, which I'd decided to christen "The Good Project." (I liked the double meaning there.)Our stated mission was to build a bridge between the developed world and the underdeveloped world—or, I should say, it was *my* stated mission, because in this early going the organization didn't extend much beyond yours truly. My mission statement was just a bunch of words on paper, untethered to any kind of action plan, but the *idea* at least was to use this new platform I found myself on to call attention to the plight of the Yanomami, and to the indigenous peoples of the world. It was an ambitious undertaking, and here in the early going there wasn't much more to it than ambition, but I knew there'd be a way to harness all the warmth and good feeling that attached to my first trip to the rainforest and put it to work in a proactive way.

A bridge? Well, yeah . . . with a foot in the developed world and another in the undeveloped world, I told myself I was the natural person to head up such an effort. And in time, I felt sure, I'd figure out how to turn that *bridge* into something more than just an easy metaphor—like, say, a path to understanding.

Right away, the administration at East Stroudsburg University took an interest in my next trip, offering to house my start-up program in its Innovation Center complex on campus. Now, I've kind of raced over my academic awakening in recounting my jungle adventure, so this is a good spot to fill in some of the blanks of what happened after I'd dropped out of high school. Somehow I managed to pick myself up from that low moment and continue with my education—a long slog that eventually took me to East Stroudsburg University. The school had played a huge role in my development, separate and apart from my time in the rainforest. I've already written how I found a way to collect my GED around the same time all my friends were graduating from high school. From there I drifted to Northampton Community College, where I discovered I had an interest in biology and the sciences, and then on to East Stroudsburg (ESU), where I continued to take courses in biology, immunology, anatomy . . . and on and on. I got mostly good grades, but I was still doing a lot of drinking early on in my college career, so every here and there you could find a blip on my transcript—a C where there should have been an A . . . that sort of thing.

I managed to graduate from ESU just before heading out for the jungle in 2011, with no immediate plans to continue on with my education, but on my way back from the territory, on a stopover at the Catholic mission, I applied for admission to the school's graduate program in biology. I did it on a whim, while I was surfing online, trying to figure out a next move, and this seemed as good an idea as any. It was a placeholder move, really—a way to move myself forward without any clear direction where I was headed. I just thought, Hey, I should advance myself in some way, so I started thinking about working toward some kind of career, maybe even as an anthropologist.

It was something to do—and now that I was getting all of this positive media attention, the university stepped up in a big way. I'd barely had time to begin my first graduate-level classes at ESU before school officials reached out to me with an offer to help launch my nascent "Good Project" initiative. This was a great windfall, but it was also a great fit, because it benefited the university as well. ESU administrators believed in the good work I might do in the region . . . but more than that, I think they saw a public relations opportunity. I was an ESU student, on the slow path to a master's degree in biology, so it made sense for them to offer me support. Why? Because any press I generated would invariably mention that I was a graduate student at the university. Best-case scenario, a shout-out on *60 Minutes* would be absolutely huge, but even if the CBS News coverage never materialized, the ESU folks had to think that whatever feel-good attention my trips to the jungle might generate in the community, in the world around, there'd be some kind of spillover effect for the university—and I was only too happy to encourage them in this thinking.

In fact, ESU officials were so pumped over the media attention that might come their way that they spent a bunch of money to help spruce up my one-room Good Project office. They blew up a couple of really nice poster-board displays from pictures I'd taken on my first trip and a couple from my father's archives. They bought some nice plants, some decent furniture . . . all so there'd be a professional-seeming backdrop for the interviews Steve Hartman wanted to conduct for the story.

But my money needs didn't end there. Now that a trip was in the offing, I went to the folks at ESU's Innovation Center with my hand out—I mean, the office plants were nice and all, but they couldn't simulate the jungles of Venezuela. The *60 Minutes* producers had some momentum going on this, so we needed to build on it right away. If it was just me, I could have waited another year or two before mounting a second expedition, but for now I moved with some urgency. I asked for six thousand dollars—a relatively small number, I realize now, but I didn't really know how to ask for money, didn't think to pad the budget in my proposal so I might settle on the number I truly needed. The first time out, I'd flown to Caracas on my savings, and my father had helped me with most of the supplies he thought I needed, and an extra infusion of cash, which I also ended up needing. I ended up charging a lot of my expenses to my credit card—a balance I was still paying off as this second trip was taking shape. This time out, I didn't want to count on my father's generosity—even though I could have counted on it, to a degree. And I didn't want to run up another big credit card bill. To me, that $6,000 ask represented a lot of money—but at the same time, $6,000 was about what it would cost if CBS News was going to cover my inland transportation.

At first, ESU said the money wouldn't be a problem, but then it was a problem—that's how it goes, right? We didn't have our 501(c)3 paperwork in order on the nonprofit, and the university wasn't crazy about the idea of funding the trip until we were a legitimate entity, but they kept telling me they could find the money, either through a grant or an outright allocation from the Innovation Center budget. They gave me their word, said to go ahead full-steam with *60 Minutes*, to make whatever preparations I needed, and to move ahead as if the money was in my pocket.

In the end, it wasn't. And when I use a phrase like "in the end," I mean it pretty much literally. The trip was ten days away, my tickets needed to be paid for, other items needed to be purchased . . . but the money never came through. The ESU folks kept putting me off and putting me off, telling me it was no problem, until I finally called them on it. I demanded the truth . . . and at last, they gave it to me: the money wasn't there.

I was stunned—and, frankly, furious. I could have put the trip off for another couple of months. I could have strung *60 Minutes* along for another while, but now all these wheels were in motion. CBS News already had its people booked on a flight from New York to Caracas, a flight I needed to be on—because, again, the camera crew was supposed to be filming me as I made my way back to my mother. So what did I do? I hit up friends and family for whatever they could afford. Twenty bucks here, fifty bucks there . . . and then of course my father kicked in a decent chunk. The head of the Innovation Center, Mary Francis, felt so guilty that her team hadn't come through with the money, she wrote me a personal check to cover my flight to Caracas, which came to about $1,400.

In this way, the trip came together. It's like it took on a momentum of its own—but we only got as far as Puerto Ayacucho, the jumping-off point for any expedition into the indigenous territory. The *60 Minutes* crew consisted of Steve Hartman and his assistant, Miles Doran, three South African camera and sound people, and the CBS News foreign deputy director, Anna Real. Also, the Venezuelan government assigned us a state photographer, four armed soldiers, and a doctor—with me, it made for an entourage of thirteen. We were like our own little invading army.

I imagined the strange scene would we make, descending on Mom's village all at once. All I could think was, My poor family.

I'D SENT WORD THROUGH the local missionaries that I was coming, so Mom had a bit of a heads-up. She didn't know exactly when I'd get there, and she had no idea of the circus I had in tow, but at least my arrival wouldn't be a total surprise. At least, to my mother it wouldn't be a total surprise. To certain individuals in the Venezuelan government . . . well, it was a surprise they wanted to avoid entirely. Why? Well, the mayoral elections were coming up—a big deal in Venezuela—and the presence of an American television news crew was perceived as some kind of threat. The issue wasn't with me, or any long-simmering issues with my father. In fact, most of the Venezuela was quite welcoming—really, they couldn't have been more accommodating. But then, as the trip approached, it was becoming more and more apparent to me and to my friends at CBS News that the Venezuelans weren't exactly laying out the welcome mat ahead of our arrival. And yet for every show of resistance we received from someone in authority, there was an equal and opposite show of support, encouraging me to return to the territory—with a camera crew in tow, if that's what I was planning. Talk about mixed signals! Going in, our "expedition" had the blessings of the Venezuelan president, Nicolás Maduro, who had succeeded Hugo Chávez earlier that year. Also, we had a letter of invitation from the leaders of my mother's village, prepared and translated by local missionaries, stating that it was okay for me to record my return visit, and that my journalist friends were welcome as long as they brought trade goods. At our hotel in Caracas, I even met the revered Venezuelan conductor Gustavo Dudamel, himself the subject of a flattering *60 Minutes* profile—so we had no reason to think the production team assigned to my story was seen as an enemy of the state.

On balance, we were more welcome than not—meaning it appeared we had the go-ahead. We were betting that it was all systems go. We had the approval of several local ministers *and* the president, so our travel plans proceeded accordingly. However, we hit a bit of a snag in Puerto Ayacucho as we were making ready to head out. Some government functionary from the Ministry of Indigenous Affairs refused to let the crew pass into the territory—the stated reason, which was completely bogus, was that the entire Yanomami tribe didn't want cameras and reporters to capture their way of life on film. The unstated reason, which was a little less bogus, was concern over how their mayoral elections might be perceived around the world. Like a lot of governments in South America—indeed, all over the world— local elections did not always hold up to world scrutiny. There's corruption everywhere, right? But this wasn't the story we were out to capture, and we made it clear that our cameras would be pointed elsewhere.

Either way, we were screwed. Or, I should say, the *60 Minutes* folks were screwed. Me, I was covered. The government couldn't keep me from entering the indigenous territory—I was Yanomami, after all, protected by the Venezuelan Constitution. I did not yet have my citizenship papers—my application was (and remains!) in progress—but I had overwhelming evidence to support that I was allowed to travel into the territory. I was Yanomami, the son of a Yanomami, and by law the government could not prevent me from traveling to visit my own mother.

Even so, there was an attempt to get a statement from one of the more prominent political Yanomami, hoping to get him to speak against me, but the guy had my back. He said, "Davi is Yanomami, same as me. He has every right to visit his family, same as me. I will not speak against another Yanomami."

This went on for several tense days. At first we thought we might work around the standoff, so I flew back to Caracas with Anna Real and Steve Hartman to sort through the mess there. The South African crew stayed back in Puerto Ayacucho and ran up a big bill at the hotel—in fact, the care and feeding of these guys, in addition to their project fees, came to about three-quarters of the CBS News budget for this piece. But they were the best of the best. They'd been all over the world. They'd been shot at, jailed, shelled by grenades . . . they'd seen it all. A brick wall of Venezuelan bureaucrats wasn't about to keep them from a story.

Or so they thought.

A couple of days later, we flew back to Puerto Ayacucho in defeat. We bought three bottles of vodka and drank our asses off—really, we just drank like animals, but in the middle of all that drinking I started to freak out, a little bit. I'd just called all this attention to myself, trying to get this news crew into the territory. And in doing so, I not only put myself on the radar of government officials here, but I'm certain I'd pissed off a few of them in the process. On my first trip, I was able to move about the country with anonymity and relative ease. On this trip, I'd become the focus of tremendous bureaucratic attention. The Venezuelan military was fully aware and fully supportive of my mission, and yet there were certain factions of the Venezuelan government that were also fully aware and fully opposed.

The stalemate scuttled the *60 Minutes* piece for the time being, but as I shot past the red tape and set out for my mother's village I could only wonder if I'd brought an unnecessary spotlight on myself and my Yanomami tribe.

I SAID MY GOODBYES to Steve and the crew in Puerto Ayacucho. Anna Real had prearranged a military transport plane for our flight to Esmeralda, and it was determined that I would still be allowed to hop on board. There was a high-ranking colonel in support of our mission who'd signed off on these arrangements, and the paperwork appeared to be in order. But before I could get on the plane, I was stopped on the tarmac by a *diputado*. I could see in her eyes that this government official was nervous, that she wasn't really comfortable in her position of authority—at least as it applied to me. Basically, she didn't want to bust my chops, but she had no choice; she was just doing her job.

She asked me a bunch of questions she already knew the answers to.

She said, "What is your business in the territory?"

I explained that I was going to visit my mother.

She said, "And after you have visited your mother, what are your plans?"

I explained that I wanted to live among my people and learn the ways of the Yanomami.

It was a bullshit interrogation, but it was bullshit I had to face. This woman had been given a script, and she was meant to follow it, even if the story made no sense. Yeah, there had been some controversy surrounding my father's time in the jungle—but that didn't seem to be the issue here. Yeah, it would have been difficult for my father to clear these bureaucratic hurdles, given his history with Venezuelan officials, who still seemed to be pretty pissed at him for marrying a Yanomami tribeswoman—but, again, this was beside the point. The people of my village, the Catholic missionaries in the region, the authorities who had followed my story, President Maduro . . . they had no issue with me. I was just a Yanomami boy, trying to make his way home to his Yanomami mother, and to reconnect with his Yanomami family.

In the moment, I was so incredibly angry at this woman—and at the ministry she claimed to represent. I felt betrayed. All along, I wanted to shout to the world how proud I was to be Venezuelan, to show American and Venezuelan television audiences what it meant to be Yanomami—in Irokai, and all the way back home, in Pennsylvania. But I would never get the chance—at least not this time.

The *60 Minutes* piece wasn't happening, but I was able to talk my way past this hurdle and onto the plane, and when we arrived in Esmeralda there weren't any crowds of Yanomami lined up in protest. There were only a dozen or so Catholic missionaries, many of whom I recognized from my previous trip. We hugged each other in greeting. They knew of all the bureaucratic forces lining up against me and convinced me that it would be smart to lie low for a couple of days at the mission compound before heading upriver, and it was there that I reconnected with my friend Andrew Lee, the son of Protestant missionaries in the territory, who had arranged for transportation to take me to my village. Andrew and I had made a meaningful connection on my first trip into the territory in 2011, in Mavaca, and he played a key role in bringing me down this second time, about a year and a half later.

A quick word on Andrew: he's one of the unsung heroes of the rainforest, a true champion of the Yanomami. He's married to a Yanomami woman, has Yanomami children. These are his people, this is his territory, and it was a revelation to me when we first met, because I saw in Andrew a chance for someone like myself, who looks like a gringo, to really make a meaningful impact in the region. He's devoted his life to the Yanomami, but even more important, they have his heart—the same way they now have mine.

Andrew essentially took the lead at this point in my trip, and I must confess, heading into the territory without my new CBS News comrades, without the strength and assurance of Hortensia Caballero, who had held my hand through the opening bars of that first trip, I felt a little vulnerable, a little lonely, a little scared.

I'd been this way before, of course—as a kid, and just a year and a half earlier. But on this trip it felt like the world was conspiring against me, like the Venezuelan government was conspiring against me, like I was on my own.

IT HAD BEEN NEARLY three full weeks since we took off with great hope from New York's LaGuardia Airport, and I still hadn't made my way upriver to my mother's village. We'd expected to hit a roadblock or two, but it felt like a dozen or more by the time Andrew Lee and I made camp with our motorist and mission guide, about a day's trek from Mom. I'd meant to be covering these last miles with the *60 Minutes* crew, but I was past that disappointment. I didn't need a camera to capture this second homecoming. There was purpose and meaning in the journey itself.

The whole way, I kept reminding myself that I was bringing great news to my mother. She was about to be a grandmother again. For all I knew, one of my half siblings in the jungle could have already made her a grandmother—and, of course, my sister, Vanessa, had already seen to this with the birth of her own children. But *I* was about to make Mom a grandmother; no, my daughter, whom we'd decided to call Naomi, would not be Mom's first *nabuh* grandchild, but she would be the first by me, and this was surely something. I was itching to tell my mother this news, but at the same time I worried she'd be a little disappointed; my last time down, she'd seemed to have her heart set on me making babies with "Layla" and "Lucy"—a true extension of her Yanomami family. And here I'd gone and sidestepped her meddling and found a way to make a baby on my own—another child that would not get to grow up among the *Irokai-teri*.

Our last night on the river was a restless one for our group. We pulled in just below the Guajaribo Rapids. Ruben, the motorist, taught me to hang a hammock from a three-point structure he'd jerry-rigged with vines, a horizontal pole, and the V of a well-placed tree. Amazingly, my version held!

The night was memorable for the distinctive hiss of a ratlike creature that rustled in the branches just above us—and (sorry, folks) for a flash memory I had as I ducked into the woods to do my business. I don't mean to be crude, but my stomach had been bothering me all that week, so it was a great relief to finally be able to let go, and as I squatted on the forest floor I thought back to another such moment some twenty years earlier. It's funny how the littlest thing, the smallest moment, can put you on a through-line reaching all the way back to childhood, and here I had a clear picture of myself in a wooded area just like this one, going through these same motions as a small boy. Then, as now, I felt a powerful sense of release—and here in *this* moment I realized I didn't have a worry in the world. All of those worries about money as I made to leave Pennsylvania . . . all those bureaucratic headaches as we made our way into the territory . . . all that discomfort I'd been having with my stomach these past few days . . . it all fell away. For the first time since leaving LaGuardia, I didn't have a worry in my head, other than the new-dad worries that would probably never go away, and this struck me just then as a great sweetness. I was completely without stress . . . and as I cleaned myself with a ready leaf, I was overcome with a sense of calm, a sense of happiness. I knew that I was not "jungle-ready," in that I did not yet have the skills I'd need to live an independent Yanomami life, but I was "jungle-ready" in the sense that my mind was receptive and open to anything that came my way.

My spirit had found its home here, I was realizing.

It was time to live.

THAT NEXT MORNING, I was like a dog with his head sticking out the window at the end of a long car ride, sensing home. There were familiar landmarks all along the way—the same way I'd catch reminders of home in Pennsylvania: a diner, a school, a street name . . . all of it lining up and welcoming me back, making me feel more secure in my own skin. Here it was the same: a bend in the river, the size and shape of the trees, the foliage dotting the shore . . . all of it leading me home.

The *Irokai-teri* spilled down to the river at the sound our wheezing motor—but not in great numbers. Compared to my first arrival on these same shores two years earlier, it was a thin turnout, but there was a reason for this. Andrew explained that the *Irokai-teri* had moved farther inland, so it took a while for news of our impending arrival to make it to the village *shabono*.

Still, it would have been nice to receive another grand welcome, so I'll admit I felt a small letdown as we throttled close to land.

Also, we had arrived during the dry season in 2011, so the river had been much lower. On this approach, the shoreline was more difficult to navigate, especially when I stepped off the boat and attempted to lug all my stuff. Happily, there were a couple of strong Yanomami males out to greet us, and they were able to haul my luggage without too much effort—and it was a good thing because the bank of the river was much softer, much sandier than I remembered. It was difficult to cross to the thick of jungle beyond the clearing—not just for me, I soon saw, but for the *Irokai-teri*, who had sculpted a small flight of stairs into the ground that had been flattened over time.

Even with help from our local "porters," it was exhausting just hauling our stuff up from the river, but we eventually made it, and when we set down the last of our gear I felt immensely alive. Spent, but alive.

It was like I'd only been gone a couple of days.

Andrew had neglected to mention just how far inland the *Irokai-teri* had moved—it took about a half hour for us to reach the village along a wet, cool, muddy trail. Mom intercepted us when we were about halfway there. She'd heard about our arrival and came dashing toward the river to greet me, and as soon as I saw her coming around a bend in the trail I dropped my bag and ran to fill the space between us. Just like last time, I felt a little awkward, because I wanted to give her a big squeeze and a kiss on the cheek, but that would have gotten the visit off to a deeply strange start.

As before, she was topless, her face decorated with the famil-iar *hii-hi* sticks. She wore a skirt, with some jungle flowers in her ears. And she wore an expression that seemed to be a mix of happy-sadness. Or sad-happiness. As we drew near to each other, I could see that she was tearing up.

I said, "Hi, Mom. I'm back." In English.

She smiled. Then she pointed to my bag, as if she meant to carry it for me. She was much stronger than I was, I'll admit, much more suited to this trail, but I waved her away and said, "*Hute.*" It's heavy.

What kind of son lets his mother carry his bags?

Almost immediately, we fell into the rhythms we'd left behind on my last expedition. It had been more than a year, but it felt like no time at all. There was Ricky Martin, out to welcome us. He had become a father since my last visit. There were my two wives, and each of them had become a mother in my absence—Wife No. 1 for the second time. There were my aunts, my uncles, my cous-ins, my spunky little niece . . . familiar faces all.

But there was no time for a prolonged family reunion. There was work to be done.

THE BIG HEADLINE SINCE my last visit? The old *shabono* had burned down—someone had left the communal fire untended while the *Irokai-teri* had gone off on a trek, and the wind kicked up and destroyed their home. So they built another, this one a little far-ther inland—about a half-hour walk from the river, at a brisk pace. I was a bit annoyed at the long walk to the *shabono*, especially with all that baggage, but it was exciting all the same.

When I arrived, the village was still in the process of clearing the land around the new communal living area. The *Irokai-teri* were cutting down trees, burning the underbrush, digging a new garden. There was a lot of work, and since my goal on this trip was to insert myself more fully into Yanomami life, I jumped right in. First, I strung my hammock by the fire I would share with my mother. Last time, I slept on the periphery, but I didn't want to be so far removed from my family. I wanted to be in the middle of everything.

Among the *Irokai-teri*, each family unit is meant to clear the swath of jungle that extends away from the family's area in the *shabono*—the rainforest equivalent of mowing your own front lawn so the neighbors don't complain. Much of the clearing was being done by the men, so I sought out Ricky Martin on this. He held a machete in his hand as I approached him one morning as he was setting to work, so I pointed to it, thinking this would explain that I wanted to help. It didn't. Next, I offered up a word in Spanish I thought might be a part of his broken vocabulary.

I said, "*Trabajo.*" Work.

Still, he didn't quite catch my meaning, so I reached for a phrase from my quiver of Yanomami phrases. I said, "*Kihami.*" Over there.

I pointed to the area he was meant to be clearing and tried a mash-up of the two languages: "*Trabajokihami.*"

Finally, he understood. He said, "Okay."

Ricky Martin handed me a machete and I went to get ready—and by *get ready* I mean I put on my shoes. I was in my boxers, shirtless, in shoes and socks, looking plainly ridiculous, but I started hacking away. It was actually a lot of fun. We just started chopping down trees, left and right, and the little kids would tail us and clear away the branches and collect them in a small pile.

It took me a while to get the hang of it. I was using a Cold Steel jungle machete, which was made of hard steel—much heavier than the machetes Dad and I tended to bring with us as trade goods. The extra weight meant there was a tremendous amount of hacking power, but you really had to give it a good swing.

I was getting into it, working up a good sweat, finding a nice rhythm to the work, when I came upon a fallen tree that had already been cut and was resting in a weird way against another tree that needed to be removed, so I went to work on this other tree. It was a decent-size tree, with a bunch of branches reaching every which way, and what looked like miles of jungle vine wrapped around the branches, the fallen log at the base, the trunk.

Those vines could be a bear, I was noticing. They were wound so tightly they would sometimes snap and recoil if you weren't careful—and, soon enough, I wasn't careful. I was tugging on a length of vine when the accompanying branch suddenly whipped back toward my face and caught me dead in the left eye. I screamed, which is not a typical display of emotion, so Ricky Martin turned to see what had happened. I had my hand over my eye, and I was shot through with adrenaline from all that hacking and sweating, so I waved him off. I'd been poked in the eye before. I thought, Okay, no big deal. I thought the sting of that first sharp pain would fade and I'd be fine.

But I wasn't fine. I tried to keep hacking, but I noticed there was this big black dot in my field of vision. And the pain, after two or three minutes, seemed to intensify. It got so bad I couldn't open my eye, so I dropped my machete and started staggering around like a Yanomami Frankenstein, my hands instinctively out in front. The others noticed and rushed to my side. Ricky Martin asked, "*Qué pasó?*"

I was in too much pain to think how to answer, but I whimpered and staggered and lumbered around our narrow forest clearing, and somehow my brother and one or two others helped me back to my hammock in the *shabono*. I couldn't open my eyes, couldn't think what to say to get the villagers to understand what had happened. Finally, I pointed to my left eye and said, "*Hii hi, nini.*" I was trying to indicate that I'd hurt my eye with a stick. I pointed to my eye again and hoped Ricky Martin would make the connection, and he did. He shouted something to the others and soon the *Irokai-teri* descended on my hammock by the dozen. People were looking at me, poking at me, trying to pry open my eyelid. I felt like I was on exhibit—better (or worse!), on the teaching unit of a jungle hospital.

The pain was just excruciating—really, I was in such agony, I couldn't think too clearly. All I could think was that something had lodged itself in my eye—a stick, or maybe a rock—and it would be a while before it occurred to me that the pain I was feeling could have been from a scratch on my cornea.

The Yanomami had some experience with this type of injury, and someone did notice bits of debris in the eye, so they set about removing it. How? By blowing on it. They took turns. Ricky Martin took a turn. The other men who'd been out clearing with us, they each took a turn. Someone had summoned my mother by this point, and she spoke to me sweetly as she leaned over my hammock and took her turn. It's like the healing turned itself into a small ritual.

In the middle of all this blowing, I heard what sounded like a disagreement. Two voices I did not recognize seemed to be arguing over what to do about my eye. The only word I could make out in the discussion was *koami*: empty, no more. In this context, it probably meant that all the debris had been cleared—or it could have meant that there was nothing more they could do for me.

I heard it again: "*Koami.*"

Meanwhile, they kept administering to me, and I was in too much agony to ask what they were doing. I couldn't see for shit, although I did manage to open my right eye at one point and see two villagers approach with a tiny stick, almost like a small straw, which had been whittled down at the tip to a fine fiber. They used this to dig out whatever debris they might have missed by just blowing, and as they dug I continued to scream and whimper. In the distance, I could hear some of the Yanomami women repeat the sounds of my whimpering, almost in a mocking way, but it must have sounded strange to them, all these noises coming from Yarima's *nabuh* son.

(I should mention here that my "good" eye didn't really do me any good—trying to open it only made my left eye twitch in unison, triggering another intense flash of pain, so I was effectively blinded.)

Next, someone took a feather and started brushing at my eyelid—I think because they wanted me to tear up, which would have helped to flush out any remaining debris.

It got so bad I couldn't take it anymore, so I waved everyone off and tried to close my eyes and will the pain away. I lay there in my hammock thinking, This is bad. Thinking, This is it, my time here is done. I was meant to stay in the jungle at least a month, and here I was, barely two weeks in, and I thought I'd have to leave. An eye trauma like this can be a dangerous thing. It might need emergency medical care, and there was no such thing as emergency care this deep in the rainforest. What if the eye gets infected? Bacterial infections, in that tropical environment, tend not to heal the way they do back home. What if the pain gets worse? As it was, it was way past intolerable. I couldn't imagine how I'd get through the night like this.

Through the pain, I remembered that I had a satellite phone, and I thought this was the time to use it. But first I'd have to find it. I couldn't open my eyes for more than a split second, just to get a little rush of vision. And remember, to open the right eye, the good eye, meant there'd be a corresponding flutter of the damaged left eye, and even the slightest movement was excruciating. So I fumbled through my things, blind, until I found my phone, and then I motioned for Mom and one of my aunts to lead me out into the open area of the *shabono*, where I thought I might pick up a signal. I did this by waving my arms like a lunatic and making a walking motion with my fingers—like from those old yellow pages "Let Your Fingers Do the Walking" commercials that used to run when I was a kid.

As we stumble-walked, I tried to remember the layout of the

phone, the menu functions, so I could work the thing with my eyes closed. I knew the very last text message I'd sent was to Chrissy, my very pregnant ex, who was like my go-between for this trip. The system we'd set up was I'd text Chrissy, and she'd pass along my message via Facebook to Andrew Lee, my missionary friend who'd dropped me off in the village. He was meant to collect me at the end of my stay, so he needed to be in on this, but I had no way to reach him by satellite phone at the Protestant mission. The only way to get to him was through this roundabout Chrissy-Facebook-Andrew circle.

Like a blind man, fumbling from memory, I sought out the text function on the phone and managed to type a brief SOS message to Chrissy—only I couldn't send it. There was no signal; the rainforest canopy was too thick, too tall. Remember, it was a relatively new *shabono*, and they'd only just started with the clearing, and I knew from my short excursions that the closest clearing was probably a ten- or fifteen-minute walk. There was no way I could make it that far with my eyes closed, one hand on Mom's shoulders for guidance. The pain was just too much. As it was, I could barely make it back to my hammock, but I slinked back in and thought the best thing to do was try to sleep it off.

I had some Advil in my gear bag, but I didn't think of taking it. Or maybe I did and realized this type of pain was beyond the healing powers of Advil.

Somehow, I got through that first night. Mom took care of me—but not the way you'd expect a mother to take care of an injured son back home. She came over to me every couple of hours, and touched my forehead, and mumbled a few words I couldn't understand, but there was nothing soothing or comforting about these checkups. Still, it was reassuring, in a way, to know that Mom was nearby and on the case—not that there was all that much she could do to help.

Throughout the night, with no other way to pass the time or distract myself from the pain, I tried to picture what my life might look like going forward. Chrissy was now about twenty-seven weeks along and really starting to show. Baby Naomi was progressing nicely, the doctor said. I wondered what she'd look like, if she'd look like me—short, with a Yanomami-round head and darkish skin. Would she have a hard time fitting in among the other girls at school? Would there be a time in her life, like me, when she'd want to find her place in the jungle?

Throughout the night, too, I could sense other bodies hovering around my hammock. I could hear some hushed conversations. If anything, the pain get worse as the night wore on—it really felt like there was a tiny stone with jagged edges lodged in my eye. I was afraid to open my eyes, so I had no idea when the night finally passed, but soon there was a thrum of early morning activity around the communal hearth, the whoosh of coming and going.

Soon after that, there was another consultation taking place alongside my hammock. All I could make out was the word *suwe*—woman. Over and over I heard this word, and then there was a kind of hush. I could feel several sets of hands on me, two or three sets about my face. Someone tried to pry open my eye, and there was a fresh rush of pain. All I could see was one big blur—I couldn't even make out any shapes. I could sense that someone was leaning over me; it felt to me like I was in shadow—and then I could feel two liquid drops gently dappling my eye. Almost immediately I felt some relief. I could actually open my eye without pain for an extended period of time. I still couldn't see; my vision remained blurry and supersensitive to light, but at least I was pain-free.

It was an amazing thing, really, because I took the soothing drops to mean there was a stash of medicine somewhere in the village. This was a tremendous relief, not just in terms of the pain, but in that the drops gave me hope as well. They helped to ease my worries about infection. I knew from my emergency medical training that one of the first things you do when you treat for eye trauma is to guard against any bacterial infection, and on this front I'd thought I was screwed. So I quite reasonably assumed that I'd just been given some antibacterial drops, and that I'd take another few doses, and eventually the crisis would pass.

I wasn't in the clear just yet, however, so I passed the rest of that next day in my hammock, keeping my eyes shut, trying to rest before the pain returned, as I feared it would. People came by and fed me plantains; Mom gave me a kind of broth; and my uncle brought some of his food to share, which he placed directly on my chest. Initially he helped me to eat, but I was feeling strong enough to feed myself, so I felt around my shirt for different items that felt familiar to my touch and brought them to my mouth. With one pinch I grabbed a couple of grub worms, thinking they were a familiar shape, a familiar texture. I'd eaten grub worms before, and actually liked them, but as soon as I realized what I'd popped into my mouth I gagged. I wasn't in the mood for grub worms just then. I wanted comfort food—ice cream, pizza, chicken soup.

I slept fitfully that night, although I did manage to dream. It was a dream that would return to me in one form or another throughout my time in the jungle on this second trip. In the dream there was Chrissy, my pregnant ex, along with all of my other ex-girlfriends: Sarah, Karen, Daisy, and on and on. It was the most curious thing, the way I kept having these wild dreams about my ex-girlfriends—not *wild* in the down-and-dirty sense, but *wild* in the weird and crazy sense. There seemed to be a theme. In every dream there came a moment when I'd ask my ex to take me back. One by one, in turn, they'd reappear to me in my dream. Each time out, I'd cry, beg, drop to my knees, like in a cliché. And in each case, in every corner of every dream, my ex would deny my pitiful appeal and reject me yet again.

It was the story of my life, coming back to bite me in the ass—subconsciously, yes, but I felt those bite marks in my sleep.

By the next morning the pain had returned, and as I lay in my hammock I once again heard the same word: *suwe*.

Once again, there were all these hands on me. Once again, someone pried open my left eyelid. Once again, it felt to me like

I was in shadow. Only this time I could make out the silhouette of a young woman leaning over my hammock as if readying to administer the eye drops, and as she leaned in closer I recognized that it was one of my wives—Wife No. 2, in fact. My first thought was, Hey, what do you know? You're the one with the medicine! Thank you!

As she leaned in closer still, I noticed that she didn't have any medicine in her hands. There was no eyedropper. Instead, she held her naked breast, which she pointed at me like a weapon. Then she pinched her nipple and squeezed, shooting a forceful stream of breast milk in the direction of my left eye.

Her aim wasn't so hot—nowhere near as dead-on as it had been the day before, although I suppose it's possible the first dose had been administered by another lactating Yanomami woman. She managed to hit her target, though, because I felt some immediate relief. I also had a face full of breast milk, but I didn't care. I would have suffered any indignity to chase away such a killing pain—and as indignities go, this wasn't much. This was just a group of jungle women holding me down on my hammock, my mother prying open my infected eyelids, and my wife, who had recently given birth to a child by another husband, showering me with breast milk and hoping that some of it might land in my eye—happens every day, right?

Of course, I was used to more sterile techniques when taking medication. A hundred questions filled my mind as I closed my eyes and waited for Wife No. 2's breast milk to do its work: Will this treatment actually cure me, or just provide temporary relief? How the hell did the Yanomami figure this out? Could the breast milk actually *increase* the risk of infection? What else did the Yanomami know about the healing powers of breast milk?

My head was all over the place, but once the pain began to subside yet again I let myself stop worrying—and this was how my injury ran its course. The breast milk treatments continued—two squirts, morning and evening. After three days I was finally able to open my eyes, but I still couldn't see too well. I had a tough time with sunlight—but here at least I could look out at the world through my undamaged right eye until the left eye adjusted to the light.

The whole time, Mom was by my side—and it was a tremendous comfort to feel her soothing touch, to know she was taking care of me. Within a week, I was back to normal, and I guess it did take a village to see me through this ordeal, but I don't know how I would have gotten through it without my mother.

She was my pain medication, my hope, my rehab.

THAT SATELLITE PHONE I was fumbling for when I was trying to text Chrissy? I did manage to put it to meaningful use on this second trip—another Flintstones-Jetsons moment that yielded an indelible memory and an unexpected lesson on what it means to be Yanomami in the context of our modern world.

The phone was a luxury, but once I was in the jungle nothing was more precious than the battery life. I figured I had about three hours of talk time on the thing, and there was no way to recharge it until I returned to the Protestant mission, so every minute counted. Trouble was, it wasn't always so easy to get a decent signal. Aside from using it to check in on Chrissy and see how her pregnancy was going, it was there as a lifeline. If there was an emergency, like the injury to my eye, it was reassuring to know I had the ability to connect with the outside world, to call for help, so I'd set up this whole semi-elaborate phone chain to keep myself in touch.

The great side benefit to the phone was the opportunity it offered to get my parents together again—this time in Mom's village, where I thought she might be more comfortable, more like herself, than she had been at the Catholic mission in Mavaca.

One afternoon after my eye injury had healed and I thought I had a better sense of where and when I might find a decent satellite signal, I took the phone from my gear bag and brought it over to Mom, who was sitting in her hammock. I pointed to the phone and said, "Talk Kenny."

She smiled to indicate she understood. She said, *"Telefono, Kenny."*

We tried to make a call right there in the *shabono*, but the signal was terrible—as in, nonexistent. Then we took the phone to a nearby garden, but we couldn't get a steady signal there, either. We kept looking and looking for a signal, but either the cloud cover was too thick, or the jungle canopy was too dense in and around the village, and after searching and searching for a signal I had to give up on the idea. I worried that I was wasting too much battery life, without even making a call. I pointed to the phone and shook my head and said, *"Bateria."* As if this would have explained anything to my mother, who was only anxious to talk to her Kenny.

For days, in idle moments, I'd get the phone out and start moving about the area, pointing it to the skies, looking for a signal. This usually happened after Mom had chased after me for a while—saying, *"Telefono, Kenny. Talk Kenny."* Once she got an idea in her head, she was all over it—a character trait that seemed to me a whole lot more American than Yanomami. Anyway, she knew where I kept the phone, knew it had these magical powers to connect her to the sound of my father's voice, so she kept after me.

I spent so much time with that damn phone, pointed skyward, that the *Irokai-teri* eventually figured out the equation of cause-and-effect. They'd pull me from whatever I was doing and look up at the clouds and say, *"Kihami kihami."* Here, here . . . Like they were making suggestions, trying to be helpful.

Finally, we were out for a trek to a new garden by the bank of the river, and I noticed there were no tall trees in the area. There was a clear shot to an open sky. We were about a twenty-minute walk from the *shabono*, but I didn't want to lose this opportunity, so I doubled back to collect the phone, and when I returned with it Mom was completely pumped. She knew what it meant. The others, they knew what it meant, too—and it occurred to me as I completed this unnecessary round-trip that they must have known what it meant all along. It was frustrating, a little. I'd never seen this garden before, this clearing with the uninterrupted path to a satellite signal, but the *Irokai-teri* all knew it was there. They knew what I was looking for, all those times I had the phone out, pointing toward the sky. At least, I *think* they knew— and yet nobody had thought to point me in this direction.

(Where oh where was the village IT guy? I wondered.)

Either way, Mom smiled, giggled, jumped up and down. She said, *"Telefono, Kenny. Talk Kenny."*

When the call went through, my father picked up immediately on the other end, and Mom's face brightened like it was lit by the moon. I'd never seen a smile so wide, so encompassing. She was overjoyed. She said, *"Kenny, ha-po. Kenny, ha-po."* Kenny, come. Kenny, come.

She wanted nothing more than for my father to return to her, after all this time—only, I'm afraid it was a practical invitation as much as an emotional one, because she started telling him everything she wanted him to bring with him to her village. She wanted fishhooks, fabrics, pots and pans. She wanted to see her Kenny, yes; but she wanted the things her Kenny could bring even more.

Even my uncle got on the phone, to make an appeal. It was an amazing thing to see, really, the way the *Irokai-teri* were able to so quickly and seamlessly understand this little piece of *nabuh* technology, the way they shot right past the novelty and started angling for what this strange machine could do for them.

"Shori," my uncle said. *"Shori, yahoriprou."* "Brother-in-law, I am poor." Then he went on to list all the things he wanted my father to bring: machetes, a motor, gasoline . . .

This, too, was the way of the Yanomami—to accept the rush of change, the approach of the modern world, and to find a way to benefit from it, and as I set the phone down after ending the call with my father I thought, Okay, lesson learned. We'd embraced the technology and put it to meaningful use; we'd found a signal and made this unlikely satellite call; but in the end the phone was also useful for the way it might deliver a few pots and pans, some yarn, some fishing line. Understand, Mom was still overjoyed to talk to my father. My uncle was pleased to hear the voice of his old friend. Their appeals in no way cheapened the affection they felt for him, the relationships they once shared.

But they still wanted those pots and pans.

INSTRUCTION IS NOT ONE of the strengths of the Yanomami—that's not how they learn. There's no tradition of a father taking his son to fish, say, and teaching him how it's done. That doesn't happen. Instead, from the day children are born, they watch the adults. They observe, they study. Their skills start with playing, mocking rituals, mimicking the world around. There is no set age or stage when a particular skill must be mastered. Boys become hunters when they are ready. Girls become mothers when they are ready. Boys become shamans when they are ready. Girls become foragers and harvesters when they are ready. There's no law or paper certificate that legitimizes an activity or certifies an acquired set of skills.

It happens when it happens—only for me, I needed someone to take me by the hand and walk me through it, and my brother Ricky Martin recognized that. He was very good at showing me how to do things in the jungle—basic survival things, like chopping down a tree, or making a fire, or hunting for tapir, or breaking open a certain kind of fruit. He even taught me to make something called *ta-te*—a banana broth-drink that very quickly became one of my very favorite things.

On my own, back home, I'd read an instruction manual, or seek out a YouTube video before heading out to try something new. But here in the jungle I didn't have such luxuries. I only had my brother Ricky Martin—Micashi. We became pals on this trip, and he took on the role of what anthropologists call an informant, which basically means he took me under his care, showed me how to survive in this part of the world, like a field guide. He taught me to shoot a bow and arrow. After just a couple tries, it got to where I could nock the arrow, pull it back, take aim at the plantain tree just across the way, and let it fly. The thud my arrow made as it hit the tree dead center was one of the most satisfying sounds in the rainforest—the sound of completion, the sound of arrival. There was a group of us out shooting, and everyone let out a rich, satisfying cry of "Awwwwww" as the arrow hit home—Ricky Martin, the loudest of all.

He also taught me to take *epena*—or, *yopo*, as it is often called. One day he took me aside and told me as a man of the village it was time for me to try it, and I could not argue. Jesus, it was painful! The blast of powder as it rocketed into my nasal cavity through that hollow tube was like nothing I'd ever experienced. It hurt like crazy. I thought my head was about to split open. After that, I was in a kind of fog, and once the pain subsided it felt like my head was about to split open in a whole bunch of other ways. It really was a mind trip, but I was clearheaded enough to observe what was going on around me. It's like I was on the very edges of the spirit world—close enough to peer across the vast expanse that separated our reality from this heightened reality, but in control enough to hang back, and I lingered on this sweet precipice for what seemed like the longest time.

On *yopo*, sounds are amplified in a beautiful, almost melodic way. It reminded me of the sustain pedal you sometimes hear on an electric guitar, the noises of the jungle stretched out so that they linger in the thick forest air, in your ears, in your memory. They echo and they don't go away.

I found myself hallucinating—only not in ways you might expect. My hallucinations were rooted in reality, a *Western* reality. For example, I'd notice all the women walking around topless, something that fails to register at all once you've been in the jungle a day or two, but the *epena* left me looking out at the world like a horny teenage boy from New Jersey. There were breasts everywhere! I could close my eyes and swear they were attacking me.

Whenever possible, I tried to be a good and patient teacher to

Ricky Martin, too. Of course, I had nothing to teach him about life in the rainforest, about the Yanomami ways, but he was desperate to learn English. He really wanted to come back with me to my *nabuh* village in America and go to school. He knew all about schooling from his time in Esmeralda, where he'd had his first taste of acculturation and started to learn the ways of the *nabuh*. One night we stayed up late while I taught him to count to sixty. It was an ambitious project—fueled along, no doubt, by another deliriously painful hit of *yopo*.

If I had to categorize this second trip to the jungle in 2013 and compare it to my first trip in 2011, I'd say the one built on the other. In 2011, the trip was mostly about finding my mother and *reconnecting* with my Yanomami family. In 2013, it was mostly about finding myself and *becoming* Yanomami.

In my head, I compared my journey to the underlying story in Robert Ludlum's Bourne books. In *The Bourne Identity*—or "The Good Identity"—the goal was to discover a sense of self. In *The Bourne Supremacy*—or "The Good Supremacy"—the goal was to master my new identity, to take control over it in some way, and that's kind of what happened for me on this second trip to my mother's village. This time out, I learned to be more Yanomami—not just in the language of the Yanomami, but in the customs, the rhythms, the pace and purpose of life in the jungle. I learned practical things, like how to hunt and fish and prepare a tapir after a kill. And I learned to think like the Yanomami, at least a little bit.

The best illustration of this is probably the clearheaded way I would wake up each morning while I was in the jungle. There's no corollary in our Western world, but in my short time with Mom I got to this place in my thinking where there wasn't even anything to think about. Does that make sense? No, I suppose it doesn't, if you're reading these words from a modern, industrialized perspective. But with a jungle mind-set, what was there to think about, really? If I was hungry, I went off in search for food. If I was tired, I rested. If I was exposed to the elements, I built a shelter. If I ran out of firewood, I went out and collected some more.

It's like one giant Nike ad—*just do it!* There's no thinking, just doing. There's no worrying, just doing. There's no second-guessing, just doing. And it took a while, but I finally got to this place in my thinking—or *not* thinking—and as I did I thought back to that comment my mother made to my father on that boat ride to Platanal, all those years ago, and wondered if I had ful-filled her vision for me.

Was I "jungle-ready," at long last? Was I Yanomami, after all?

THREE WEEKS INTO THIS second trip, I started to think the land around the *shabono* would never be cleared. The jungle was so deep, so thick it seemed to swallow up the constant efforts of the *Irokai-teri* to hack away at it. I wondered if it was always like this, if the men always busied themselves with the business of pushing back the jungle—a job that was never finished.

Once my eye was fully healed, I decided to get back to helping out with this never-ending chore. My time in the territory was coming to a close, and I wanted to make as much of a contribu-tion as I could before it came time to leave. Each time out, I got a little better at this clearing business—my efforts were a little less embarrassing, a little more proficient. However, the very first time I picked up a machete following my injury, Mom flashed me this look of maternal worry. It was like she was one of my friends' moms back home, from childhood, telling me not to run with scissors. She didn't say anything, but I could see in her look that she didn't trust me not to hurt myself.

So I answered her worry in English. I said, "It's okay, Mom. I'll cut the trees like this." Then I cupped my hand and placed it over my left eye, like an eye patch, while I pantomimed a hacking motion with my right hand.

She laughed—everyone did.

But Ricky Martin took some extra time with me, to help me get my rhythm back. He told me where to cut, when to cut, how to cut. As always, he was a good and patient teacher, and as we moved farther and farther from the village, he seemed to get more and more into it. He expected more and more from me. Soon he wasn't just teaching me to master the hacking motion, but also the proper way to howl like a true Yanomami as I worked.

You see, the howling is a big part of it—almost like a battle cry, to inspire us as we work. Absolutely, the joyful, exuberant sounds of the Yanomami hacking away at the brush surrounding the *shabono* were like sweet music—the rainforest was filled with the sounds of progress and purpose, effort and release . . . all of that good, good stuff.

Ricky Martin didn't like the way I yelled at first. He teased and said I yelled like a *nabuh*, which I took as a great insult. When the Yanomami men howl, it comes across in a high-pitched way, almost like a singsong shriek. My voice didn't quite project in the same way; it came across in a sad, low tone that sounded more like scolding than a satisfying, uninhibited howling.

Each time I yelled, Ricky Martin corrected me.

He howled, *"Eh . . . eh . . . ahuuuu!"* And this seemed to please him.

In answer, I howled, *"Eh . . . eh . . . ahuuu!"* And this didn't please him at all.

Every time we headed out to continue with the clearing, he had me practice my howl. He was determined that I get it right—and finally, just a couple of days before I was due to leave, I did.

And it's a good thing, too, because Ricky Martin was beginning to get frustrated with me—not angry, but it felt to me like he was coming to a boil. My hacking, I should mention, was improving—Mom would have been proud of me, I thought as I worked, building up a heavy sweat. And yet no matter how I tried to mimic my brother's howling as I worked, I couldn't seem to get it right, to where he eventually started screaming at me.

He howled, the right way.

I howled, and could only get close to it.

This went on for a while, until finally I hit just the right tone, with just the right inflection, just the right mix of joy and abandon. It's like it came from someplace deep down inside me, a place I no longer had to think about. And I didn't need to hear from Ricky Martin that I'd gotten it right, because I *felt* it.

"*Eh . . . eh . . . ahuuuu!*" I howled. "*Eh . . . eh . . . ahuuuu!*" Over and over and over. And with each full-throated cry I got this rush of pure energy, and the accompanying swings of my machete sliced through the thick jungle air like nothing at all.

To see me hack away at these trees in this way, to sing out in this way, to dance across the jungle floor in this way . . . you could have sworn I was Yanomami.

CHAPTER EIGHT

The Good Project

SO HERE I AM, PUTTING the finishing touches to this book in my Pennsylvania apartment, as my daughter, Naomi, sleeps in the next room—a fine setting, I think, for me to reflect on what these past years have meant and the place I seem to have made for myself among the Yanomami.

Already, the nonprofit organization I started to imagine on my first trip to the Amazon has become a reality. We're not firing on all cylinders just yet, but the Good Project is poised to become a powerful voice on behalf of the world's indigenous population. We'll shine particular light on the *Irokai-teri*, but we'll also turn our attention to other villages, other tribes, other regions. As of this writing, we've completed our first two service trips to Costa Rica, working with student groups from East Stroudsburg University among the Cabecar tribe and helping to build an all-important cross-cultural alliance—and I'm actually packing for my third trip to the region.

The idea behind the Good Project is to raise money, raise awareness, raise the platform a little bit so that we can look on at each other in an elevated way. What do I mean by that exactly? Well, we're out to

give the indigenous peoples of the world more of a voice—that's
the easy description. My thinking is, now that my story has captured a certain amount of attention, I want to deflect some of
that and get people thinking of ways to champion the causes of
these remote tribes—in the rainforest and beyond. There are all
kinds of ways to bring some of the benefits of the modern word
to these good people without asking them to give up any of their
time-honored customs, their way of life. We can help by gently
integrating technology, by sharing new irrigation techniques, by
bringing in much-needed medicines and clothing and supplies.
We'll do this one project at a time, because while I'm really out
to make a difference I recognize that the only way to change the
big picture is through a series of small strokes. If we see a specific
need, we'll move to fill it.

Already I've got a board of directors in place, and a support
network of organizations doing good work in some of the most
remote corners of the planet, and in the coming years I hope to
build a bridge between the developed world and the undeveloped
world. Just how we'll go about doing that . . . well, we're figuring
it out as we go along, as we look for "good" projects to get behind.

For now, I can only share my family's story and trust that it
offers a path to understanding the Yanomami of today. I'm no
expert, but I do believe I'm uniquely qualified to weigh in on
this—so that's the plan, starting out. The book you hold in your
hands is a part of that effort, so before I sign off in these pages
I want to share some final thoughts on the changing face of my
people—and first, the changing face of my family.

AS I REFLECT ON my time in the jungle I'm especially happy with
the way I was able to reconnect my parents after all this time.
Granted, it was only a Skype connection, only a short satellite
phone call, but these were important markers in the life of my
family. Progress can be a good thing, right? In a million years,
my father could never have imagined speaking Yanomami to my

mother in *Irokai-teri*, to his good friends. He told me when I got back that these calls gave him a sense of closure—but I didn't really press him on what he meant, the same way I didn't really press Mom on why she left Danny on that runway and disappeared into the forest. My thinking is, The past is the past. I don't care about it. All that matters to me is the present, and here in the present we all managed to find each other again . . . and I consider this a win-win, all around.

You see, I went to the Amazon to find my mother. I went to the Amazon to find my indigenous heritage. I went to the Amazon to find myself. And yet my journey of self-discovery did not end when I left the jungle. It continues here in the United States. I've become closer and more open with my family. I might have gone looking for my mother, but in a lot of ways it took looking for Mom for me to finally find my father. Really, Dad and I have become companions and great friends on the back of my journey—I don't mean to diminish the good and important work he's done throughout his career, but in some ways we interact as colleagues. No, I don't even get close to his experience, his level of insight—but at least we're working the same puzzle. We sometimes spend hours and hours sharing our stories, our observations. I look at how we are with each other now and have a hard time recognizing how things used to be between us, back when I would shut down at the mere mention of my mother or the Yanomami people. Today I embrace every chance I get to talk about Mom. I want to drink it all in—and, happily, my father is an endless resource.

He's been through a lot, my father. He was judged and scrutinized for marrying the woman he loved. In a lot of ways, marrying a Yanomami woman and having three children with her inhibited his anthropological career. He didn't have time to research and publish. His abilities as an impartial, scientific observer of the Yanomami were thrown into question. But he doesn't regret the choices he made as a young man. "How could I?" he asks me, when I put the question to him. "I have three wonderful children. I have wonderful memories."

Like me, my father recognizes the drastic changes that have taken place in the jungle since his time among the Yanomami. He wholeheartedly supports my mission of providing assistance to indigenous peoples struggling to stand tall against the encroaching pressures of the modern world. Just recently, a Yanomami male was ruthlessly beaten to death by police officers in Puerto Ayacucho—a story that left my father deeply saddened. He grieved not only for this one individual and his family, but for his people. For the longest time, Dad had a hard time reconciling the incident with the Yanomami he knew and loved in the most remote parts of the jungle, keeping to their traditional lifestyles and customs.

Of course, he knows that change is inevitable, and that "progress" is unavoidable. His frustration is that he's been out of the loop for so long. For a time he was one of the foremost experts on traditional Yanomami culture—and he remains a leading authority in this area, even as traditional Yanomami culture is undergoing these radical shifts.

My journey also brought about a deepening in my relationships with my siblings. My brother Daniel—we no longer call him "Danny"—has recently graduated with a degree in nutritional science from West Chester University, in Pennsylvania. I am so enormously proud of him and his accomplishments—but what's interesting to me is that he had a very different relationship with the memory of our mother as kids. We each struggled, but in our own ways, with our own issues, and I'll leave it to Daniel to share his feelings on growing up Yanomami, if he so chooses. But now that I've reconnected with Mom in this way, now that I've reconnected with Dad in this way, Daniel and I have been coming together in this way, too. Not long after I returned from my second visit to the rainforest, the two of us sat down and got to talking over a couple of beers. Talk turned naturally to Mom— and when I say *naturally*, you have to realize we'd never really talked about her before, so what might have seemed natural in other families was completely new in ours.

Daniel told me what a great thing it was that I had trekked all the way down to Venezuela and somehow made my way to Mom. I told him I'd love it if he wanted to join me on one of my next trips, and make the same journey himself, but only when he is ready. Of course, *ready* can mean different things to different people, even if they're part of the same family, with some of the same experiences. In my case, I wasn't *ready* until I was twenty-four years old, when all the elements of the cosmos were in just the right place. Who can say when that moment will come for my brother—but when it does, *if* it does, I'm determined to be there for him, to help him along in his quest.

He liked this idea—and so we toasted to it.

Vanessa, she's another story. We've been talking more and more about Mom these days. Now that she's a mother herself, she seems to want to understand what was going on with Mom when she dashed back into the jungle. I think Vanessa processed it one way when she was a child, but she's got a different perspective now, and I know a part of her would love to find a way to reach out to Mom, across these many miles, across these vast linguistic and cultural barriers, and find a way to talk about it. In fact, she's recently expressed an interest in joining me on one of my upcoming expeditions. But the reality is, with two little kids of her own, we'll have to figure out how a trip like that could work; what that trip might mean to Vanessa personally, I can only imagine.

But, again, that is her story to tell—all I can do, as her brother, is be around to help her see it through.

And then there's my renewed relationship with my mother—a relationship at the very heart of this odyssey. I find myself missing her deeply. I often wonder, as I'm driving to work along Route 80, what she might be doing in that exact moment. Is she collecting firewood? Is she out crabbing with the other women? Is she harvesting plantains? Every now and then I imagine her sitting down by the side of the creek and pulling out the bundle of family photos she keeps safely stored in a small bag she's taken to carrying with her. I can see her looking at pictures of me, Vanessa,

Daniel. I can see her looking at pictures of my father. I can see her tearing up—wondering, perhaps, when I might return to her.

It makes me sad to think of her in this way—but at the same time, selfishly, it fills me with this tremendous sense of connection. All those years, I never knew if she was thinking about us at all, off somewhere in the jungle, doing her thing. And now I know. There is a place for us in her heart.

There is a place for *me*.

Another sad thing: I catch myself thinking more and more of the passage of time. Mom's getting old—there's no looking away from this difficult truth. No, the Yanomami don't keep track of things like chronological age, but jungle life is harsh. It cheats you from a bunch of years, and in the back of my mind I wonder how many more visits we'll be able to share. I wonder, and I worry. It's one of the great frustrations of this new phase of my life that I cannot move so easily, so freely, back and forth to and from the jungle. But life is complicated in our so-called civilized world. I have to keep working to keep ahead of my bills. I have to lay in the foundation for some kind of career. I have to make sure I have food, gasoline, clothing, health insurance . . . all the little things we need to survive in the wilds of Pennsylvania. It's not like it is in the jungle, where everything you need is right there. And now, on top of everything else, I have a daughter to take care of, so I can't simply take off for the jungle—the thought of being apart from my beautiful Naomi makes my heart skip.

So in those low moments when I'm imagining Mom looking at pictures, wondering when I might return, I catch myself thinking how great it would be if I could somehow place a satellite phone in that small bag. If I could somehow reach out to her and let her know I'm on my way—because I'm working on it.

UNTIL I'M ABLE TO return to the rainforest, I figure the thing to do is to keep my focus on the territory, to build on the experiences I shared with my Yanomami family. After all, we are no longer the isolated people my father came upon all the way back in 1975, when my father first made contact with the people of Mom's village.

One of the key problems I've seen since I started studying the region and on my two extended visits to the territory is that Westerners are inclined to think of the Yanomami as one homogeneous tribe. Also, we tend to exoticize them—meaning, to paint them with a single, romantic brush and imagine that *all* Yanomami are unspoiled, naked, pristine, primitive . . . just as they first appeared to us in the Western media back in the 1950s.

In reality, they are a dynamic, evolving people that have experienced a wide spectrum of acculturation. And yet this tendency to exoticize the Yanomami . . . it makes it easy for Westerners to forget that they are human beings. They are not zoo animals confined within impervious walls. They are not creatures to be studied or evaluated. No, they are a caring, feeling, spirited group of willful, prideful people, engaging and interacting with other tribes and with Westerners, picking up new skills, technologies, ideologies along the way.

In this way, they are just like you and me.(Okay, so maybe they're a little more like *me*, and a little less like *you*, but you get the idea . . .)

Today, many Yanomami live in mud huts with metal roofs. Some live in brick houses. And yes, a great many continue to live in the ancient *shabono* structures of their ancestors. You will find that the degree of acculturation increases the closer you get to the mission compounds that now dot the territory, and to small settlement cities like Esmeralda. Many Yanomami speak Spanish and have received some form of Western-style education; some are getting involved in local politics and policymaking. There are Yanomami who own their own boats and motors. More and more, Yanomami villages have some form of electricity, and a select few have been blessed with running water. And there are numerous villages that can boast their own schools, with classes very often taught by their own Yanomami teachers.

I think it's fair to say that the Yanomami are experiencing one of the fastest rates of acculturation in their rich, noble history, and on some level I have to believe this is a welcome thing. I've chosen my words carefully here; when I say "I have to believe," I mean I have no other choice; to believe otherwise would be to consign my people to a lifetime of frustration and decline. And yet the truth remains that I'm not entirely convinced that all of these changes have been entirely positive, and so on some *other* level, I'm afraid I must hold back. Absolutely, in a vacuum, each development brings with it an exciting string of prospects. Access to education, the acquisition of modern technology (such as laptops and cell phones), the increased mobility afforded by newer forms of transportation . . . it all adds up to a time of enormous opportunity, but taken together this sea change also raises a string of troubling questions: Can the Yanomami keep up with this rapid rate of change? What does it mean for the Yanomami to face the future? Do they even know what it means to look toward the future? Can they imagine what's possible?

Consider: my mother's village has been relatively unaffected by this age of transformation, but in neighboring villages the influences of the twenty-first century are everywhere apparent. It's remarkable, really, when you think that as recently as twenty or thirty years ago, these people were living the way their ancestors had lived for generations, for centuries. Now the postmodern Yanomami youth are clothed, listening to music, learning math, reading books . . . so there is an ever-widening gap between the generations. As a result, a great many young Yanomami are dealing with their own kinds of identity crises. Who are they? In what world do they truly belong?

Sadly, there are many Yanomami who grapple with all these questions—and, as a consequence, many are renouncing their heritage. In many cases, they don't even want to be called Yanomami; they'd rather be known as Venezuelan.

I look on at these developments with a heavy heart—but then, who am I to judge? Me, of all people? Me, who was so quick to renounce my own Yanomami roots. Let's face it, I spent my whole life running from my indigenous past. Now I'm running toward it, and it saddens me to see so many members of my tribe running the other way. We share the same blood and yet we're at cross-purposes.

This is the baggage, the fine print that comes with the Westernization of the Yanomami, and I could see it in an in-your-face way during my time in Esmeralda. In all, I spent several weeks in the settlement, on my way into and out of the territory. It was a place to refresh, reflect, and recharge my batteries—literally *and* figuratively. While in Esmeralda, I passed the time in the company of other young Yanomami, about the same age as me. I walked around a lot, took in the sights, snapped tons of pictures, talked to as many people as I could. I really wanted to get a sense of the place—not as a tourist or an outsider, but as a full-fledged Yanomami, just passing through.

It was amazing to see so many Yanomami boys and girls in their school uniforms, scurrying to make it to their classrooms ahead of the school bell—quite a contrast to the memories I carried of the Yanomami boys and girls of my home village, who ran naked in the jungle, splashing in the creek, soaking up the ways of their parents and grandparents.

One day toward the end of my stay in the settlement, I was walking back to my room from lunch when I noticed a group of a dozen or so young Yanomami boys crowded around Father Arroldo. I walked over and asked what was going on. Father Arroldo explained that these boys wanted to know who I was.

"They are too nervous to approach you," he said. "Can you please speak to them?"

Of course I agreed. I faced the boys and told them I was Yanomami, same as them, only I had a *nabuh* father and a mother from Hasupuwe. They looked at me like I was trying to mess with their heads.

"*Peheti?*" one of them asked—meaning, Is that really true?

"*Awei,*" I said. Yes.

Now the boys were intrigued. I offered to go inside and show them pictures on my laptop—dozens of shots of my Yanomami family and our village. This I did. Then I showed them pictures of my American home—together with images of skyscrapers, cars, winter landscapes.

They were dumbstruck. For a few moments, no one spoke. Finally, one of the boys broke the silence. He said, *Why are you really here? You are* nabuh. *You have everything you need. Why would you come to this place?*

I said, "I am here because I have the blood of the Yanomami. I am here because this is my home. My family is here. My mother is here. I am here because these are my lands. These are *our* lands. I am proud to be Yanomami, proud to be the son of a Yanomami woman. Yes, I am *nabuh*, but someday I will learn the ways of the Yanomami. I will hunt. I will fish. I will garden.

"*Yanomami keya!*"

As I spoke, I paid close attention to this one boy who'd asked the question. I watched his eyes become wider as I told him of my life in the United States. He was astonished. And as he listened to what I had to say, his face brightened in a smile—ear to ear, wide enough to hold a plantain on its side. For a connecting moment, we both shared a pride in who we were, in what we could become.

In this way, I connected with these boys—and I realized I could build on this connection and find a way to reach out to other Yanomami youth. I'm not so full of myself to think I might stand as a role model—truth be told, some of the choices I made early on in my life show me as someone who behaved terribly, even recklessly, someone who disrespected his parents and his heritage at every turn. And yet I was able to overcome my own bad behavior and find a way to embrace my birthright, to make it my own.

These boys were doing mostly okay. They were in school; they were expanding their horizons. But I worried about some of the other Yanomami, caught between the ancient ways of my moth-er's village and some of the more acculturated villages. All across the territory, there were hundreds of postmodern Yanomami losing their way, our young people especially, and this terrifies me. It puts me in mind of a *New York Times* article I happened upon as I was finishing this book—on the remote Guarani tribe in western Brazil, where the suicide rate has soared in the past decade. According to a local pediatrician with the Ministry of Health in the Brazilian state of Mato Grosso do Sul, there have been about 500 suicides among this tribe of 45,000 in the last ten years. That's an alarming number—and some experts suggest the true number is even higher.

In the article, there's a quote from a Guarani anthropologist named Tonico Benites that I found troubling: "At some point, many people I knew, friends, had lost their autonomy, their way of supporting themselves. So they end up thinking about death."

What does this mean for the Yanomami? Well, I take it to mean that the more things change, the more apparent it becomes to these young people what they have done so long without. They begin to lose hope. The more they see, the more they see what they're missing. As they are exposed more and more to the developed world, they'll start to lose themselves in feelings of despair, disconnection. Over time, I imagine, this can lead to a rejection of their Yanomami ways, spreading across an entire generation, as young people begin to hate the very blood that flows through their veins. I know how this works. I've been there. They will sink into a deep, dark place that can only lead to depression, self-destruction, self-loathing.

Naturally, this troubles me as well. Why? Because the acculturated Yanomami know where they are at the bottom of the social status totem pole. They know that many people who come to study them, trade with them, and "welcome" them to their missions and developed communities still consider them unintelligent, backward. Despite their many advances, they remain "primitive savages" in the eyes of the world. Indeed, in some parts of the world, in modern Venezuela especially, the term *Yanomami* is often used as a pejorative, a way to insult someone. (*What are you, Yanomami?*) In my own travels, I've met physicians in the territory—scientists who should know better—who've referred to my fellow Yanomami as lazy and ignorant. That pisses me off. But I can only work to change these misconceptions—not by subjecting these arrogant physicians and wrong-minded relief workers and sleazy bureaucrats to sensitivity training, but by helping them to see the majestic beauty of my people, their inherent wisdom, the strength of their character.

And there is also this—a relatively new phenomenon regarding the mobility of the Yanomami. Many are now leaving their territory, moving away from the missions and resettling in cities like Puerto Ayacucho. They're quitting the jungle entirely and leaving their old ways behind. Some are being trained in field medicine; others are hired as translators for local and field hospitals; and many are involved in missionary work. Unfortunately, many don't make it. They get involved in crime, drugs, alcohol, prostitution . . . all the dangers of modern life that find us in the developed world. These are the supposed "fruits" of our Western civilization.

Is this what it means to assimilate? Is this what it means to embrace technology and other modern advances? Or does it simply represent the collateral damage that happens in the face of the Yanomami's Westernization process—a small price to pay for the greater good?

I don't know. Really, I don't. I only know that these things trouble me—that they are something to think about. The frantic pace of change . . . it doesn't sit right with me, as I close out this chapter in my life and look ahead to the next one. And so here I am, a newly minted Yanomami-American, reawakened to my rainforest roots after a lifetime of turning away from them, and now I can only fear for the future of the Yanomami. My Yanomami. I fear that the diffusion of these dangerous, demeaning aspects of Western culture will seep deeper and deeper into the Yanomami territory.

To my family.

As I sit and worry and wonder, I think of psychologist Abraham Maslow's famous "hierarchy of needs" and how important it is to have the sense of belonging. It's paramount—so much so that it can override your physical and psychological needs and leave you struggling, scrambling. In my case, as a young man coming to terms with who I was, who I was meant to be, it left me mired in a deep, dark depression—even suicidal at times. This is what I fear for my Yanomami brothers and sisters.

But it is not too late for them. No. I *cannot* believe it's too late. I can only hope that by shining some important new light on the territory, the Yanomami of today can find a way to survive and thrive in their changing world. I've only just begun to explore my Yanomami side. As I told those boys in Esmeralda, I am proud to be Yanomami, proud to be the son of a Yanomami woman. But it is a new sort of pride—you can still smell the fresh paint on it. Yes, I am *nabuh*, but someday I will learn the ways of the Yanomami. Someday, I will return to my mother's village with my daughter, Naomi, and introduce her to the *Irokai-teri*—and we will live as our ancestors have lived, as future generations will live . . . in what ways we can.

Acknowledgments

THERE ARE SO MANY PEOPLE I'd like to thank for helping me discover myself and encouraging me to write this book. Unfortunately (or, I guess, fortunately), the list is too long for me to mention everyone's name here. I'd need a whole other volume. But these people know who they are. *You* know who you are—and you know you have my never-ending gratitude. But this is not just my story. It's my mother's story and my father's story. It's my family's story. It's America's story. It's Venezuela's story. It's *our* story. I want to especially thank all those involved in the creation of this memoir. A special shout-out to Steven Hartman, who opened the door to Jenny Bent, my literary agent, and to her colleague John Silbersack. I'd like to thank Mark Chait, for bringing this project on at HarperCollins, and Denise Oswald, my editor, for so capably and so thoughtfully seeing it through. In addition, I want to thank the entire Dey Street/HarperCollins team, including Heidi Richter, Kendra Newton, Andrea Molitor, and Tom Pitoniak for putting my story out into the world in such a beautiful way. And of course, a thousand thanks to my friend Daniel Paisner. I couldn't have done this without him.